Finding a Voice

Personal response to A level English

Finding a Voice

Personal response to A level English

Mike Royston

Stanley Thornes (Publishers) Ltd

Text © Mike Royston 1998

Original line illustrations © Stanley Thornes (Publishers) Ltd 1998

First published in 1998 by:
Stanley Thornes (Publishers) Ltd
Ellenborough House
Wellington Street
CHELTENHAM GL50 1YW
England

98 99 00 01 02 / 10 9 8 7 6 5 4 3 2 1

A catalogue record for this book is available from the British Library.

ISBN 0-7487-3373-6

Printed and bound in Great Britain by Scotprint Ltd, Musselburgh, Scotland
Typeset by Tech Set Limited, Gateshead, Tyne & Wear
Illustrated by Jane Taylor
Cover photo: Stock Market

For Ruth Harris, most generous of friends

Acknowledgements

The author gratefully acknowledges the contribution to this book of several 'generations' of sixth form students at Finham Park School, Coventry, and at The Billericay School, Essex. Their commitment to independent learning has informed the book's methodology; the examples it contains of A level work are theirs.

The author and publishers wish to thank the following for permission use copyright material:

Accelerated Learning Systems Ltd for advertising material; Anvil Press Poetry for Carol Ann Duffy, 'Telegrams' from *Selling Manhattan* (1987); The Associated Examining Group and Northern Examinations and Assessment Board, the Oxford and Cambridge Examinations and Assessment Council, the University of Cambridge Local Examinations Syndicate, for extracts from A level question papers and Examiners' reports; Carcanet Press Ltd for Gillian Clarke, 'Miracle on St David's Day' from *Selected Poems* (1985); Gerald Duckworth and Company Ltd for material from Dorothy Parker, 'I Live on Your Visits' from *The Dorothy Parker Omnibus*; Faber and Faber Ltd for Sylvia Plath, 'Morning Song' from 'Ariel' in *Collected Poems*; Ted Hughes, 'The Horses' from *The Hawk in the Rain*; Norman Nicholson, 'Rising Five' from *Selected Poems 1940–1982*; Seamus Heaney, 'Follower' from 'Door into the Dark' in *New Selected Poems 1966–1987*; and an extract from Timberlake Wertenbaker, 'Our Country's Good' in *Plays One*; Guardian Media Group plc for Decca Aitkenhead, 'Now the Army steps down into the gutter', *The Guardian*, October 1997; A M Heath & Co Ltd on behalf of the Estate of the author for an extract from George Orwell, *The Road to Wigan Pier*, Martin Secker and Warburg Ltd. Copyright © Mark Hamilton as the Literary Executor of the Estate of the Late Sonia Brownell Orwell; David Higham Associates on behalf of the author for Charles Causley, 'Ballad of the Breadman' from *Collected Poems*; and on behalf of the Estate of the author for an extract from Graham Greene, *A Gun for Sale*, Heinemann; Icon Books Ltd for material from Peter Pugh and Carl Flint, *Thatcher for Beginners* (1997) pp. 172–3; R R Knudson, on behalf of the Literary Estate of the author, for May Swenson, translator, 'Under a Ramshackle Rainbow' by Ingemar Gustafson; Macmillian Publishers for Thomas Hardy, 'The Darkling Thrush' from *The Complete Poems of Thomas Hardy*, ed. James Gibson (1976) Papermac; Newspaper Publishing plc for Michael Glover, 'And the word was with Norman', *The Independent*; 24.9.97; and Stevie Morgan, 'Diary of a divorce', *The Independent*, Sept. 1997; The Orion Publishing Group for R S Thomas, 'A Blackbird Singing' from *Collected Poems*, J M Dent; and material from Alan Clark, *Diaries*, Weidenfeld and Nicolson (1993); Oxford University Press for David Coward, translator, 'Country Living' from *A Day in the Country and Other Stories* by Guy de Maupassant. Copyright © David Coward, 1990; Penguin UK for an extract from L P Hartley, *The Go-Between*, Hamish Hamilton (1953) pp. 44–5, 101–2, 153–4, 211–2. Copyright © L P Hartley, 1953; and Marge Piercy, 'Rape poem' from *Eight Chambers of the Heart*, Michael Joseph, 1995. Copyright © Middlemarsh Inc, 1995; Casarotto Ramsay Ltd on behalf of The University of the South, Sewanee, Tennessee for an extract from Tennessee Williams, *A Streetcar Named Desire*, New Directions. Copyright © 1947, 1953 by Tennessee Williams renewed 1975, 1981. The University of the South. All rights whatsoever in this play are strictly reserved and application for performance etc., must be made before rehearsal to Casarotto Ramsay Ltd., National House, 60–66 Wardour Street, London W1V 4ND. No performance may be given unless a licence has been obtained; Random House UK Ltd for Maeve Binchy, 'Chancery Lane' from *Central Line* (1983) Century; and for material from David Lodge, *Nice Work*, Martin Secker & Warburg; and Anita Brookner, *Hotel du Lac* (1984) Jonathon Cape; Rogers, Coleridge and White Ltd on behalf of the author for Edward Lucie-Smith, 'The Lesson' from *A Tropical Childhood and Other Poems*, OUP. Copyright © Edward Lucie-Smith 1961; Audrey Salkeld for 'On shaky ground', *The Sunday Times*, 14.9.97; Sheil Land Associates Ltd on behalf of the author for Peter Ackroyd, 'She was sick and wicked', *The Times*, 19.9.97; A P Watt Ltd on behalf of the author for Nadine Gordimer,

'Country Lovers' from *A Soldier's Embrace*; and on behalf of Michael Yeats for W B Yeats, 'The Song of Wandering Aengus' from *Collected Poems of W B Yeats*;

The Women's Press Ltd for material from Joan Ryan, 'Epilogue' from *Little Girls in Pretty Boxes: the making and breaking of elite gymnasts and figure skaters* (1996) pp. 216–20.

The author and publishers also wish to thank the following for permission to reproduce copyright photographs:

Anvil Press Poetry, p.30; Mary Evans Picture Library, pp.48 & 83; The Ronald Grant Archive, p.78; The Shakespeare's Centre Library, Stratford-upon-Avon, The Merchant of Venice, RST, 1997, p.88; King Lear, RST, 1968, p.97; Shakespeare's Globe, John Tramper, p.82.

Every effort has been made to trace the copyright holders but if any have been inadvertently overlooked the publishers will be pleased to make the necessary arrangement at the first opportunity.

Contents

To the student

Active learning, personal response

A recent Chief Examiner's report on A level English states:

> Examiners commented that the best responses produced beautifully presented, well thought out and cohesive work that would put some real text books to shame and were deeply impressed that this was achieved even in examination conditions. Many candidates demonstrated immense creativity and originality that gave great pleasure to their readers.

Notice the emphasis on 'originality' and on candidates' willingness to think things out for themselves. This is the key to success. A level English is not principally a 'content' subject. It is a *process* of personal enquiry into the language and literature set, or chosen, for study.

What you learn from your course can only be learned by your own active involvement in this process. If you choose to remain passive and let someone else do your thinking for you, the most you will learn is how to be a parrot.

For this reason, *Finding a Voice* is based on the premise that knowledge and understanding about English must be *personally made*. The 'meaning' of a text is what it means *to you*. It can't be handed down from on high.

Other voices – your teachers', your fellow students', academic commentators' – will be important in shaping your personal response. But you will find your *own* voice most readily by taking part in a dialogue with theirs, as well as with the writers whose novels, plays, poems and non-fiction you study.

The purpose of *Finding a Voice* is to help you build and sustain this learning dialogue. It is not a 'crib' book for set texts, nor an all-purpose survey of English writing. Much of the material it contains can be incorporated directly into your A level course. Its main use, however, is to demonstrate a range of study techniques which can be applied to texts across the spectrum of English/English Literature.

These techniques may not all work for you. The ones that do will increase your confidence in tackling the content of your syllabus. Confidence doesn't come in a kit or from combing through commercial study notes. It develops gradually as you learn to trust your own response through reading, talking and writing about challenging texts.

Finding a voice capable of saying what you want to say is the difficult route – but it's the only one that provides the motivation, the awareness and (above all) the enjoyment necessary for you to reach your full A level potential. Keep faith with it.

Chapter 1 Helping yourself to A level

 1.1 **Beyond GCSE: two levels of response to the same material**

Main text: *Nice Work*, David Lodge

 1.2 **Responding to characters' voices in fiction**

Main text: 'Chancery Lane', Maeve Binchy

 1.3 **Responding to the author's voice**

Main text: 'The Kiss', Kate Chopin

 1.4 **Voices on and off stage**

Main text: *Our Country's Good*, Timberlake Wertenbaker

 1.5 **Making your own voice heard**

Main text: 'Carnation', Katherine Mansfield

The purpose of this chapter is to introduce you to some basic A level requirements which build on, rather than leave behind, the ways of working that you used at GCSE. The activities encourage you to ask and answer your own questions on a number of typical A level texts instead of relying solely on your teacher. Each of the five sections focuses on a particular skill and begins with a brief description of why it will prove to be important as you progress through your course.

Beyond GCSE: two levels of response to the same material

The purpose of this section is to identify some basic differences between working on a literary text for GCSE and studying at A level. The activity below will help you judge for yourself the 'difficulty factor' involved in moving from one to the other.

Read the passage below, which is the opening of a modern novel. The central character, Vic Wilcox, is managing director of a Midlands engineering firm.

> ➤⊣◆⊱·◯·⊰◆⊢≺

from Nice Work
by David Lodge

Monday, January 13th, 1986. Victor Wilcox lies awake, in the dark bedroom, waiting for his quartz alarm clock to bleep. It is set to do this at 6:45. How long he has to wait he doesn't know. He could easily find out by groping for the clock, lifting it to his line of vision, and pressing the button that illuminates the digital display. But he would rather not know. Supposing it is only six o'clock? Or even five? It could be five. 5
Whatever it is, he won't be able to get to sleep again. This has become a regular occurrence lately: lying awake in the dark, waiting for the alarm to bleep, worrying.

Worries streak towards him like enemy spaceships in one of Gary's video games. He flinches, dodges, zaps them with instant solutions, but the assault is endless: the Avco account, the Rawlinson account, the price of pig-iron, the value of the pound, the 10
incompetence of his Marketing Director, the vandalizing of the toilets in the fettling shop, the pressure from his divisional boss, last month's accounts, the quarterly forecast, the annual review …

In an effort to escape this bombardment, perhaps even to doze awhile, he twists on to his side, burrows into the warm plump body of his wife, and throws an arm around her 15
waist. Startled, but still asleep, drugged with Valium, Marjorie swivels to face him. Their noses and foreheads bump against each other; there is a sudden flurry of limbs, an absurd pantomime struggle. Marjorie puts her fists up like a boxer, groans and pushes him away. An object slides off the bed on her side and falls to the floor with a thump. Vic knows what it is: a book entitled *Enjoy Your Menopause*, which one of Marjorie's friends at the 20
Weight Watchers' club has lent her, and which she has been reading in bed, without much show of conviction, for the past week or two. On retiring to bed Vic's last action is normally to detach a book from Marjorie's nerveless fingers, tuck her arms under the covers and turn out her bedside lamp, but he must have neglected the first of these chores last night, or perhaps *Enjoy Your Menopause* was concealed under the coverlet. 25

He rolls away from Marjorie, who, now lying on her back, begins to snore faintly. He envies her that deep unconsciousness, but cannot afford to join her in it. Once, desperate for a full night's sleep, he had accepted her offer of a Valium, sluicing it down with his usual nightcap, and moved about the next morning like a diver walking on the seabed. He made a mistake of two percentage points in a price for steering-boxes for 30
British Leyland before his head cleared. *You shouldn't have mixed it with whisky, Marjorie said. You don't need both.* Then I'll stick to whisky, he said. *The Valium lasts longer,* she said. Too bloody long, if you ask me, he said. I lost the firm five thousand pounds this morning, thanks to you. *Oh, it's my fault, is it?* she said, and her lower lip began to tremble. Then to stop her crying, anything to stop that, he had to buy her the 35
set of antique-look brass fire-irons she had set her heart on for the lounge, to give an extra touch of authenticity to the rustic stone fireplace and the imitation-log gas fire.

Marjorie's snores become louder. Vic gives her a rude, exasperated shove. The snoring stops but, surprisingly, she does not wake. In other rooms his three children are also asleep. Outside, a winter gale blusters against the sides of the house and swishes the branches of trees to and fro. He feels like the captain of a sleeping ship, alone at the helm, steering his oblivious crew through dangerous seas. He feels as if he is the only man awake in the entire world.

The alarm clock cheeps.

Vic sighs, hits the Off button on the clock, switches on his bedside lamp (its dimmer control turned low for Marjorie's sake), gets out of bed and paddles through the deep pile of the bedroom carpet to the *en suite* bathroom, making sure the connecting door is closed before he turns on the light inside.

Vic pees, a task requiring considerable care and accuracy since the toilet bowl is low-slung and tapered in shape. He does not greatly care for the dark purplish bathroom suite ('Damson', the estate agent's brochure had called the shade) but it had been one of the things that attracted Marjorie when they bought the house two years ago – the bathroom, with its kidney-shaped handbasin, its goldplated taps and sunken bath and streamlined loo and bidet. And, above all, the fact that it was 'en suite'. *I've always wanted an* en suite *bathroom*, she would say to visitors, to her friends on the phone, to, he wouldn't be surprised, tradesmen on the doorstep or strangers she accosted in the street. You would think '*en suite*' was the most beautiful phrase in any language, the lengths Marjorie went to introduce it into her conversation. If they made a perfume called *En Suite*, she would wear it.

>─┤◄►─·─O─·─◄►┤─◄

GCSE level task

1. *What do you learn about the characters of Vic and Marjorie from this passage?*
2. *What impressions have you formed of their marriage?*

Using whatever method suits you best, make notes in answer to these questions. Do not convert them into a formal written commentary. Take up to half an hour.

When you have finished, compare your own understanding and response with at least two other people's.

A level task

Examine carefully the way in which this passage is written. How does the author direct our attitude towards Vic and Marjorie and to their relationship?

Do not write anything. Discuss with a partner, or in a group, what this task requires you to do that the GCSE task did not.

Working together, talk about the style and structure of the first two paragraphs of the passage, using the following questions as prompts:

Paragraph 1

- Does the way in which the first sentence is written suggest anything important about Vic?
- Vic is described as 'groping' for the alarm clock. Thinking of the passage as a whole, suggest why the author may have chosen this word (as opposed to, say, 'reaching' or 'feeling').

- Look at the four sentences from 'Supposing it is ...' to '... get to sleep again' (lines 5-6). From whose point of view are these sentences written? Suggest why.

- The author ends the paragraph with the word 'worrying', straight after a comma. Why?

Paragraph 2

- Vic's worries are compared with 'enemy spaceships in one of Gary's video games'. What is implied here about Vic's feelings about life in general?

- This paragraph contains only two sentences. Paragraph 1 contains eleven. Suggest reasons for this difference.

- Look at the two items in Vic's 'worry list' that come immediately before and after 'the vandalizing of the toilets in the fettling shop'. What do you notice about this *sequence* of worries? What does it suggest about Vic's state of mind?

Work together through the remaining six paragraphs of the passage, asking and answering similar questions of your own. Do not write anything. Put forward your responses as fully as possible, paying close attention to (a) the author's choice of words, and (b) the way in which he constructs his sentences and paragraphs.

General

- What have you noticed about the way the author (a) uses humour, and (b) builds up the *whole* passage to guide our responses to Vic and Marjorie?

Comparing tasks

With your teacher, discuss what you have gathered from this activity about the requirements made on you by A level. How 'different' *are* they? How far is it a question of 'looking at the same things in a different way'?

For your own reference, it may be useful to write down the conclusions you draw from this discussion.

Responding to characters' voices in fiction

This section asks you to form your own impression of the characters in a story where they speak only for themselves, without the author's narrative voice to guide your response. You will need to be alert to the characters' differing speech styles and to what these reveal about their relationships with each other: a vital A level skill.

The following short story by the Irish author, Maeve Binchy, is made up entirely of letters. Read the letters aloud, either with a partner or in a group. Take them one by one: it is not important which 'character' you read.

>─┼─◄►─○─◄►─┼─◄

Chancery Lane
by Maeve Binchy

Dear Mr Lewis,

I'm sure you will think this very, very odd and you will spend the rest of your life refusing to talk to strange women at parties in case something of the sort should happen again. We met briefly at the Barry's last week. You mentioned you were a barrister and I mentioned the Lord knows what because I was up to my eyebrows in gin. I was the one who was wearing a blue dress and what started out as a feather boa, but sort of moulted during the night. Anyway, your only mistake was to let me know where you worked, and my mistakes that night were legion. 5

I know nobody else at all in the legal world and I wonder if you could tell me where to look. In books people open yellow pages and suddenly find exactly the right kind of lawyer for themselves, but I've been looking in the windows of various solicitors' offices and they don't seem to be the kind of thing I want. They're full of files and girls typing. You seemed to have a lot of style that night, and you might know where to direct me. 10

I want to sue somebody for a breach of promise. I want to take him for everything he's got. I want a great deal of publicity and attention drawn to the case and photographs of me leaving the court to appear in the newspapers. What I would really like is to see all the letters involved published in the papers, and I want to be helped through the crowds by policemen. 15

But what I don't know is how to begin. Do I serve something on him, or send him a writ or a notice to prosecute? I feel sure the whole thing will gather its own momentum once it starts. It's the beginning bit that has me worried. If you could write back as soon as possible and tell me where to start, I should be for ever grateful. 20

I feel it would be unprofessional to offer you a fee for this service, but since it's a matter of using your knowledge and experience for my benefit, I should be very happy to offer you some of mine in return. You may remember that I am a tap-dancing teacher (I probably gave several exhibitions to the whole room that night). So, if ever you want a lesson, I'd be delighted to give you one. 25

Yours sincerely,
Jilly Twilly

Dear Tom,   30

Thanks belatedly for a wonderful party last week. I don't know what you put in those
drinks but it took me days to get over it all. I enjoyed meeting all your friends. There was
a woman with the impossible name of Jilly Twilly, I think, but perhaps I got it wrong. She
wore a blue dress and a feather boa of sorts. I seem to have taken her cigarette-lighter
by mistake, and I was wondering if you could let me have her address so that I could   35
return it. She seemed a lively sort of girl, have you known her long?

Once more, thanks for a great party.
John Lewis

Dear John,

Glad you enjoyed the party. Yes, I gather her name is Jilly Twilly, unlikely as it sounds. I   40
don't know her at all. She came with that banker guy, who is a friend of Freddy's so he
might know. Pretty spectacular dance she did, wasn't it? The women were all a bit sour
about it, but I thought she was great.

Greetings to all in chambers,
Tom   45

Dear Ms Twilly,

Thank you for your letter. Unfortunately you have approached the wrong person.
Barristers are in fact briefed by solicitors in cases of this kind. So what you must do if you
have a legal problem is to consult your family solicitor. If his firm does not handle the
kind of litigation you have in mind, perhaps he may recommend a firm who will be able   50
to help you.

I enjoyed meeting you at the party, and do indeed remember you very well. You
seemed a very cheerful and happy person, and I might point out that these breach of
promise actions are rarely satisfactory. They are never pleasant things for anyone, and I
cannot believe that you would actually crave the attendant publicity.   55

I urge you to be circumspect about this for your own sake, but please do not regard this
as legal advice, which it certainly is not.

I wish you success in whatever you are about to do, but with the reservation that I think
you are unwise to be about to do it all.

Kind wishes,   60
John Lewis

Dear Mr Lewis,

Thank you very much for your letter. I knew I could rely on you to help me, and despite
all those stuffy phrases you used I can see you will act for me. I understand completely
that you have to write things like that for your files. Now, this is the bones of the story.   65
Charlie, who is the villain of the whole scene and probably of many other scenes as well,
is a very wealthy and stuffy banker, and he asked me to marry him several times. I gave
it some thought and though I knew there would be problems, I said yes. He bought me
an engagement ring and we were going to get married next June.

Because you are my lawyer and can't divulge anything I tell you, I will tell you privately that I had a lot of doubts about it all. But I'm not getting any younger, I haven't been in so many shows recently, and I teach dancing when I'm not in shows. I thought it would be fairly peaceful to get married and not to worry about paying the rent and all that. So Charlie and I made a bargain. I was to behave nicely in front of his friends, and he was to behave unstuffily in front of mine. It worked fine, a bit gruesome at some of those bank things. Merchant bankers en masse are horrific and Charlie did his best with my friends. I wasn't going to let him down in his career and he wasn't going to interfere in mine. If I got a dancing part, so long as I wasn't naked, I could take it.

And it was all fine until Tom Barry's party, and when I woke up Charlie wasn't there, he had left a note and taken my engagement ring, the rat. He said … Oh well I'll make a photostat of the note, we'll probably need it as evidence. I'll also write out his address and you could get things going from your end.

I suppose it will be all right to pay you from the proceeds. I don't have any spare cash just now.

Warm wishes,
Jilly Twilly

Photostat of note:

Jilly,

Now I've finally had enough. Your behaviour tonight is something that I would like obliterated from my mind. I do not want to see you again. I've kept my part of the bargain, you have failed utterly in yours.

Perhaps it is as well we discovered this before we were married. I am too angry to thank you for the undoubtedly good parts of our relationship because I cannot recall any of them.

I have reclaimed my ring. Your may keep the watch.

Charles

Dear Ms Twilly,

You have utterly misunderstood my letter. I really cannot act for you in any way in your projected action against Mr Benson. As an acquaintance, may I take the liberty of reminding you once again of how unwise you would be to start any such proceedings? You are an attractive young woman, you seem from my short meeting with you to be well able to handle a life which does not contain Mr Benson. My serious and considered advice to you, not as a lawyer but as a fellow guest at a party, is to forget it all and continue to live your own life without bitterness. And certainly without contemplating a litigation that is unlikely to bring you any satisfaction whatsoever.

Yours sincerely,
John Lewis

Dear John,

Stop telling me what to do with my life, it *is* my life. If I want to sue I'll sue. Please have the papers ready or I will have to sue you for malpractice. You have wasted quite a lot of time already. I am enclosing a copy of the letter where Charlie mentions my marrying him. It will probably be exhibit A at the trial.

110

Kind wishes and hurry up,
Jilly

Darling Jilly,

You must know that the bank can't put any money into the ridiculous venture you suggest. I didn't come to America to meet show-biz people and interest them in your little troupe of dancers. I know that it must be disheartening for you not to get any backing, but in six months' time we will be married and you won't need to bother your pretty little head or your pretty little feet about a career. I love you, Jilly, but I wish you wouldn't keep telephoning the bank here on reverse charges, because I am only here for a conference and it looks badly to get several calls a day, all about something which we haven't the slightest intention of doing.

115

120

Look after yourself if you can,
Charles

Dear Ms Twilly,

125

These Chambers will have no further correspondence with you about any legal matters whatsoever. Kindly go through the correct channels, and approach a solicitor who will if necessary brief counsel for you.

Yours faithfully,
John Lewis

130

Dear John,

What have I done? Why is this kind of thing always happening to me? I thought we got on so well that night at Tom Barry's party. Did I tell you by the way that Charlie was quite wrong? Tom Barry was not one of his friends, he was a mutual new friend that we had met with Freddie who was one of Charlie's friends. So I didn't break any bargain by behaving badly.

135

I just thought that the publicity of a big breach of promise case might give me some chance of being noticed. People would hear of me, I'd get more jobs. You see without Charlie or my ring or anything I have so little money, and I was only trying to claw at life with both hands.

140

It's fine for you, you are a wealthy, settled barrister. What would you do if you were a fast-fading, poor little dancer betrayed by everyone? I'm nearly 26, my best years of dancing are probably over.

It was my one chance of hitting back at life, I thought I should grab it. Anyway, I'm sorry, I seem to have upset you. Goodbye.

145

Jilly

Dear Jilly,

My letter may have seemed harsh. I do indeed see what you mean about grabbing at life, and I admire your pluck, believe me I do. What you need is not so much a court action, it's much more a good friend to advise you about your career and to cheer you up. I don't think you should get involved with anyone like Charlie, your worlds are too different. I only vaguely remember him from the party at Tom Barry's but I think he was a little buttoned up. 150

You need somebody younger than Charlie Benson.

Perhaps you and I might meet for a meal one evening and discuss it all, totally as friends and in no way in a client–lawyer relationship. If you would like this please let me know. 155

Cordially,
John

Dear Monica,

I'm afraid I won't be able to make the week-end after all. Rather an important case has come up and I can't leave London just now. I know you will be disappointed, still we did agree that I should do everything possible to advance my career, so that is what I'm doing. I hope the week-end goes awfully well, looking forward to seeing you soon. 160

Love,
John 165

Dear John,

I was sorry about the week-end. Daddy and Mummy were sorry you were kept in London. Daddy kept saying that all work and no play … you know the way Daddy does.

I came to London last Tuesday. You weren't in Chambers and you weren't in your flat, even though I phoned you there lots of times up to midnight. Maybe Daddy is right and although we all want to advance your career, perhaps it is a question of all work and no play. 170

Love anyway darling,
Monica

Darling John, 175

How can I thank you for the lovely, lovely week-end. I always wanted to go to Paris and it really cheered me up. It was such a relief to be able to talk to someone so understanding. I'm afraid you must have spent a fortune but I did enjoy myself.

See you next week-end,
love Jilly 180

Dear Monica,

I must say I thought your phone-call to the office today was hysterical and ill-timed. I was in consultation and it was very embarrassing to have to discuss my private life in front of others. I do not know where and why you have got this absurd notion that we had an understanding about getting married. From my side certainly we have no such thing. I always regarded you as a good friend, and will continue to do so unless prevented by another phone-call like today's.

185

You may check your letters from me to see whether any such 'understanding' was mentioned. I think you will see that nowhere do I mention marriage. I find this an embarrassing topic so will now close.

190

John

Dear Tom,

I appreciate your intentions in writing to me with what you consider a justifiable warning. I realise you did this from no purposes of self-interest.

Still, I have to thank you for your intention and tell you that your remarks were not well-received. Ms Twilly and I are to be married shortly, and I regard your information that she has had seven breach of promise actions settled out of court as utterly preposterous. In fact I know for a certainty that the lady is quite incapable of beginning a breach of promise action, so your friend's sources cannot be as accurate as he or you may think.

195

Under other circumstances I would have invited you to our wedding but, as things are, I think I can thank you for having had the party where I was fortunate enough to meet my future bride and wish you well in the future.

200

Sincerely,
John Lewis

Public and private voices

There are seventeen letters altogether. Number them in sequence. Make brief notes about the *purpose*, the *style* and the *character* of the writer in any **six** of the letters, as if on the back of the envelope in which it was sent:

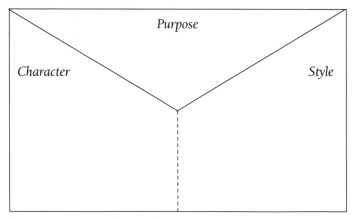

Letter 1: Jilly to John Lewis

Pay most attention to the following:

- The purpose of the letters, that is, the effect each correspondent intends his/her letter to have on the person it's sent to. This is not always what it seems to be on the surface: you will often have to read 'between the lines'.

- The way in which Jilly and John are presented in a changing light as the letters progress.

- The way in which the style of each letter reflects the feelings and the character of its writer. In your notes, try to pin down the writer's *tone*, quoting any phrases which make this particularly clear.

Suggestions for writing

✧ Assume that Jilly and Charlie Benson have plotted together from the start to lure John into marriage. (He is obviously rich!) Choose a point somewhere in the second half of the story and write a letter from Jilly to Charlie telling him how the plot is going. Use a suitable tone.

✧ Write Monica's reply to the last letter John writes her. Use your knowledge of Monica from letters 13, 14 and 16 to help you establish her character and the style in which she will write.

Responding to the author's voice

The story featured in this section is very short, but every word counts in revealing the characters' feelings (spoken and unspoken) and the author's view of them. When studying longer works for A level, you will need to appreciate how writers direct your response to their subject matter through the use of what appears to be minor detail. The activities in this section give you practice in this aspect of appreciation.

Read the following short story by the American author, Kate Chopin. It was written in 1898.

The Kiss

by Kate Chopin

It was still quite light out of doors, but inside with the curtains drawn and the smouldering fire sending out a dim, uncertain glow, the room was full of deep shadows.

Brantain sat in one of these shadows; it had overtaken him and he did not mind. The obscurity lent him courage to keep his eyes fastened as ardently as he liked upon the girl who sat in the firelight.   5

She was very handsome, with a certain fine, rich colouring that belongs to the healthy brune type. She was quite composed, as she idly stroked the satiny coat of the cat that lay curled in her lap, and she occasionally sent a slow glance into the shadow where her companion sat. They were talking low, of indifferent things which plainly were not things that occupied their thoughts. She knew that he loved her – a frank, blustering   10 fellow without guile enough to conceal his feelings, and no desire to do so. For two weeks past he had sought her society eagerly and persistently. She was confidently waiting for him to declare himself and she meant to accept him. The rather insignificant and unattractive Brantain was enormously rich; and she liked and required the entourage which wealth could give her.   15

During one of the pauses between their talk of the last tea and the next reception the door opened and a young man entered whom Brantain knew quite well. The girl turned her face toward him. A stride or two brought him to her side, and bending over her chair – before she could suspect his intentions, for she did not realise that he had not seen her visitor – he pressed an ardent, lingering kiss upon her lips.   20

Brantain slowly arose; so did the girl arise, but quickly, and the new-comer stood between them, a little amusement and some defiance struggling with the confusion in his face.

'I believe,' stammered Brantain, 'I see that I have stayed too long. I – I had no idea – that is, I must wish you good-by.' He was clutching his hat with both hands, and probably   25 did not perceive that she was extending her hand to him, her presence of mind had not completely deserted her; but she could not have trusted herself to speak.

'Hang me if I saw him sitting there, Nattie! I know it's deuced awkward for you. But I hope you'll forgive me this once – this very first break. Why, what's the matter?'

'Don't touch me; don't come near me,' she returned angrily. 'What do you mean by   30 entering the house without ringing?'

'I came in with your brother, as I often do,' he answered coldly, in self-justification. 'We came in the side way. He went upstairs and I came in here hoping to find you. The explanation is simple enough and ought to satisfy you that the misadventure was unavoidable. But do say that you forgive me, Nathalie,' he entreated, softening.

35

'Forgive you! You don't know what you are talking about. Let me pass. It depends upon – a good deal whether I ever forgive you.'

At the next reception which she and Brantain had been talking about she approached the young man with a delicious frankness of manner when she saw him there.

'Will you let me speak to you a moment or two, Mr Brantain?' she asked with an engaging but perturbed smile. He seemed extremely unhappy; but when she took his arm and walked away with him, seeking a retired corner, a ray of hope mingled with the almost comic misery of his expression. She was apparently very outspoken.

40

'Perhaps I should not have sought this interview, Mr Brantain; but – but, oh, I have been so very uncomfortable, almost miserable since that little encounter the other afternoon. When I thought how you might have misinterpreted it, and believed things' – hope was plainly gaining ascendancy over misery in Brantain's round, guileless face – 'of course, I know it is nothing to you, but for my own sake I do want you to understand that Mr Harvy is an intimate friend of long standing. Why, we have always been like cousins – like brother and sister, I may say. He is my brother's most intimate acquaintance and often fancies that he is entitled to the same privileges as the family. Oh, I know it is absurd, uncalled for, to tell you this; undignified even,' she was almost weeping, 'but it makes so much difference to me what you think of – of me.' Her voice had grown very low and agitated. The misery had all but disappeared from Brantain's face.

45

50

'Then you do really care what I think, Miss Nathalie? May I call you Miss Nathalie?' They turned into a long, dim corridor that was lined on either side with tall, graceful plants. They walked slowly to the very end of it. When they turned to retrace their steps Brantain's face was radiant and hers was triumphant.

55

* * *

Harvy was among the guests at the wedding; and he sought her out in a rare moment when she stood alone.

60

'Your husband,' he said, smiling, 'has sent me over to kiss you.'

A quick blush suffused her face and round polished throat. 'I suppose it's natural for a man to feel and act generously on an occasion of this kind. He tells me he doesn't want his marriage to interrupt wholly that pleasant intimacy which has existed between you and me. I don't know what you've been telling him,' with an insolent smile, 'but he has sent me here to kiss you.'

65

She felt like a chess player who, by clever handling of his pieces, sees the game taking the course intended. Her eyes were bright and tender with a smile as they glanced up into his; and her lips looked hungry for the kiss which they invited.

'But, you know,' he went on quietly, 'I didn't tell him so, it would have seemed ungrateful, but I can tell you. I've stopped kissing women; it's dangerous.'

70

Well, she had Brantain and his million left. A person can't have everything in the world; and it was a little unreasonable of her to expect it.

Internal voices

Copying the framework set out below, note down what Kate Chopin reveals about the thoughts and feelings of Brantain and Nathalie at different points in the story.

This activity is more effective if you work with a partner. One person should 'track' Brantain's thoughts and feelings, the other Nathalie's.

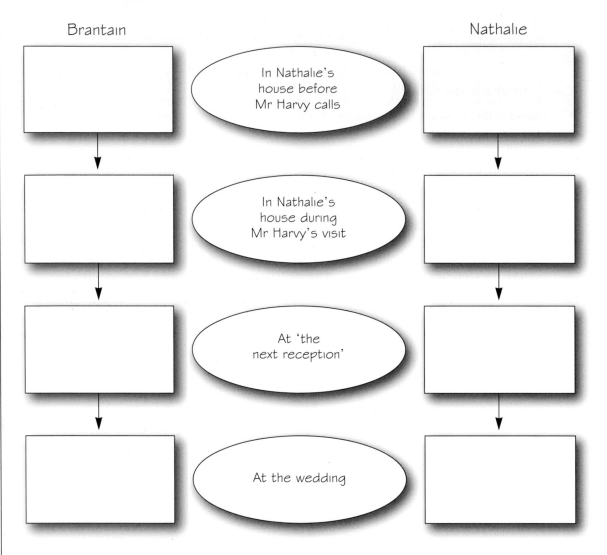

Brantain   Nathalie

In Nathalie's house before Mr Harvy calls

In Nathalie's house during Mr Harvy's visit

At 'the next reception'

At the wedding

Compare your notes on Brantain and Nathalie. Which character understands the other better? Use your notes to predict how their marriage will work out: imagine it a year after the wedding.

The narrator's voice

Consider how Kate Chopin's narrative technique provides an insight into her two central characters. Use the following prompts:

● At the start of the story, 'the room was full of deep shadows' and Brantain 'sat in one of these'. Nathalie 'idly stroked the satiny coat of the cat that lay in her lap'. What differences in character and feeling do these early descriptions suggest?

- What is implied about Nathalie by the italicised words in this sentence: '… she liked and *required* the *entourage* which wealth could give her'?

- Before the wedding, Brantain and Mr Harvy use different names for Nathalie. What are they? Why do you think Kate Chopin draws our attention to this?

- Look again at the paragraph beginning 'Perhaps I should not have sought this interview …' (lines 44–54). Comment on the style of speech Nathalie uses to Brantain here. What does it show about her nature?

- What is indicated by the italicised words in this sentence: 'When they turned to retrace their steps Brantain's face was *radiant* and hers was *triumphant*'?

- Do you feel that Kate Chopin directs the reader's sympathies in this story? If so, towards whom – and by what means does she do it?

- The story's title sounds very commonplace. To what extent do you consider it to be apt?

Suggestions for writing

◇ Use your understanding of the story to write two entries in Nathalie's diary: the first on the day Brantain proposes to her, the second several months after the wedding.

◇ 'She felt like a chess player who, by clever handling of his pieces, sees the game taking the course intended.' Examine the way in which Kate Chopin presents Nathalie to us as 'a chess player' in this story. In your view, how skilful a 'player' is she?

Voices on and off stage

This section focuses on one complete scene from a contemporary play. The activities encourage you to respond to it as a piece of live theatre written for the stage rather than as a 'drama text' for classroom study. This approach to plays, including Shakespeare's, is crucial if you are to explore fully the way in which they communicate and the unique way in which they 'work'.

Read to yourself the scene below from Timberlake Wertenbaker's play *Our Country's Good*, first performed in 1988 at the Royal Court Theatre in London. Then read the scene aloud with a partner, as if in rehearsal.

Our Country's Good is set in 1789. It is about the first group of convicts to be transported to Botany Bay in New South Wales for crimes committed in England. Its female playwright notes: 'Transportation allowed England to dump its "criminal class" on the other side of the world, there to be forgotten, with the added advantage that returning ships could carry raw material home to equip the navy.'

The Governor-in-Chief of New South Wales, Captain Arthur Phillip, is interested in rehabilitating the convicts as well as in punishing them. Despite strong opposition from his fellow officers, he proposes that the convicts should stage their own production of a play (*The Recruiting Officer*, a popular 18th-century comedy) in order to educate them in something other than crime.

This scene begins with Second Lieutenant Ralph Clark writing in his diary. At first, his thoughts are with his young wife across the sea in England. He is joined by Harry Brewer, a former embezzler, who has earned the trust of the Governor under whom he served in the navy. He has been appointed the colony's executioner and has recently had to hang a convict, Handy Baker. Harry now sleeps with Baker's whore – a teenage convict nicknamed Duckling, who was transported for thieving.

from Our Country's Good

by Timberlake Wertenbaker

Scene 4: The loneliness of men

Ralph Clark's tent. It is late at night. Ralph stands, composing and speaking his diary.

Ralph   Dreamt, my beloved Alicia, that I was walking with you and that you was in your riding-habit – oh my dear woman when shall I be able to hear from you –

All the officers dined with the Governor – I never heard of any one single person having so great a power vested in him as Captain Phillip has by his commission as Governor-in-Chief of new South Wales – dined on a cold collation but the Mutton which had been killed yesterday morning was full of maggots – nothing will keep 24 hours in this dismal country I find –

Went out shooting after breakfast – I only shot one cockatoo – they are the most beautiful birds – 10

Major Ross ordered one of the Corporals to flog with a rope Elizabeth Morden for being impertinent to Captain Campbell – the Corporal did not play with her but laid it home which I was very glad to see – she has long been fishing for it –

On Sunday as usual, kissed your dear beloved image a thousand times – was 15 very much frightened by the lightning as it broke very near my tent – several of the convicts have run away.

He goes to his table and writes in his journal.

If I'm not made 1st Lieutenant soon …

Harry Brewer has come in. 20

Ralph Harry –

Harry I saw the light in your tent –

Ralph I was writing my journal.

Silence.

Is there any trouble? 25

Harry No. (*Pause.*) I just came.

Talk, you know. If I wrote a journal about my life it would fill volumes. Volumes. My travels with the Captain – His Excellency now, no less, Governor-in-Chief, power to raise armies, build cities – I still call him plain Captain Phillip. He likes it from me. The war in America and before that, 30 Ralph, my life in London. That would fill a volume on its own. Not what you would call a good life.

Pause.

Sometimes I look at the convicts and I think, one of these could be you, Harry Brewer, if you hadn't joined the navy when you did. The officers may look 35 down on me now, but what if they found out that I used to be an embezzler?

Ralph Harry, you should keep these things to yourself.

Harry You're right, Ralph.

Pause.

I think the Captain suspects, but he's a good man and he looks for different 40 things in a man –

Ralph Like what?

Harry Hard to say. He likes to see something unusual. Ralph, I saw Handy Baker last night.

Ralph You hanged him a month ago, Harry. 45

Harry He had a rope – Ralph, he's come back.

Ralph It was a dream. Sometimes I think my dreams are real – But they're not.

Harry We used to hear you on the ship, Ralph, calling for your Betsey Alicia.

Ralph Don't speak her name in this iniquitous shore!

Harry Duckling's gone silent on me again. I know it's because of Handy Baker. I saw him as well as I see you. Duckling wants me, he said, even if you've hanged me. At least your poker's danced its last shindy, I said. At least it's young and straight, he said, she likes that. I went for him but he was gone. But he's going to come back, I know it. I didn't want to hang him, Ralph, I didn't.

Ralph He did steal that food from the stores.

Pause.

I voted with the rest of the court those men should be hanged, I didn't know His Excellency would be against it.

Harry Duckling says she never feels anything. How do I know she didn't feel something when she was with him? She thinks I hanged him to get rid of him, but I didn't, Ralph.

Pause.

Do you know I saved her life? She was sentenced to be hanged at Newgate for stealing two candlesticks but I got her name put on the transport lists. But when I remind her of that she says she wouldn't have cared. Eighteen years old, and she didn't care if she was turned off.

Pause.

These women are sold before they're ten. The Captain says we should treat them with kindness.

Ralph How can you treat such women with kindness? Why does he think that?

Harry Not all the officers find them disgusting, Ralph – haven't you ever been tempted?

Ralph Never! (*Pause.*) His Excellency never seems to notice me.

Pause.

He finds time for Davey Collins, Lieutenant Dawes.

Harry That's because Captain Collins is going to write about the customs of the Indians here – and Lieutenant Dawes is recording the stars.

Ralph I could write about the Indians.

Harry He did suggest to Captain Tench that we do something to educate the convicts, put on a play or something, but Captain Tench just laughed. He doesn't like Captain Tench.

Ralph A play? Who would act in a play?

Harry The convicts of course. He is thinking of talking to Lieutenant Johnston, but I think Lieutenant Johnston wants to study the plants.

Ralph I read *The Tragedy of Lady Jane Grey* on the ship. It is such a moving and uplifting play. But how could a whore play Lady Jane?

Harry	Some of those women are good women, Ralph, I believe my Duckling is good. It's not her fault – if only she would look at me, once, react. Who wants to fuck a corpse!
	Silence. 90
	I'm sorry. I didn't mean to shock you, Ralph, I have shocked you, haven't I? I'll go.
Ralph	Is His Excellency serious about putting on a play?
Harry	When the Captain decides something, Ralph.
Ralph	If I went to him – no. It would be better if you did, Harry, you could tell His 95 Excellency how much I like the theatre.
Harry	I didn't know that Ralph, I'll tell him.
Ralph	Duckling could be in it, if you wanted.
Harry	I wouldn't want her to be looked at by all the men.
Ralph	If His Excellency doesn't like *Lady Jane* we could find something else. 100
	Pause.
	A comedy perhaps …
Harry	I'll speak to him, Ralph. I like you.
	Pause.
	It's good to talk … 105
	Pause.
	You don't think I killed him then?
Ralph	Who?
Harry	Handy Baker
Ralph	No, Harry. You did not kill Handy Baker. 110
Harry	Thank you, Ralph.
Ralph	Harry, you won't forget to talk to His Excellency about the play?

✂━◄►•○•◄►━✂

Planning a performance

You are directing a performance of *Our Country's Good*. Make production notes for this scene using the model overleaf. These should include:

- the different tones of voice in which both characters speak as the scene goes on, so that their feelings are clear to the audience;

- any gestures and movements on stage that Ralph and Harry might make at particular points in the scene.

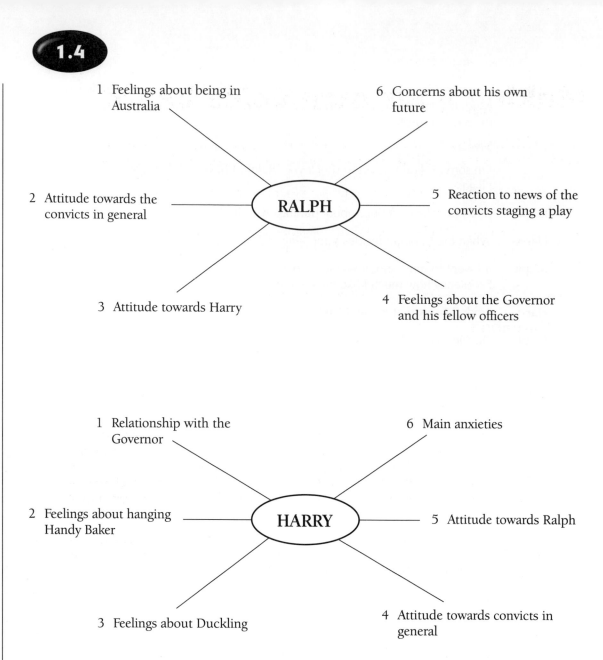

1 Feelings about being in Australia

6 Concerns about his own future

2 Attitude towards the convicts in general

RALPH

5 Reaction to news of the convicts staging a play

3 Attitude towards Harry

4 Feelings about the Governor and his fellow officers

1 Relationship with the Governor

6 Main anxieties

2 Feelings about hanging Handy Baker

HARRY

5 Attitude towards Ralph

3 Feelings about Duckling

4 Attitude towards convicts in general

You may like to direct two members of your class in a workshop performance of this scene.

Text and sub-text

Scene 4 is sub-titled 'The loneliness of men'. Near its end, Harry says: 'It's good to talk.' As the play's director, how would you bring out the fact that, for much of the scene, Ralph and Harry are in effect talking to *themselves* rather than to each other?

With your teacher, consider the distinction in drama between text and sub-text.

Making your own voice heard

This final section encourages you to respond in an entirely personal way to a piece of writing open to a wide variety of interpretations. It is in this spirit that you will do your best and most enjoyable A level work – as long as you are prepared to trust, and justify, your own ideas. To this end, the activities on page 23 suggest a way of working with your teacher which should prove fruitful as you progress through the A level course.

The story below was written by the New Zealand author Katherine Mansfield in 1917. Read it once to yourself. Then straight afterwards read it aloud with a partner: divide it up between you in any way you wish.

Carnation

by Katherine Mansfield

On those hot days Eve – curious Eve – always carried a flower. She snuffed it and snuffed it, twirled it in her fingers, laid it against her cheek, held it to her lips, tickled Katie's neck with it, and ended, finally, by pulling it to pieces and eating it, petal by petal.

'Roses are delicious, my dear Katie,' she would say, standing in the dim cloak-room, with a strange decoration of flowery hats on the hat pegs behind her – 'but carnations are simply divine! They taste like – like – ah well!' And away her little thin laugh flew, fluttering among those huge, strange flower heads on the wall behind her. (But how cruel her little thin laugh was! It had a long sharp beak and claws and two beady eyes, thought fanciful Katie.) 5

Today it was a carnation. She brought a carnation to the French class, a deep, deep red one, that looked as though it had been dipped in wine and left in the dark to dry. She held it on the desk before her, half shut her eyes and smiled. 10

'Isn't it a darling?' said she. But –

'*Un peu de silence, s'il vous plaît,*' came from M. Hugo. Oh, bother! It was too hot! Frightfully hot! Grilling simply! 15

The two square windows of the French Room were open at the bottom and the dark blinds drawn half-way down. Although no air came in, the blind cord swung out and back and the blind lifted. But really there was not a breath from the dazzle outside.

Even the girls, in the dusky room in their pale blouses, with stiff butterfly-bow hair ribbons perched on their hair, seemed to give off a warm, weak light, and M. Hugo's white 20 waistcoat gleamed like the belly of a shark.

Some of the girls were very red in the face and some were white. Vera Holland had pinned up her black curls *à la japonaise* with a penholder and a pink pencil; she looked charming. Francie Owen pushed her sleeves nearly up to the shoulders, and then she inked the little blue vein in her elbow, shut her arm together, and then looked to see the mark it made; 25 she had a passion for inking herself; she always had a face drawn on her thumb nail, with black, forked hair. Sylvia Mann took off her collar and tie, took them off simply, and laid them on the desk beside her, as calm as if she were going to wash her hair in her bedroom at home. She *had* a nerve! Jennie Edwards tore a leaf out of her notebook and wrote 'Shall we ask old Hugo-Wugo to give us a thrippenny vanilla on the way home!!!' and passed it 30 across to Connie Baker, who turned absolutely purple and nearly burst out crying. All of them lolled and gaped, staring at the round clock, which seemed to have grown paler, too; the hands scarcely crawled.

'*Un peu de silence, s'il vous plaît,*' came from M. Hugo. He held up a puffy hand. 'Ladies, as it is so 'ot we will take no more notes today, but I will read you' – and he paused and smiled a broad, gentle smile – 'a little French poetry.' 35

'Go-od God!' moaned Francie Owen.

M. Hugo's smile deepened. 'Well, Mees Owen, you need not attend. You can paint yourself. You can 'ave my red ink as well as your black one.'

How well they knew the little blue book with red edges that he tugged out of his coat-tail 40 pocket! It had a green silk marker embroidered in forget-me-nots. They often giggled at it when he handed the book round. Poor old Hugo-Wugo! He adored reading poetry. He would begin, softly and calmly, and then gradually his voice would swell and vibrate and gather itself together, then it would be pleading and imploring and entreating, and then rising, rising triumphant, until it burst into light, as it were, and then – gradually again, it 45 ebbed, it grew soft and warm and calm and died down into nothingness.

The great difficulty was, of course, if you felt at all feeble, not to get the most awful fit of the giggles. Not because it was funny, really, but because it made you feel uncomfortable, queer, silly, and somehow ashamed for old Hugo-Wugo. But – oh dear – if he was going to inflict it on them in this heat …! 50

'Courage, my pet,' said Eve, kissing the languid carnation.

He began, and most of the girls fell forward, over the desks, their heads on their arms, dead at the first shot. Only Eve and Katie sat upright and still. Katie did not know enough French to understand, but Eve sat listening, her eyebrows raised, her eyes half veiled, and a smile that was like the shadow of her cruel little laugh, like the wing shadows of that cruel 55 little laugh fluttering over her lips. She made a warm, white cup of her fingers – the carnation inside. Oh, the scent! It floated across to Katie. It was too much. Katie turned away to the dazzling light outside the window.

Down below, she knew, there was a cobbled courtyard with stable buildings round it. That was why the French Room always smelled faintly of ammonia. It wasn't unpleasant; it was 60 even part of the French language for Katie – something sharp and vivid and – and – biting!

Now she could hear a man clatter over the cobbles and the jing-jang of the pails he carried. And now *Hoo-hor-her! Hoo-hor-her!* as he worked the pump and a great gush of water followed. Now he was flinging the water over something, over the wheels of a carriage perhaps. And she saw the wheel, propped up, clear of the ground, spinning round, flashing 65 scarlet and black, with great drops glancing off it. And all the while he worked the man kept up a high, bold whistling that skimmed over the noise of the water as a bird skims over the sea. He went away – he came back again leading a cluttering horse.

Hoo-hor-her! Hoo-hor-her! came from the pump. Now he dashed the water over the horse's legs and then swooped down and began brushing. 70

She *saw* him simply – in a faded shirt, his sleeves rolled up, his chest bare, all splashed with water – and as he whistled, loud and free, and as he moved, swooping and bending, Hugo-Wugo's voice began to warm, to deepen, to gather together, to swing, to rise – somehow or other to keep time with the man outside (Oh, the scent of Eve's carnation!) until they became one great rushing, rising triumphant thing, bursting into light, and then – 75

The whole room broke into pieces.

'Thank you ladies,' cried M. Hugo, bobbing at his high desk, over the wreckage.

And 'Keep it, dearest,' said Eve. '*Souvenir tendre,*' and she popped the carnation down the front of Katie's blouse.

Either with a partner or in a small group, talk about your reaction to this story *without your teacher's involvement*. What interests you most about it? What do you think Katherine Mansfield's purposes were in writing it? Do you feel it is written effectively?

Assume that your teacher does not know the story. Make a list of no more than five 'prompt' questions based on your own close reading of the text which are designed to draw out her/his personal response to it. Invite her/him to make notes on these for homework. In a future lesson, you could compare interpretations.

Chapter 2 How to read and write about poems

 2.1 How 'different' is poetry?

Main texts: 'Rape Poem', Marge Piercy
'The Garden of Love', William Blake
'Ballad of the Bread Man', Charles Causley
'The Song of Wandering Aengus', W.B. Yeats
'Telegrams', Carol Ann Duffy

 2.2 First responses: working your way around and into a poem

Main texts: 'Under a Ramshackle Rainbow', Ingemar Gustafson
'Death the Leveller', James Shirley
'The Send-Off', Wilfred Owen

 2.3 Writing up a critical analysis: from plan to essay

Main texts: 'The Send-Off' (continued)
'Morning Song', Sylvia Plath

 2.4 Patterns of meaning: commenting on verse form

Main texts: 'The Lesson', Edward Lucie-Smith
'Requiescat', Oscar Wilde

 2.5 Weighing every word: the poet's choice of language

Main texts: 'The Horses', Ted Hughes
'Miracle on St David's Day', Gillian Clarke
'La Belle Dame Sans Merci', John Keats
'In Time of Pestilence', Thomas Nashe

How 'different' is poetry?

What is your reaction to the following statements about poetry – specifically, poetry at A level? Talk about them in a small group.

1. Unlike novels and plays, poems don't usually tell a story. This makes them (a) less interesting and (b) more difficult to understand.

2. Poems always seem more compressed than other forms of literature. This means they have to be pored over and dissected for a long time before it becomes clear what they are about.

3. Poetry from the past is a particular sticking-point. The language is old-fashioned. Poets like the Romantics and the Metaphysicals were writing within 'conventions' which sometimes seem remote from modern readers.

4. What seems to be required at A level is 'detailed analysis' of a poem's style. In order to answer exam questions, there's a lot of work to be done on such things as imagery, rhyme schemes, metre, alliteration, etc.

5. Apparently there is a special jargon for writing about poetry that isn't needed for writing about novels. This jargon is often obscure: 'quatrain', 'enjambment', 'assonance', 'hexameter' and the like. It comes as rather a shock after GCSE, when there was less emphasis on poetry anyway.

These statements reflect the concerns of many A level students. Perhaps you share some of them. They are echoed by Liz Lochhead, a modern poet whose work is set for A level. She remembers her school experience of poetry like this:

> For most of school I had quite a strong distaste for poetry. ''Tis', ''Twas', 'Oh!', 'O!', 'Ah!', 'Wert', ludicrous inversions of normal word order, 'thou', 'thee', odes to skylarks, nightingales or Grecian urns, a prickling embarrassment and irritation against those airy-fairy beings who *refused just to put things down in plain English* … No wonder I preferred plays, stories, novels!

As a class, use the comments above to discuss with your teacher:

● why you think A level exam boards make the study of poetry compulsory;

● whether it *is* more 'difficult' to respond to poems than to other literary forms – and, if so, why;

● whether you feel that poets can communicate with their readers in ways that prose writers and playwrights cannot.

What is a poem anyway?

On the following pages are four poems commonly found on A level syllabuses. Read them through to yourself, one after the other. Simply try to be as open as possible to what each poet is trying to say.

Rape Poem

There is no difference between being raped
and being pushed down a flight of cement steps
except that the wounds also bleed inside.

There is no difference between being raped
and being run over by a truck   5
except that afterwards men ask if you enjoyed it.

There is no difference between being raped
and being bit on the ankle by a rattlesnake
except that people ask if your skirt was short
and why you were out alone anyhow.   10

There is no difference between being raped
and going head first through a windshield
except that afterwards you are afraid
not of cars
but half the human race.   15

The rapist is your boyfriend's brother.
He sits beside you in the movies eating popcorn.
Rape fattens on the fantasies of the normal male
like a maggot in garbage.

Fear of rape is a cold wind blowing   20
all of the time on a woman's hunched back.
Never to stroll alone on a sand road through pine woods,
never to climb a trail across a bald
without that aluminum in the mouth
when I see a man climbing toward me.   25

Never to open the door to a knock
without that razor just grazing the throat.
The fear of the dark sides of hedges,
the back seat of the car, the empty house
rattling keys like a snake's warning.   30

The fear of the smiling man
in whose pocket is a knife.
The fear of the serious man
in whose fist is locked hatred.

All it takes to cast a rapist is to be able to see your body   35
as jackhammer, as blowtorch, as adding-machine-gun.
All it takes is hating that body
your own, your self, your muscle that softens to flab.

All it takes is to push what you hate,
what you fear on to the soft alien flesh.   40
To bucket out invincible as a tank
armoured with treads without senses
to possess and punish in one act,
to rip up pleasure, to murder those who dare
live in the leafy flesh open to love.   45

Marge Piercy

The Garden of Love

I went to the Garden of Love,
And saw what I never had seen:
A Chapel was built in the midst,
Where I used to play on the green.

And the gates of this Chapel were shut,   5
And 'Thou shalt not' writ over the door;
So I turn'd to the Garden of Love
That so many sweet flowers bore;

And I saw it was filled with graves,
And tomb-stones where flowers should be;   10
And priests in black gowns were walking their rounds,
And binding with briars my joys and desires.

William Blake

Ballad of the Bread Man

Mary stood in the kitchen
　　Baking a loaf of bread.
An angel flew in through the window.
　　'We've a job for you,' he said.

'God in his big gold heaven,   5
　　Sitting in his big blue chair,
Wanted a mother for his little son.
　　Suddenly saw you there.'

Mary shook and trembled,
　　'It isn't true what you say.'   10
'Don't say that,' said the angel,
　　'The baby's on its way.'

Joesph was in his workshop
　　Planing a piece of wood.
'The old man's past it,' the neighbours said.   15
　　'That girl's been up to no good.'

'And who was that elegant fellow,'
　　They said, 'in the shiny gear?'
The things they said about Gabriel
　　Were hardly fit to hear.   20

Mary never answered,
　　Mary never replied.
She kept the information,
　　Like the baby, safe inside.

It was election winter.   25
　　They went to vote in town.
When Mary found her time had come
　　The hotels let her down.

The baby was born in an annexe
　　Next to the local pub.   30
At midnight, a delegation
　　Turned up from the Farmers' Club.

They talked about an explosion
    That made a hole in the sky,
Said they'd been sent to the Lamb and Flag   35
    To see God come down from on high.

A few days later a bishop
    And a five-star general were seen
With the head of an African country
    In a bullet-proof limousine.   40

'We've come,' they said, 'with tokens
    For the little boy to choose.'
Told the tale about war and peace
    In the television news.

After them, came the soldiers   45
    With rifle and bomb and gun,
Looking for enemies of the state.
    The family had packed and gone.

When they got back to the village
    The neighbours said, to a man,   50
'That boy will never be one of us,
    Though he does what he blessed well can.'

He went round to all the people
    A paper crown on his head.
Here is some bread from my father.   55
    Take, eat, he said.

Nobody seemed very hungry.
    Nobody seemed to care.
Nobody saw the god in himself
    Quietly standing there.   60

He finished up in the papers,
    He came to a very bad end.
He was charged with bringing the living to life.
    No man was that prisoner's friend.

There's only one kind of punishment   65
    To fit that kind of crime.
They rigged a trial and shot him dead.
    They were only just in time.

They lifted the young man by the leg,
    They lifted him by the arm,   70
They locked him in a cathedral
    In case he came to harm.

They stored him safe as water
    Under seven rocks.
One Sunday morning he burst out   75
    Like a jack-in-the-box.

Through the town he went walking.
    He showed them the holes in his head.
Now do you want any loaves? he cried.
    'Not today,' they said.   80

Charles Causley

The Song of Wandering Aengus

I went out to the hazel wood,
Because a fire was in my head,
And cut and peeled a hazel wand,
And hooked a berry to a thread;
And when white moths were on the wing,   5
And moth-like stars were flickering out,
I dropped the berry in a stream
And caught a little silver trout.

When I had laid it on the floor
I went to blow the fire a-flame,   10
But something rustled on the floor,
And someone called me by my name:
It had become a glimmering girl
With apple blossom in her hair
Who called me by my name and ran   15
And faded through the brightening air.

Though I am old with wandering
Through hollow lands and hilly lands,
I will find out where she has gone,
And kiss her lips and take her hands;   20
And walk among long dappled grass,
And pluck till time and tides are done,
The silver apples of the moon,
The golden apples of the sun.

W.B. Yeats

⊱┤⧫⟩⧽⭘⧼⟨⧫├⭤

As a class, consider:

- the ways in which any *two* of these poems could have been written as short stories or as drama;

- whether the writers' choice of poem-form helps them to convey their subject matter particularly well – or whether it makes no real difference. Focus on any aspects of form and style that you want.

In small groups, devise 'Five Tips for New Students of Poetry'. (Others before you have come up with things like 'Always read a poem in sentences, not line-by-line.') Write them down. Then present them to the whole class. Evaluate each one in turn, using the poems in this section to illustrate and justify what you say. End by agreeing on a class-list of 'Tips' in order of their importance.

Round off this section by discussing as a class whether the piece of writing below is a poem or a literary gimmick. Say whether you think its *form* helps to convey its theme, as you understand it.

⊱┤⧫⟩⧽⭘⧼⟨⧫├⭤

Telegrams

URGENT WHEN WE MEET COMPLETE STRANGERS DEAR STOP
THOUGH I COUNT THE HOURS TILL YOU ARE NEAR STOP
WILL EXPLAIN LATER DATE TILL THEN CANT WAIT STOP C

COMPLETELY FOGGED WHAT DO YOU MEAN BABY? STOP
CAN'T WE SLOPE OFF TO MY PLACE MAYBE? STOP   5
NOT POSS ACT NOT MET WITH RAISON DETRE STOP B

FOR GODS SAKE JUST TRUST ME SWEETHEART STOP
NATCH IT HURTS ME TOO WHEN WERE APART STOP
SHIT WILL HIT FAN UNLESS STICK TO PLAN STOP C

SHIT? FAN? TRUST? WHAT'S GOING ON HONEY? STOP
IF THIS IS A JOKE IT ISNT FUNNY STOP
INSIST ON TRUTH LOVE YOU BUT STRUTH! STOP B

YES I KNOW DARLING I LOVE YOU TOO STOP
TRY TO SEE PREDIC FROM MY POINT OF VIEW STOP
IF YOU DONT PLAY BALL I WONT COME AT ALL STOP C

PLEASE REPLY LAST TELEGRAM STOP
HAVE YOU FORGOTTEN THAT NIGHT IN MATLOCK? C

NO WAS TRYING TO TEACH YOU LESSON PET STOP
ALSO BECAUSE OF THESE AM IN DEBT STOP
TRUST WHEN NEXT MEET WILL PASSIONATELY GREET STOP B

NO NO NO NO GET IT THROUGH YOUR THICK HEAD STOP
IF SEEN WITH YOU AM AS GOOD AS DEAD STOP
THE WIFE WILL GUESS WEVE BEEN HAVING SEX STOP C

SO YOURE MARRIED? HA! I MIGHT HAVE GUESSED STOP
THOUGHT IT ODD YOU WORE STRING VEST STOP
AS SOON AS I MET YOU I WENT OVER THE TOP
NOW DO ME A FAVOUR PLEASE PLEASE STOP STOP B

Carol Ann Duffy

Now look back to Liz Lochhead's comment on her distaste for poetry when she was at school (page 25 above). It would be unfair to leave it unfinished. She goes on to say: 'At the time I didn't realize that the poet is *always* trying to put things down in plain, the *plainest* English, in as short and as clear and as *true* a way as possible.'

Have any of the poems in this section made you feel that this is an accurate description of what writing poetry is about? Give your honest opinion, either in a class discussion or in small groups.

First responses: working your way around and into a poem

Read the poem below to yourself, twice.

Work with a partner. First make yourselves enlarged photocopies of the poem. On the photocopied page – *not* on a separate sheet of paper – jot down anything which strikes you, interests you, puzzles you or pleases you about the poem.

Decide for yourselves how much conversation you want to have as you work. Annotate the poem in any way you wish: underline, circle, write on or alongside the text, use arrows, fill up the margins … Take between 20 and 30 minutes.

Under a Ramshackle Rainbow

A dead tree.
On a rotten branch sit two wingless birds. Among leaves
on the ground a man is searching for his hands.
It is fall.

A stagnant marsh.   5
On a mossy stone sits the man angling. The hook
is stuck in the waterlily.
The waterlily is stuck in the mud.

An overgrown ruin.
In the grass the man sleeps sitting up. A raindrop descends   10
in slow-motion through space.
Somewhere in the grass a pike flounders.

A dry well.
At the bottom lies a dead fly. In the wood nearby
a spider gropes through the fog.   15
The man is trapped in the spiderweb on the horizon.

An abandoned ant hill.
Above a little woodmarsh floats the man. The sun
is just going down. The man has already stopped growing.
The ants gather on the shore.   20

Ingemar Gustafson
translated from the Swedish by May Swenson

Now form a small group. Ideally, it should not include the partner with whom you have already worked. Compare your responses to the poem. The extent to which you draw on your jottings and annotations is up to you. Take as much time as you like.

The questionnaire below is designed to help you think about the way in which you have worked on 'Under a Ramshackle Rainbow'. Make a photocopy of it and tick the appropriate box opposite each question.

	Yes	No	Not sure
Do you feel that writing comments on the photocopied sheet helped you to 'get inside' the poem?			
Was it helpful to your response to have time to think things out for yourself?			
Did you benefit from asking your own questions as opposed to answering your teacher's?			
After you had spent 20–30 minutes jotting, did you find that you were starting to lose interest?			
Did your group discussion help to clarify responses you had already made to the poem?			
Did the discussion help you to take your insights into the poem further?			
Would you rather have conducted your discussion in a whole-class context than in a group?			
Are you used to working on poems in this way?			

Use your completed questionnaire to contribute to a class discussion on the merits/demerits of this method of starting out to study a poem at A level. Include in the discussion your thoughts about what other preparation may be needed if you were now asked to write a critical analysis of Ingemar Gustafson's poem.

Finally, in the light of this activity, discuss the way you are currently working on any of your poetry set texts. Do your answers to the questionnaire raise any issues you want to explore further?

Moving towards a written response

The poem below has been set by different examining boards as an A level 'unseen'. Make a first response to it, either by using the same approach as you took to 'Under a Ramshackle Rainbow' or by using a method which, as a class, you agree is the most helpful to you.

Death the Leveller

The glories of our blood and state
    Are shadows, not substantial things;
There is no armour against Fate;
    Death lays his icy hand on kings;
        Sceptre and Crown   5
        Must tumble down,
And in the dust be equal made
With the poor crooked scythe and spade.

Some men with swords may reap the field,
    And plant fresh laurels where they kill: 10
But their strong nerves at last must yield;
    They tame but one another still:
        Early or late
        They stoop to Fate,
And must give up their murmuring breath   15
When they, pale captives, creep to death.

The garlands wither on your brow;
    Then boast no more your mighty deeds!
Upon Death's purple altar now
    See where the victor-victim bleeds;   20
        Your heads must come
        To the cold tomb;
Only the actions of the just
Smell sweet, and blossom in their dust.

James Shirley

Moving from 'first response' to 'written analysis' is initially a matter of selecting and organising your material. With any poem, this process will become more manageable if you get into the habit of asking yourself these three key questions about the poem as a whole:

- What are the main ideas/feelings the poet is trying to express to me?

- How do the poem's form, style and language help to convey its ideas/feelings to me?

- How effective are the poem's form, style and language in conveying its ideas/feelings to me?

These questions provide you with a framework for planning and writing a poetry analysis. The plan on pages 36–7 demonstrates how to build up such a framework for analysing the poem below, which describes a platoon of First World War army recruits being sent from England to fight at the front line in France. Study both the poem and the plan before coming back to 'Death the Leveller'.

The Send-Off

Down the close, darkening lanes they sang their way
To the siding-shed,
And lined the train with faces grimly gay.

Their breasts were stuck all white with wreath and spray
As men's are, dead.   5

Dull porters watched them, and a casual tramp
Stood staring hard,
Sorry to miss them from the upland camp.
Then, unmoved, signals nodded, and a lamp
Winked to the guard.   10

So secretly, like wrongs hushed-up, they went.
They were not ours:
We never heard to which front these were sent.

Nor there if they yet mock what women meant
Who gave them flowers.   15

Shall they return to beatings of great bells
In wild train-loads?
A few, a few, too few for drums and yells,
May creep back, silent, to still village wells
Up half-known roads.   20

Wilfred Owen

Now turn your attention back to James Shirley's poem 'Death the Leveller' on page 34.

Whichever method you have used for making a first response, draw on it to construct a plan, similar to the one on 'The Send-Off', for writing about Shirley's poem. Base your plan on the three key questions (page 34). Include in it a substantial amount of quotation: you will find this invaluable when you come to write up your analysis in essay form.

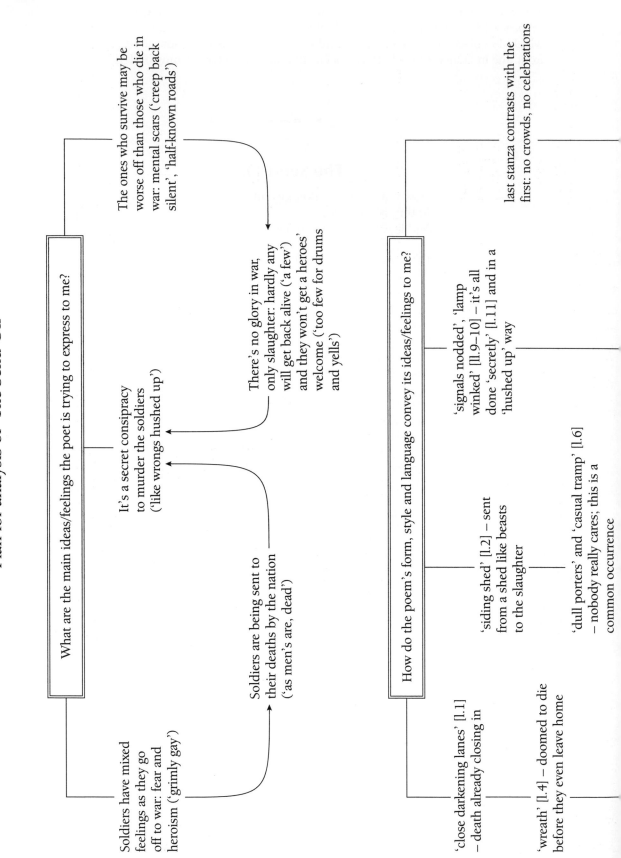

Plan for analysis of 'The Send-Off'

What are the main ideas/feelings the poet is trying to express to me?

The ones who survive may be worse off than those who die in war: mental scars ('creep back silent', 'half-known roads')

It's a secret consipracy to murder the soldiers ('like wrongs hushed up')

There's no glory in war, only slaughter: hardly any will get back alive ('a few') and they won't get a heroes' welcome ('too few for drums and yells')

Soldiers are being sent to their deaths by the nation ('as men's are, dead')

Soldiers have mixed feelings as they go off to war: fear and heroism ('grimly gay')

How do the poem's form, style and language convey its ideas/feelings to me?

last stanza contrasts with the first: no crowds, no celebrations

'signals nodded', 'lamp winked' [ll.9–10] – it's all done 'secretly' [l.11] and in a 'hushed up' way

'siding shed' [l.2] – sent from a shed like beasts to the slaughter

'dull porters' and 'casual tramp' [l.6] – nobody really cares; this is a common occurrence

'close darkening lanes' [l.1] – death already closing in

'wreath' [l.4] – doomed to die before they even leave home

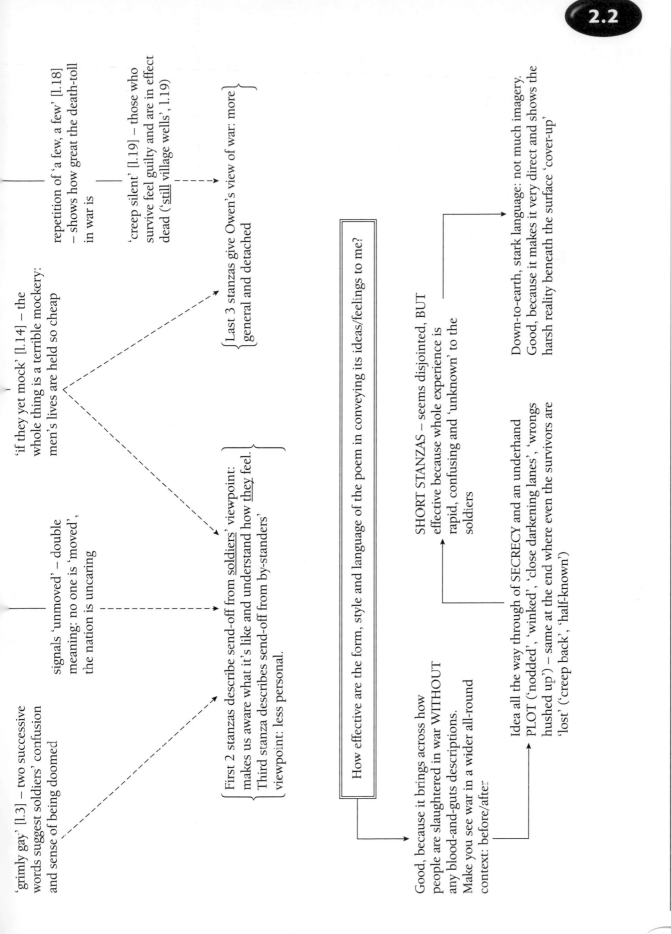

'grimly gay' [l.3] – two successive words suggest soldiers' confusion and sense of being doomed

signals 'unmoved' – double meaning: no one is 'moved', the nation is uncaring

'if they yet mock' [l.14] – the whole thing is a terrible mockery: men's lives are held so cheap

repetition of 'a few, a few' [l.18] – shows how great the death-toll in war is

'creep silent' [l.19] – those who survive feel guilty and are in effect dead ('still village wells', l.19)

{ Last 3 stanzas give Owen's view of war: more general and detached

{ First 2 stanzas describe send-off from soldiers' viewpoint: makes us aware what it's like and understand how they feel. Third stanza describes send-off from by-standers' viewpoint: less personal.

How effective are the form, style and language of the poem in conveying its ideas/feelings to me?

Good, because it brings across how people are slaughtered in war WITHOUT any blood-and-guts descriptions. Make you see war in a wider all-round context: before/after

Idea all the way through of SECRECY and an underhand PLOT ('nodded', 'winked', 'close darkening lanes', 'wrongs hushed up') – same at the end where even the survivors are 'lost' ('creep back', 'half-known')

SHORT STANZAS – seems disjointed, BUT effective because whole experience is rapid, confusing and 'unknown' to the soldiers

Down-to-earth, stark language: not much imagery. Good, because it makes it very direct and shows the harsh reality beneath the surface 'cover-up'

Writing up a critical analysis: from plan to essay

The first part of this section demonstrates how to turn the plan on pages 36–7 into a 'critical analysis' essay about 'The Send-Off'.

There is no such thing as a perfect essay: nor does anyone, including an examiner, expect you to write one. The point of the example below is to illustrate an end-product with which A level examiners would be more than satisfied. Read it slowly and carefully, referring back frequently to the plan. At the end of the essay, there are a number of 'points arising' to which you should pay close attention.

A critical analysis of 'The Send-Off' by Wilfred Owen

In 'The Send-Off', Wilfred Owen describes a group of army recruits beginning their journey by train to fight abroad at the front line. It quickly emerges that they are actually being 'sent off' to their almost certain deaths by a nation which cares nothing for their fate. Owen makes clear that the recruits are the victims of a sinister conspiracy, mere cannon fodder for the trenches. Few will return. Those who do may be less fortunate, Owen suggests, than their slaughtered comrades: the poem ends with a disturbing image of a handful of survivors whose minds are permanently scarred by what they have been through. Overall, the poem is a strongly felt, bitter protest against the way in which the nation's young men are inhumanly sacrificed in the name of a false and hollow patriotism.

The opening stanza depicts the recruits on the first stage of their journey. They march 'down close darkening lanes', an image which suggests not only that dusk is falling but also that death is already closing in on them, inescapably. They sing to keep their spirits up and board the train 'with faces grimly gay'. Already, perhaps, they know inside themselves that they are doomed, an impression strengthened by the emphasis on 'grimly'.

This feeling is reinforced in the next stanza. To decorate their tunics, the soldiers are given flowers which include 'wreath' as well as 'spray'. The choice of wreath is morbidly ironic : it anticipates their likely deaths, as Owen stresses further by his simile 'As men's are, dead'. It is noticeable that they do not board the military train from a main-line platform but from a 'siding-shed'. The impression given here is that they are being transported secretly, and also (since it is a 'shed') like animals being sent to the slaughter. The fact that they are cannon fodder has to be kept from public attention for obvious reasons.

The nation's indifference to the soldiers is underlined by the way in which they are watched only by 'dull' porters and 'a casual tramp'. This is certainly not a triumphal or a heroic send-off. Owen implies that they are not the first, and will not be the last, platoon to be ferried off to war 'secretly'. The routine seems well-established. There is something sinister and underhand about the way 'the signals nodded' and 'a lamp / Winked at the guard'. With a 'nod and a wink' the soldiers are ushered to their deaths, missed only by a passing tramp.

5

10

15

20

25

30

At this point, roughly half way through the poem, Owen changes the perspective and gives his own view of what is being done to the soldiers. The poem now becomes more explicit about the fact that the whole affair is 'hushed-up'. The simile 'like wrongs' suggests two things. The soldiers are being treated as if they have committed a crime for which they must be punished, when in fact they are innocent. Owen also hints that the military authorities are guilty of 'wrongs' in treating them so callously. The soldiers are never heard of again – 'We never heard to which front these were sent'. Their lives are held so cheap by those in command that the flowers they were given to celebrate their departure become merely a mockery: 'Nor there if they yet mock what women meant'. What the women, presumably wives and sweethearts, 'meant' was love and concern; what the authorities have in mind is precisely the opposite.

The poem ends with a contrast. Instead of the celebration which the soldiers perhaps imagined – 'great bells … wild train loads' – those who do return will be greeted only by silence and strangeness. There will not be many of them, as the repetition of 'A few, a few, too few …' emphasises. They will 'creep back' furtively, as if feeling guilty to be alive when so many of their comrades are dead. It may also be that they are now aware of how the nation saw them as expendable and so feel that they have no 'home' to come back to.

What is certain is that the survivors will be changed for ever by war. Owen portrays them as 'silent'. They have been traumatised by what they have experienced. After living through such horror, what is there to say to families and friends? They are pictured returning to where they lived – 'village wells' – but they feel like strangers: once-familiar roads are now only 'half known' to them. Their horrific experience on the battlefield means that, in a sense, they will always 'live' there.

The poem is very compressed. It is written in short stanzas which, on first reading, make it seem rather disjointed. This may be deliberate on Owen's part, reflecting the way in which the whole process has been rapid, confusing and disorientating for the men. They were whisked away 'under cover', and the few who survive feel estranged from their former selves.

Owen's style is direct and the language is stark. This is appropriate in a poem which strips away the 'hushed-up' layers of secrecy and shows us the truth about how the nation's youth was betrayed. There are no graphic descriptions of carnage or bloodshed, just a 'before and after' approach to the subject. This is effective because it makes us see war in a wider context. After reading 'The Send-Off', we know why so many men were casually slaughtered in World War I. The fact that they were 'killed' by their own country makes Owen's poem particularly chilling.

>╶┤╺◀╸╴○╴╶▶╺┤╸◀

Points arising

If this analysis were being assessed by an A level examiner, the aspects of it listed below would gain considerable credit. Read them through carefully – and learn from them.

- **First paragraph.** This presents a summary, or overview, of the poem's main themes. It is general but not vague. It provides a clear outline of the key points which will be explored in detail as the essay develops.

- **Subsequent paragraphs.** These combine insights into the poet's ideas and feelings with comment on aspects of his style and language. Examples from the text are given to exemplify the points being made. 'Themes' and 'style' are not treated separately but together: the writer is simultaneously drawing on material from points gathered under key questions 1 and 2 in the plan.

- **Paragraph links.** The writer reflects the development of ideas and feelings in the poem by the way in which the essay's paragraphs progress in a connected way. (See, for example, the progression from paragraph 2 to 3 and that from 6 to 7). Where the poem takes a 'new turn', the paragraphing also reflects this: see the beginning of paragraph 5.

- **Topic sentences.** Each paragraph begins with a statement which signals what the essential subject matter of that paragraph will be. This usually takes the form of a concise, straightforward observation such as 'What is certain is that the survivors will be changed for ever by war' (paragraph 7).

- **Reference and quotation.** All the way through, the writer remains close to the text of the poem. No general statement is made without being either reached through, or supported by, close examination of the text and textual reference. Quotation is built into the writer's own sentences, so that it is integral to the analysis rather than 'tacked on' as an after-thought. Normally, a short phrase quoted from the poem, or even a single word, will be adequate: quoting a block of five lines gives away the fact that you probably have nothing to say about them.

- **Key question 3:** 'How effective are the form, style and language of the poem …?'. The last two paragraphs address this question explicitly. However, judgements about the poem's effectiveness are also being made implicitly throughout the whole essay. Check to see.

- **Personal response.** As you read, you should be aware of a personal intelligence and an individual interpretation emerging from the writer's close focus on the text. It is not necessary constantly to repeat 'I think …' or 'In my opinion …' to demonstrate that you are responding 'personally': this will be self-evident if you think clearly about the details in the text as you write the whole essay.

- **Terminology.** Little, if anything, in the writer's expression will strike you as being drawn from a 'special' language-bank of jargon. A level examiners are neither impressed by, nor likely to give credit for, highly technical terminology for its own sake. What they require most is a clear, concise essay style. (There is more advice on this in Chapter 9.)

Discuss with your teacher any other 'points arising' from this example. Prepare for doing so by making your own list of matters you would like to address.

In practice

Use what you have learned about writing a critical analysis either to turn your plan on 'Death the Leveller' into an essay or, if you feel confident enough, to plan and write an analysis of the poem below. It was written by Sylvia Plath following the birth of her first child.

>─┤◄►·◎·◄►┤─◄

Morning Song

Love set you going like a fat gold watch.
The midwife slapped your footsoles, and your bald cry
Took its place among the elements.

Our voices echo, magnifying your arrival. New statue.
In a drafty museum, your nakedness
Shadows our safety. We stand round blankly as walls.

5

I'm no more your mother
Than the cloud that distils a mirror to reflect its own slow
Effacement at the wind's hand.

All night your moth-breath   10
Flickers among the fat pink roses. I wake to listen:
A far sea moves in my ear.

One cry, and I stumble from bed, cow-heavy and floral
In my Victorian nightgown.
Your mouth opens clean as a cat's. The window square   15

Whitens and swallows its dull stars. And now you try
Your handful of notes;
The clear vowels rise like balloons.

Sylvia Plath

Patterns of meaning: commenting on verse form

How to write meaningfully about verse form: a common sense approach

What do examiners expect when they ask you to 'comment on verse form'? There is only one answer, and it is a simple one:

Show how the form in which the poem is written helps to convey its meaning.

If you learn to do this, writing in a clear and straightforward way, you will earn full credit. During the A level course, you will absorb from your teacher(s) all the 'terminology' you need. It does not resemble a foreign language.

The form or 'patterning' (a more helpful word) of a poem is part of its meaning. This is why a competent analysis will always take some account of the pattern/shape which the poet creates. Your starting-point should always be to get a 'feel' of the patterning of any poem, that is, of the way in which the whole poem is constructed and of the way in which the parts of the pattern combine together to build up an overall shape. Then go on to (a) describe it, and (b) relate it to the ideas and feelings the poet is trying to express.

The rest of this section suggests a method of doing this.

Sectioning a poem

As a class, read and discuss the poem below. It is about the feelings of a ten-year-old boy when news of his father's death is brought to him at the private school where he is a boarding pupil.

>─┤◄►•─O─►┤◄

The Lesson

'Your father's gone,' my bald headmaster said.
His shiny dome and brown tobacco jar
Splintered at once in tears. It wasn't grief.
I cried for knowledge which was bitterer
Than any grief. For there and then I knew   5
That grief has uses – that a father dead
Could bind the bully's fist a week or two;
And then I cried for shame, then for relief.

I was a month past ten when I learned this:
I still remember how the noise was stilled   10
In school-assembly when my grief came in.
Some goldfish in a bowl quietly sculled
Around their shining prison on its shelf.
They were indifferent. All the other eyes
Were turned towards me. Somewhere in myself   15
Pride, like a goldfish, flashed a sudden fin.

Edward Lucie-Smith

>─┤◄►•─O─►┤◄

When you have worked through to a clear sense of the various feelings that his father's death causes, turn your attention to Lucie-Smith's patterning of the poem. Make this the focus of the last phase of your discussion.

Now look at the method demonstrated below for describing the form and structure of this poem. It is based on:

- tracing the development of ideas/feelings in the poem as a whole;

- identifying the keynotes of each stanza;

- pin-pointing any oppositions or tensions which emerge in the course of the poem;

- sectioning the poem in diagram form so that its pattern is clearly 'visible' on the page.

Poem-sectioning diagram

The Lesson

Stanza 1	KEYNOTES	DEVELOPMENTS	OPPOSITIONS
'Your father's gone,' my bald headmaster said. His shiny dome and brown tobacco jar Splintered at once in tears. It wasn't grief.	CRIED	News of death: sudden shock and sadness	Adult/Child
I cried for knowledge that was bitterer Than any grief. For there and then I knew That grief has uses – that a father dead Could bind the bully's fist a week or two;	'knowledge'	Death stops the bullying: feels happy	Sad/Happy
And then I cried for shame, then for relief.	'shame, relief'	Guilt follows from self-knowledge	Shame/Relief

Stanza 2			
I was a month past ten when I learned this:	PRIDE		
I still remember how the noise was stilled In school-assembly when my grief came in.	'noise was stilled'	Self-importance on a formal occasion	Public setting/ Private feeling
Some goldfish in a bowl quietly sculled Around their shining prison on its shelf.			
They were indifferent. All the other eyes Were turned towards me. Somewhere in myself	'turned towards me'	Centre of attention	Collective response/ Personal response
Pride, like a goldfish, flashed a sudden fin.	LEARNED 'The Lesson'	School celebrity: enjoys this	Child/Adult (within himself)

Study the diagram closely. How does it attempt to relate the form of the poem to its meaning? Does it take you any further than you got in your discussion?

Now describe the form and structure of the poem below by 'sectioning' it on a photocopy in a similar way. Remember that your purpose is to relate its pattern to whatever ideas/feelings you think the poet is trying to express.

>─┤◄►─·─○─·◄►├─◄

Requiescat*

Tread lightly, she is near
    Under the snow;
Speak gently, she can hear
    The daisies grow.

All her bright golden hair   5
    Tarnished with rust,
She that was young and fair
    Fallen to dust.

Lily-like, white as snow,
    She hardly knew   10
She was a woman, so
    Sweetly she grew.

Coffin-board, heavy stone,
    Lie on her breast;
I vex my heart alone,   15
    She is at rest.

Peace, peace; she cannot hear
    Lyre[†] or sonnet;
All my life's buried here.
    Heap earth upon it.   20

Oscar Wilde

* **Requiescat**: Latin: 'rest in peace'; the occasion of this poem was the death of Wilde's 13-year-old sister
[†] **Lyre**: an ancient harp, often played to accompany a mournful song; the lyre-flower is also called 'bleeding heart'

Weighing every word: the poet's choice of language

Why this word rather than that?

The majority of marks for a critical analysis are given for your ability to comment on the poet's choice of language (or 'diction' as it is sometimes called). Good poets, like good writers of anything, deliberate long and hard about the words they choose: you have to assume that no words that reach print get there by accident or through some airy-fairy process of 'inspiration'. Whether you judge them to be used effectively is another matter – and one of the more interesting challenges of analysing a poem.

Not surprisingly, students are often uncertain what to say about a poet's 'choice of language'. There it is, the complete poem, staring at you from the page: what is there to say? Your starting-point is to remember that once the page was blank. For every word the poet finally decided on, many more possible words were considered – and rejected. Ask yourself, then: why does s/he use *this* word (or phrase) rather than scores of alternatives that could have been chosen? This deceptively simple question will lead to you being able to make relevant and perceptive comments on language choice.

Practise asking, and answering, the question by discussing as a class the opening part of Ted Hughes's poem 'The Horses', in which he describes a pre-dawn walk though the Yorkshire countryside.

from The Horses

I climbed through woods in the hour-before-dawn dark.
Evil air, a frost-making stillness,

Not a leaf, not a bird, –
A world cast in frost. I came out above the wood

Where my breath left tortuous statues in the iron light.   5
But the valleys were draining the darkness

Till the moorline – blackening dregs of the brightening grey –
Halved the sky ahead. And I saw the horses:

Huge in the dense grey – ten together –
Megalith-still. They breathed, making no move,   10

With draped manes and tilted hind-hooves,
Making no sound.

I passed: not one snorted or jerked its head.
Grey silent fragments

Of a grey silent world.   15

Ted Hughes

To get your discussion started:

● Why might the air seem 'evil'?

● Why are the woods a 'world' – and why does Hughes describe this world as being 'cast' in frost?

● 'Statues' seems a strange word to apply to breath. Give your opinion about why Hughes does so.

In the poem on page 46, Gillian Clarke describes visiting a mental hospital to read poetry to a group of patients. With a partner, consider the effect of the words and phrases printed in bold type.

Miracle on St David's Day

An afternoon yellow and **open-mouthed**
with daffodils. The sun **treads** the path
among cedars and enormous oaks.
It might be a country house, guests strolling,
the rumps of gardeners between nursery shrubs.   5

I am reading poetry to the insane.
An old woman, interrupting, offers
as many buckets of coal as I need.
A beautiful **chestnut**-haired boy listens
entirely absorbed. A schizophrenic   10

on a good day, they tell me later.
In a **cage of first March sun** a woman
sits not listening, not seeing, not feeling.
In her neat clothes the woman is **absent**.
A big, mild man is tenderly led   15

to his chair. He has never spoken.
His labourer's hands on his knees, he **rocks**
gently to the rhythm of the poems.
I read to their presences, absences,
to the big, dumb labouring man as he rocks.   20

He is suddenly standing, silently,
huge and mild, but I feel afraid. Like slow
movement of spring water or the first bird
of the year in the **breaking darkness**,
the labourer's voice recites 'The Daffodils'*.   25

The nurses are **frozen**, alert; the patients
seem to listen. He is hoarse but word-perfect.
Outside the daffodils are **still as wax**,
a thousand, ten thousand, their **syllables**
unspoken, their creams and yellows still.   30

Forty years ago, in a Valleys school,
the class recited poetry by rote.
Since the dumbness of misery **fell**
he has remembered there was a **music**
of speech and that once he had something to say.   35

When he's done, before the applause, we **observe**
the flowers' silence. A thrush sings
and the daffodils are **aflame**.

Gillian Clarke

* 'The Daffodils': the well-known poem by Wordsworth

You will have found that paying close attention to Gillian Clarke's choice of language actually 'opens up' the whole poem for you. This is not just a question of identifying the main ideas and feelings in the poem. You should by now have started to be aware of other aspects of the poet's craft covered in previous sections: the patterning of the poem, the development of its theme, the effectiveness of the way it is written, and so on. Starting your study of any poem with the question 'Why this word/phrase rather than that?' is, therefore, a method that will pay off.

Use it to plan and write a full critical analysis of one of the two poems that follow. Draw on what, to you, has been the most helpful guidance for reading and writing about poems given in this chapter.

>──<◆>──○──<◆>──<

La Belle Dame Sans Merci

O what can ail thee, knight-at arms,
    Alone and palely loitering?
The sedge has withered from the lake,
    And no birds sing.

O what can ail thee, knight-at-arms,   5
    So haggard and so woe-begone?
The squirrel's granary is full,
    And the harvest's done.

I see a lily on thy brow
    With anguish moist and fever-dew,   10
And on thy cheeks a fading rose
    Fast withereth too.

'I met a lady in the meads,
    Full beautiful – a faery's child,
Her hair was long, her foot was light,   15
    And her eyes were wild.

'I made a garland for her head,
    And bracelets too, and fragrant zone,
She looked at me as she did love,
    And made sweet moan.   20

'I set her on my pacing steed,
    And nothing else saw all day long,
For sideways would she lean, and sing
    A faery's song.

'She found me roots of relish sweet,   25
    And honey wild, and manna dew,
And sure in language strange she said –
    'I love thee true!'

'She took me to her elfin grot,
    And there she wept and sighed full sore,   30
And there I shut her wild, wild eyes
    With kisses four.

'And there she lullèd me asleep,
    And there I dreamed – ah! woe betide!
The latest dream I ever dreamed   35
    On the cold hill's side.

'I saw pale kings, and princes too,
      Pale warriors, death-pale were they all;
They cried – 'La belle Dame sans merci
      Hath thee in thrall!'   40

I saw their starved lips in the gloam,
      With horrid warning gapèd wide,
And I awoke and found them here,
      On the cold hill's side.

And this is why I sojourn here,   45
      Alone and palely loitering,
Though the sedge is withered from the lake,
      And no birds sing.'

John Keats

The poem below was written in 1593 when the plague, or 'pestilence', wiped out roughly a fifth of London's population.

In Time of Pestilence

Adieu, farewell earth's bliss!
This world uncertain is:
Fond* are life's lustful joys,
Death proves them all but toys.
None from his darts can fly;   5
I am sick, I must die –
      Lord, have mercy on us!

Rich men, trust not in wealth,
Gold cannot buy you health;
Physic himself must fade,   10
All things to end are made;
The plague full swift goes by;
I am sick, I must die –
      Lord, have mercy on us!

* **Fond**: foolish

Beauty is but a flower   15
Which wrinkles will devour;
Brightness falls from the air;
Queens have died young and fair;
Dust hath closed Helen's eye;
I am sick, I must die –   20
          Lord, have mercy on us!

Strength stoops unto the grave,
Worms feed on Hector brave;
Swords may not fight with fate;
Earth still holds ope her gate;   25
Come, come! the bells do cry;
I am sick, I must die –
          Lord, have mercy on us!

Haste therefore each degree*
To welcome destiny;   30
Heaven is our heritage,
Earth but a player's stage.
Mount we unto the sky;
I am sick, I must die –
          Lord, have mercy on us!   35

Thomas Nashe

* **degree**: class of person

>−!−<>−·−O−·−<>−!−<

Looking further …

The purpose of this chapter has been to suggest some ways of thinking, talking and writing your way into poems. The intention is not to provide you with an all-purpose A level course in poetry appreciation. As you work on 'set' poetry texts in class, you will need to develop further skills, such as recognising and commenting on the effects that poets achieve through their use of imagery, sound, rhythm, rhyme and so on. These skills are best acquired in the context of studying the work of particular poets for whatever syllabus you are following.

In Chapter 5 of this book you will find guidance for tackling unseen poems under exam conditions. Chapter 9 will help to extend your vocabulary when writing about literature in general and poetry in particular: you may wish to glance ahead to it now.

Extensions

Section 5 of Chapter 5 gives detailed guidance on *comparing* poems with a similar theme. At a later stage, you could return to some of the poems in this chapter for practice in making comparisons. The following would be particularly suitable:

- 'The Song of Wandering Aengus' and 'La Belle Dame Sans Merci';
- 'Death the Leveller' and 'In Time of Pestilence'.

Chapter 3 Studying a novel in less than six months

 3.1 Inside out, outside in: two ways of 'doing' novels in English

Main text: *Animal Farm*, George Orwell

 3.2 Landmark maps and character-tracking

Main texts: *Animal Farm* (continued)
The Go-Between, L.P. Hartley

 3.3 Interrogations: freeze-framing the text

Main texts: 'Country Lovers', Nadine Gordimer
'Country Living', Guy de Maupassant

 3.4 Networks: selecting material, exploring links

Main texts: 'Country Lovers' (continued)
Mansfield Park, Jane Austen

Inside out, outside in: two ways of 'doing' novels in English

The 'inside out' method

A Year 12 class, 'doing' Jane Austen's novel *Mansfield Park* as a set text for A level, worked through the book with their teacher, chapter by chapter, for more than six months. Their notes were extremely thorough: one student compiled a total of over 40,000 words! Not surprisingly, they felt that they had 'covered everything' they could possibly be asked in the exam.

They had other feelings too. This is a selection of them, quoted *verbatim* from written comments they made after taking their A level, in which their results on the whole were excellent:

- The way we did the book killed it for me. If I'd read it outside the exam course, I'd probably have enjoyed it … I've read *Emma* and I quite liked that … but *Mansfield* got to be a mountain we had to climb week after week, just because it was there for the exam. Like Everest.

- I'll never read another book by Jane Austen in my life. And I say that after getting a Grade B in English, which must sound pretty ungrateful …

- I can't say I actually enjoyed it … but the way we did it gave me confidence that we'd done it properly. I've got friends at [another school] who were just told to read the book by themselves and make their own notes on it – so really we were lucky, I suppose.

- After a while, I just switched off and wrote down what our teacher said. I did English because I like to put my own point of view forward – and I know that was how a lot of us felt … but if we had discussed everything in it, it would have us taken even longer to get through it than it did.

- Boring! That's not a criticism of Mr _____ . If the examiners want us to know the book inside out and back to front, I suppose that slogging through it is the only way. You're doing A level to get a good grade, so … It was a shame, though. It spoiled the lessons, really.

In a group, discuss your reactions to these comments. Do you identify with any of them?

Think seriously about the reasons why you are taking A level English. Can you suggest any ways of studying a novel apart from 'slogging through it' in class?

The 'outside in' method

A level students often admit to becoming 'bogged down' or confused by a lengthy novel. More often than not, the reason is that they wrestle with a mass of textual detail before mentally constructing a general frame into which such detail can be fitted. In other words, they lose sight of the wood for the trees.

The 'outside in' method is designed to reverse this situation. It is based on the following common-sense principles:

- The priority is to establish a clear idea of the shape or pattern of any novel as a whole before further work on it gets under way.

- For readers to make sense of a novel, an understanding of its overall shape must grow out of their own response to it rather than other people's.

- Once a novel's 'whole shape' is clearly fixed in the reader's mind, working on the details of the text – in class discussion, for instance – will be:
  - easier to understand;
  - able to be done more quickly;
  - likely to be done with more confidence;
  - and, above all, more enjoyable.

Discuss these principles with your teacher. What might be the advantages and/or disadvantages for studying novels at A level of the approach that they imply?

A basic example: working on Animal Farm for GCSE

The example of the 'outside in' method that follows has been chosen precisely because it was not done at A level, nor by students who were likely to aspire to A level. Judge for yourselves how effectively it works. The example is based on George Orwell's *Animal Farm*, a synopsis of which is given below.

> The animals on Manor Farm are treated oppressively by Farmer Jones. Inspired by three pigs – Old Major, Snowball and Napoleon – they succeed in driving out their human masters. After a famous victory at the Battle of the Cowshed, seven animal Commandments are formulated to guarantee that All Animals Are Equal.
>
> Gradually, however, things start to go wrong. Napoleon recruits and trains his own private 'army' of dogs, banishes Snowball and moves into the farmhouse where he lives in luxury. The other animals, notably Boxer, the strong and willing horse, are treated with increasing tyranny by the pigs, who are secretly trading with neighbouring farmers. After the animals lose the Battle of the Windmill, Boxer dies and is sold to the knacker's yard by the pigs for their own private profit. By the end of the book, the pigs have become indistinguishable from humans with whom they now share the commercial ownership of the farm. The other animals are again treated as slaves; they are back where they started.
>
> Some animals, it transpires, are More Equal Than Others.

The GCSE students in question were a Year 10 class. Most of them had learning difficulties and needed considerable help in reading *Animal Farm*. As a coursework assignment they were asked:

> *What makes the animals' rebellion go well at first? Why does it fail in the end?*

In small groups, they worked on getting clear the novel's whole shape by making 'notes' as if *Animal Farm* were a board game. Look carefully at what they produced (page 53). Then discuss with your teacher:

- What evidence is there that the students understood the book as a whole?

- What attitude do you think they had towards 'making notes' on it?

- How far do you think their 'notes' helped them to write on the question they were set?

- In your opinion, is this approach any more than just a gimmick suitable for 'slow learners' – as opposed, say, to A level students?

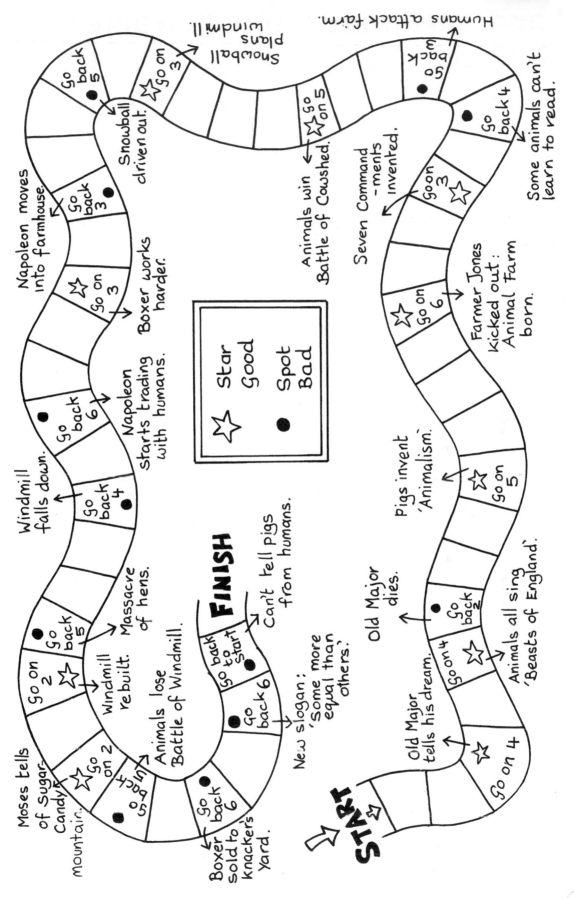

Humans attack farm.

Snowball plans windmill.

Go on 3

Go back 5

Go back 4

Go back 4

Go on 5

Go on 3

Animals win Battle of Cowshed.

Seven Command-ments invented.

Snowball driven out.

Go back 3

Napoleon moves into farmhouse.

Go on 3

Boxer works harder.

Go on 6

Farmer Jones kicked out: Animal Farm born.

Go back 6

Napoleon starts trading with humans.

☆ Star Good

● Spot Bad

Pigs invent 'Animalism'.

Go back 4

Windmill falls down.

Go on 5

Go on 2

Go back 5

Windmill rebuilt.

Massacre of hens.

Animals lose Battle of Windmill.

FINISH

Can't tell pigs from humans.

Old Major dies.

Go back 2

Go on 2

Go back 6

New slogan: 'Some more equal than others'.

Animals all sing 'Beasts of England'.

Moses tells of Sugar Candy mountain.

Go on 2

Go back 5

Go back 6

Boxer sold to Knacker's Yard.

Old Major tells his dream.

Go on 4

Go on 4

START

Landmark maps and character-tracking

After one straight read-through of a novel, it is helpful to draw out its overall 'plan' or pattern in diagram form. Decide on just a few key episodes – no more than four or five – which, for you, represent the most important landmarks in the plot. Make a simple 'map' to show (a) exactly what these landmarks are, and (b) how they connect up with one another.

Inevitably, what you produce will over-simplify the novel's plot. At this early stage, that doesn't matter: you can refine it later as, with further work in class, your knowledge of the book increases. This kind of map serves three principal purposes:

- You will establish a clear outline of major events in the whole book.

- You will accurately identify links between the main episodes in the story.

- You will avoid becoming bogged down in what, after your first encounter with a novel, often seems like distracting detail.

Most students find this to be a more useful and accessible form of note-making than lengthy chapter-summaries or points scribbled down during class discussion.

On page 55 is an example of a map for *Animal Farm* in the form of a simple flow diagram. It was produced by a Year 12 A level student working on the novel as an example of satirical writing (see the assignment title at the head of the flow-chart). It took a week to produce and went through three drafts. Once completed to her satisfaction, however, it provided the basis for an essay which turned out to be of a very high standard. She made no other notes.

Look at it, preferably with your teacher, and consider why the student may have found it so useful. Bearing in mind the topic she was exploring, list the advantages of this form of note-making as opposed to others which could have been used.

Tracking character development

Trace the development of X's character during the course of the novel, making clear the most important influences on him/her.

This is a demand familiar from GCSE, and one that you will meet again at A level. The mapping activity below gives you practice in tackling this typical kind of task.

You will be concentrating on four landmarks from L.P. Hartley's novel *The Go-Between* (1953). Read carefully the brief synopsis of its plot which follows, even if you are already familiar with the book.

> Set in 1900, the story centres on Leo, a twelve-year-old boy whose invitation to spend the summer holiday with an upper-class family in Norfolk introduces him to a completely new style of life. It also confronts him with a set of circumstances far beyond his previous experience. Marian, the elder daughter of the family, is conducting a secret affair with Ted Burgess, a tenant-farmer on their Brandham Hall estate. For social reasons, she is expected to marry the aristocratic Lord Trimingham: their engagement is about to be announced.
>
> Marian and Ted hit on the idea of using Leo as a 'go-between' to send letters to one another in which they arrange sexual meetings. At first, Leo has no suspicion of what he is caught up in. He accepts the story that they need to correspond privately on 'business' matters. Even when

Flow-chart demonstrating how the events in *Animal Farm* show human equality to be 'an impossible ideal, not a practical reality'

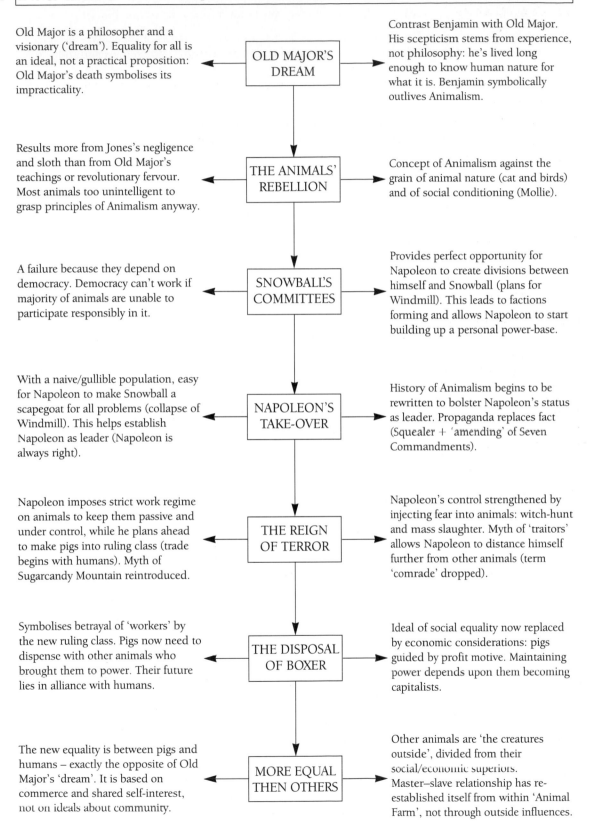

Old Major is a philosopher and a visionary ('dream'). Equality for all is an ideal, not a practical proposition: Old Major's death symbolises its impracticality.

OLD MAJOR'S DREAM

Contrast Benjamin with Old Major. His scepticism stems from experience, not philosophy: he's lived long enough to know human nature for what it is. Benjamin symbolically outlives Animalism.

Results more from Jones's negligence and sloth than from Old Major's teachings or revolutionary fervour. Most animals too unintelligent to grasp principles of Animalism anyway.

THE ANIMALS' REBELLION

Concept of Animalism against the grain of animal nature (cat and birds) and of social conditioning (Mollie).

A failure because they depend on democracy. Democracy can't work if majority of animals are unable to participate responsibly in it.

SNOWBALL'S COMMITTEES

Provides perfect opportunity for Napoleon to create divisions between himself and Snowball (plans for Windmill). This leads to factions forming and allows Napoleon to start building up a personal power-base.

With a naive/gullible population, easy for Napoleon to make Snowball a scapegoat for all problems (collapse of Windmill). This helps establish Napoleon as leader (Napoleon is always right).

NAPOLEON'S TAKE-OVER

History of Animalism begins to be rewritten to bolster Napoleon's status as leader. Propaganda replaces fact (Squealer + 'amending' of Seven Commandments).

Napoleon imposes strict work regime on animals to keep them passive and under control, while he plans ahead to make pigs into ruling class (trade begins with humans). Myth of Sugarcandy Mountain reintroduced.

THE REIGN OF TERROR

Napoleon's control strengthened by injecting fear into animals: witch-hunt and mass slaughter. Myth of 'traitors' allows Napoleon to distance himself further from other animals (term 'comrade' dropped).

Symbolises betrayal of 'workers' by the new ruling class. Pigs now need to dispense with other animals who brought them to power. Their future lies in alliance with humans.

THE DISPOSAL OF BOXER

Ideal of social equality now replaced by economic considerations: pigs guided by profit motive. Maintaining power depends upon them becoming capitalists.

The new equality is between pigs and humans – exactly the opposite of Old Major's 'dream'. It is based on commerce and shared self-interest, not on ideals about community.

MORE EQUAL THEN OTHERS

Other animals are 'the creatures outside', divided from their social/economic superiors. Master–slave relationship has re-established itself from within 'Animal Farm', not through outside influences.

he realises they are lovers, his naivety prevents him from being aware of what is really at stake. Only at the very end of the novel, when he sees Marian and Ted making love, does Leo understand what their 'forbidden' relationship means for everyone – including himself.

The novel's central theme is the pre-adolescent Leo's growing awareness of sexuality – as well as other aspects of the adult world, such as the intricate connection between marriage and social class.

Your first landmark is Extract 1, from the novel's third chapter. Read it to yourself twice.

>─┼─◄►──○──◄►─┼─◄

from **The Go-Between**
by L.P. Hartley

Leo has recently arrived at Brandham Hall. He feels rather ill-at-ease, partly because the weather is very hot and he has brought only his winter clothes. Marian takes him to Norwich to buy a summer outfit. In this extract, the light suit she has chosen for him is being generally admired.

(1) My spiritual transformation took place in Norwich: it was there that, like an emerging butterfly, I was first conscious of my wings. I had to wait until tea for the public acknowledgement of my apotheosis*. My appearance was greeted with cries of acclaim, as if the whole party had been living for this moment. Instead of gas-jets, fountains of water seemed to spring up around me. I was made to stand on a chair and 5 revolve like a planet, while everything of my new outfit that was visible was subjected to admiring or facetious comment.

'What a cool customer he looks!' said someone, wittily. 'Yes,' said another, 'just like a cucumber, and the same shade of green!'

They discussed what kind of green it was. 'Lincoln green!' said another voice. 'He 10 might be Robin Hood!' I was delighted by that, and saw myself roaming the greenwood with Maid Marian. 'Don't you *feel* different?' somebody asked me, almost as indignantly as if I had denied it. 'Yes,' I exclaimed, 'I feel quite another person!' – which was less than the truth.

They all laughed at this. The talk drifted away from me, as it does from children, 15 and I got down awkwardly from my pedestal, realizing that my moment was over; but what a moment it had been.

The purpose of your map will be to chart Leo's character development throughout the novel. On the basis of the synopsis and a close reading of Extract 1, the map could begin to be constructed like this:

Leo's feelings about himself	Leo's attitude towards Marian	Leo's relationship to the adult world
Changed: feels more confident ('like an emerging butterfly, I was first conscious of my wings') and grown up. His self-esteem increases ('I feel quite another person').	Grateful to her: by taking him to Norwich, she has made possible his 'transformation'. Infatuated with her in a childish way: he imagines her as his paramour ('roaming the greenwood with Maid Marian').	Noticed and approved of by the adults at tea-time ('greeted with cries of acclaim'). Accepted as part of their social circle ('my moment . . . what a moment it had been').

---

*apotheosis: glorification

Now read straight through Extracts 2, 3 and 4 which follow. Your task will be to complete the map on the basis of what you read. For the moment, though, concentrate only on getting clear in your mind an outline of the novel's events in sequence.

> Marian encourages Leo's devotion to her by making a fuss of him: the more she does so, the more eager he will be to carry letters between herself and Ted. On one occasion, she leaves a letter unsealed. While he is taking it to Ted's farm, Leo is overcome by curiosity . . .

(2) I would not take the letter out of the envelope: I would only read the words that were exposed, and three of them were the same, as I could see from upside down.

> 'Darling, darling, darling, same place, same time, this evening. But take care not to —'

The rest was hidden by the envelope.   5

Not Adam and Eve, after eating the apple, could have been more upset than I was.

I felt utterly deflated and let down: so deep did my disappointment and disillusion go that I lost all sense of where I was, and when I came to it was like waking from a dream.

They were in love! Marian and Ted Burgess were in love! Of all the possible   10
explanations, it was the only one that had never crossed my mind. To think how I had been taken in! My world of high intense emotions collapsing around me, released not only the mental strain but the very high physical pressure under which I had been living; I felt I might explode. My only defence was, I could not have expected it of Marian. Marian who had done so much for me, Marian who knew how a boy felt, Marian the   15
Virgin of the Zodiac – how could she have sunk so low? To be what we all despised more than anything – soft, soppy – hardly, when the joke grew staler, a subject for furtive giggling.

That Marian of all people should have done this! No wonder she wanted to keep it secret. Instinctively, to cover her shame, I thrust the letter deep into the envelope and   20
sealed it.

> In the second half of the novel, Marian and Lord Trimingham (Hugh) become engaged. With plans for their wedding in progress, Leo assumes that he will be carrying no more letters to and from Ted's farm. He is taken aback when, in this extract, Marian asks a favour of him . . .

(3) 'Hullo, Leo! Just the man I was looking for' – and there she was, in every other way so like my vision of her that it almost surprised me she was not carrying something – but she was: I saw it now, a letter.

> 'Will you do something for me?' she said
> 'Oh yes. What shall I do?'   5
> 'Just take this letter.'

It shows how little thought I had of Ted in connexion with her that I said,
> 'Who to?'
> 'Who to? Why, to the farm you silly,' she answered, half laughing, half impatient.

The scaffolding of my life seemed to collapse: I was dumbfounded.   10
> 'Oh, I can't.'
> 'You can't?' she echoed, mystified. 'Why not?'
> 'It's because of Hugh'.

'Hugh?' she said. 'What has Hugh to do with it?'

I gave her a despairing look.   15

'He might be upset.'

At that her eyes blazed. She came a step forward and stood over me, her nose hawk-like, her body curved to pounce.

'What has he got to do with it?' she repeated. 'I told you, this is a business matter between me and . . . and Mr Burgess. Do you understand, or are you too stupid?'   20

I stared at her in terror.

'You come into this house, our guest,' she stormed, 'we take you in, we know nothing about you, we make a great fuss of you – I suppose you wouldn't deny that? – I know I have – and then I ask you to do a simple thing which a child in the street that I'd never spoken to would do for the asking – and you have the infernal cheek to say   25 you won't! We've spoiled you. I'll never ask you to do anything for me again, never! I won't speak to you again!'

I made some gesture with my hands to try to stop her – to push her away from me or to bring her closer – but she almost struck out at me in her fury: I thought – and it was a moment of relief – that she was actually going to hit me.   30

All at once her manner changed; she seemed to freeze.

'You want paying, that's what you want,' she said quietly, 'I know.' She produced her purse from somewhere and opened it. 'How much do you want, you little Shylock?'

But I had had enough: I snatched the letter which she still held crumpled in her hand, and ran away from her as fast as I could.   35

In an attempt to smooth the way for Marian's marriage to Lord Trimingham, her family 'arrange' for Ted to join the army and fight in the Boer War. Marian is distraught. In this extract from near the end of the novel, she breaks down in front of Leo – who naively offers her a solution . . .

---

(4)   'Marian, why don't you marry Ted?'

It was only for a moment, but in that moment her face reflected all the misery she had been going through; it was a heart's history in a look. 'I couldn't, I couldn't!' she wailed. 'Can't you see why?'

I thought I did, and since so many barriers between us were being overturned, I   5 added – it seemed only logical:

'But why are you going to marry Hugh if you don't want to?'

'Because I must marry him,' she said. 'You wouldn't understand. I *must*. I've *got* to!' Her lips trembled and she burst into tears.

I had seen grown-up people with red eyes, but I had never seen a grown-up   10 person cry before, except my mother. My mother when she cried became unrecognizable. Marian didn't: she was just Marian in tears. But there was a change – in me. For when she cried she was not Marian the deceiver, Marian who for her own purposes had taken me in and then called me green, but the Marian of the first days, who had rescued me from being laughed at, Marian who had curtsied to me at the concert, Marian of the   15 Zodiac, Marian whom I loved.

The sight of her tears loosened mine and I cried too. How long we cried I do not know . . . She rose and kissed me; she had never kissed me before.

'And you won't mind taking our notes as usual?'

'No,' I breathed.   20

'Bless you,' she said. 'You're a friend in a thousand.'

Completing the route

Re-read, and think carefully about, Extract 4 in the light of what you now know about *The Go-Between* as a whole. Then make an enlarged copy of the map below. Complete the route of Leo's character development in the novel by filling in the boxes at the foot of the page. Look for signs of Leo's growing awareness of the situation in which Marian finds herself and of how this affects his feelings.

This activity works best if you do it first by yourself, then compare your responses with those of others during class discussion.

The Go-Between: Leo's development in the course of the novel

Leo's feelings about himself	Leo's attitude towards Marian	Leo's relationship to the adult world
Extract 2 Feels hurt and cheated ('utterly deflated and let down'): in his foolishness, he's let himself be exploited ('how I had been taken in').	His imagined ideal view of her collapses ('how could she have sunk so low?').	Becomes aware that grown-ups are not a race of exalted creatures ('Virgin of the Zodiac') but ordinary and fallible.
Comes down to earth from the elevated dream world in which he's been living ('My world of high intense emotions collapsing around me').	Feels she has betrayed both him and – worse still – herself ('to cover *her* shame, I thrust the letter deep into the envelope').	Confronted by the evidence of adult love but still far from understanding what it implies ('a subject for furtive giggling').
Extract 3 Feels totally out of his depth: mystified by M's anger towards him ('you little Shylock').	His relationship with her seems broken for ever by her 'fury' at him ('I won't speak to you again').	Finds that adults can be volatile, unpredictable and cruel ('I stared at her in terror').
Terrified: he's doing what he thinks is right but all it provokes is violent rage ('her body curved to pounce').	Thinks she now sees him only as an ungrateful and ignorant little boy ('are you too stupid?').	Having seen adult character in a new and frightening light, he wants to escape back to the security of childhood ('ran away . . . as fast as I could').
Extract 4		

This page may be photocopied for use within the purchasing institution only

Mapping a familiar novel

Choose three or four episodes from a novel you are studying for A level which, in your opinion, mark key points in a major character's development. Make a landmark map like the one for *The Go-Between*, or one that you devise yourself, to show how and why the character changes in the course of the story.

Whichever kind of map you construct, it must fit on to one sheet of paper and incorporate quotations from the text.

What about conventional note-making?

Glance back to the opening sub-sections of this chapter (pages 51 and 52). The purpose of working in the ways demonstrated above, and in the rest of the chapter, is to provide a manageable frame for the detailed study of a novel, not to throw out the baby with the bathwater. If you feel more secure making conventional notes at every stage of your work on a set book, do so – *as long as your notes don't become a substitute for thinking for yourself.*

Mapping and modelling can be used flexibly for almost any aspect of your work on a text – including, of course, drama. They help you to sort out your first responses to a new book; they facilitate essay planning; they are particularly valuable for revision in the run-up to an exam. It is much easier to share maps with other members of the class: they allow you to work together more readily and they can be exchanged (or collated into a class file) very easily.

In short, they are a powerful tool for study. The more you use them, the more uses you will find for them.

Interrogations: freeze-framing the text

Having achieved a clear overview of the 'shape' of any novel, you will then need to establish links between the whole and the part. This section suggests various ways of doing so which encourage you to be active and exploratory in questioning the text yourself. Of necessity, the sample materials are short stories rather than whole novels. However, the 'freeze- frame' techniques for working on them are all readily transferable to full-length fiction.

Read the story below, which was written by the South African author Nadine Gordimer in 1980.

>━┃━◄►━•━○━•━◄►┃━◄

Country Lovers

by Nadine Gordimer

The farm children play together when they are small; but once the white children go away to school they soon don't play together any more, even in the holidays. Although most of the black children get some sort of schooling, they drop every year farther behind the grades passed by the white children; the childish vocabulary, the child's exploration of the adventurous possibilities of dam, koppies, mealie lands and veld – there comes a time when the white children have surpassed these with the vocabulary of boarding-school and the possibilities of inter-school sports matches and the kind of adventures seen at the cinema. This usefully coincides with the age of twelve or thirteen; so that by the time early adolescence is reached, the black children are making, along with the bodily changes common to all, an easy transition to adult forms of address, beginning to call their old playmates *missus* and *baasie* – little master.

The trouble was Paulus Eysendyck did not seem to realise that Thebedi was now simply one of the crowd of farm children down at the kraal, recognisable in his sisters' old clothes. The first Christmas holidays after he had gone to boarding-school he brought home for Thebedi a painted box he had made in his wood-work class. He had to give it to her secretly because he had nothing for the other children at the kraal. And she gave him, before he went back to school, a bracelet she had made of thin brass wire the and grey-and-white beans of the castor-oil crop his father cultivated. (When they used to play together, she was the one who had taught Paulus how to make clay oxen for their toy spans.) There was a craze, even in the *platteland* towns like the one where he was at school, for boys to wear elephant-hair and other bracelets beside their watch straps; his was admired, friends asked him to get similar ones for them. He said the natives made them on his father's farm and he would try.

When he was fifteen, six feet tall, and tramping round at school dances with the girls from the 'sister' school in the same town; when he had learnt how to tease and flirt and fondle quite intimately these girls who were the daughters of prosperous farmers like his father; when he had even met one who, at a wedding he had attended with his parents on a nearby farm, had let him do with her in a locked storeroom what people did when they made love – when he was as far from his childhood as all this, he still brought home from a shop in town a red plastic belt and gilt hoop ear-rings for the black girl, Thebedi. She told her father the missus had given these to her as a reward for some work she had done – it was true she sometimes was called to help out in the farmhouse. She told the girls in the kraal that she had a sweetheart nobody knew about, far away, away on another farm, and they giggled, and teased, and admired her. There was a boy in the kraal called Njabulo who said he wished he could have bought her a belt and ear-rings.

5

10

15

20

25

30

35

When the farmer's son was home for the holidays she wandered far from the kraal and her companions. He went for walks alone. They had not arranged this; it was an urge each followed independently. He knew it was she, from a long way off. She knew that his dog would not bark at her. Down at the dried-up river-bed where five or six years ago the children had caught a leguaan one great day – a creature that combined ideally the size and ferocious aspect of the crocodile with the harmlessness of the lizard – they squatted side by side on the earth bank. He told her traveller's tales: about school, about the punishments at school, particularly, exaggerating both their nature and his indifference to them. He told her about the town of Middleburg, which she had never seen. She had nothing to tell but she prompted with many questions, like any good listener. While he talked he twisted and tugged at the roots of white stinkwood and Cape willow trees that looped out of the eroded earth around them. It had always been a good spot for children's games, down there hidden by the mesh of old, ant-eaten trees held in place by vigorous ones, wild asparagus bushing up between the trunks, and here and there prickly-pear cactus sunken-skinned and bristly, like an old man's face, keeping alive sapless until the next rainy season. She punctured the dry hide of a prickly-pear again and again with a sharp stick while she listened. She laughed a lot at what he told her, sometimes dropping her face on her knees, sharing amusement with the cool shady earth beneath her bare feet. She put on her pairs of shoes – white sandals, thickly Blanco-ed against the farm dust – when he was on the farm, but these were taken off and laid aside, at the river-bed.

One summer afternoon when there was water flowing there and it was very hot she waded in as they used to do when they were children, her dress bunched modestly and tucked into the legs of her pants. The schoolgirls he went swimming with at dams or pools on neighbouring farms wore bikinis but the sight of their dazzling bellies and thighs in the sunlight had never made him feel what he felt now, when the girl came up the bank and sat beside him, the drops of water beading off her dark legs the only points of light in the earth-smelling, deep shade. They were not afraid of one another, they had known one another always; he did with her what he had done that time in the storeroom at the wedding, and this time it was so lovely, so lovely, he was surprised . . . and she was surprised by it, too – he could see in her dark face that was part of the shade, with her big dark eyes, shiny as soft water, watching him attentively: as she had when they used to huddle over their teams of mud oxen, as she had when he told her about detention weekends at school.

They went to the river-bed often through those summer holidays. They met just before the light went, as it does quite quickly, and each returned home with the dark – she to her mother's hut, he to the farmhouse – in time for the evening meal. He did not tell her about school or town any more. She did not ask questions any longer. He told her, each time, when they would meet again. Once or twice it was very early in the morning; the lowing of the cows being driven to graze came to them where they lay, dividing them with unspoken recognition of the sound read in their two pairs of eyes, opening so close to each other.

He was a popular boy at school. He was in the second, then the first soccer team. The head girl of the 'sister' school was said to have a crush on him; he didn't particularly like her, but there was a pretty blonde who put up her long hair into a kind of doughnut with a black ribbon round it, whom he took to see films when the schoolboys and girls had a free Saturday afternoon. He had been driving tractors and other farm vehicles since he was ten years old, and as soon as he was eighteen he got a driver's licence and in the holidays, this last year of his school-life, he took neighbours' daughters to dances and to the drive-in cinema that had just opened twenty kilometres from the farm. His sisters were married, by then; his parents often left him in charge of the farm over the weekend while they visited the young wives and grandchildren.

When Thebedi saw the farmer and his wife drive away on a Saturday afternoon, the boot of their Mercedes filled with fresh-killed poultry and vegetables from the garden that it was part of her father's work to tend, she knew that she must come not to the river-bed but up to the house. The house was an old one, thick-walled, dark against the heat. The kitchen was its lively thoroughfare, with servants, food supplies, begging cats and dogs, pots boiling over, washing being damped for ironing, and the big deep-freeze the missus had ordered from town, bearing a crocheted mat and a case of plastic irises. But the dining-room with the bulging-legged heavy table was shut up in its rich, old smell of soup and tomato sauce. The sitting-room curtains were drawn and the TV set silent. The door of the parents' bedroom was locked and the empty rooms where the girls had slept had sheets of plastic spread over the beds. It was in one of these that she and the farmer's son stayed together whole nights – almost: she had to get away before the house servants, who knew her, came in at dawn. There was a risk someone would discover her or traces of her presence if he took her to his own bedroom, although she had looked into it many times when she was helping out in the house and knew well, there, the row of silver cups he had won at school.

When she was eighteen and the farmer's son nineteen and working with his father on the farm before entering a veterinary college, the young man Njabulo asked her father for her. Njabulo's parents met with hers and the money he was to pay in place of the cows it is customary to give a prospective bride's parents was settled upon. He had no cows to offer; he was a labourer on the Eysendyck farm, like her father. A bright youngster; old Eysendyck had taught him brick-laying and was using him for odd jobs in construction, around the place. She did not tell the farmer's son that her parents had arranged for her to marry. She did not tell him, either, before he left for his first term at the veterinary college, that she thought she was going to have a baby. Two months after her marriage to Njabulo, she gave birth to a daughter. There was no disgrace in that; among her people it is customary for a young man to make sure, before marriage, that the chosen girl is not barren, and Njabulo had made love to her then. But the infant was very light and did not quickly grow darker as most African babies do. Already at birth there was on its head a quantity of straight, fine floss, like that which carries the seeds of certain weeds in the veld. The unfocused eyes it opened were grey flecked with yellow. Njabulo was the matt, opaque coffee-grounds colour that has always been called black: the colour of Thebedi's legs on which beaded water looked oyster-shell blue, the same colour as Thebedi's face, where the black eyes, with their interested gaze and clear whites, were so dominant.

Njabulo made no complaint. Out of his farm labourer's earnings he bought from the Indian store a cellophane-windowed pack containing a pink plastic bath, six napkins, a card of safety pins, a knitted jacket, cap and bootees, a dress, and a tin of Johnson's Baby Powder, for Thebedi's baby.

When it was two weeks old Paulus Eysendyck arrived home from the veterinary college for the holidays. He drank a glass of fresh, still-warm milk in the childhood familiarity of his mother's kitchen and heard her discussing with the old house-servant where they could get a reliable substitute to help out now that the girl Thebedi had had a baby. For the first time since he was a small boy he came right into the kraal. It was eleven o'clock in the morning. The men were at work in the lands. He looked about him, urgently; the women turned away, each not wanting to be the one approached to point out where Thebedi lived. Thebedi appeared, coming slowly from the hut Njabulo had built in white man's style, with a tin chimney, and a proper window with glass panes set in straight as walls made of unfired bricks would allow. She greeted him with hands brought together and a token movement representing the respectful bob with which she was accustomed to acknowledge she was in the presence of his father or mother. He lowered his head under the doorway of her home and went in. He said, 'I want to see. Show me.'

She had taken the bundle off her back before she came out into the light to face him. 140
She moved between the iron bedstead made up with Njabulo's checked blankets and
the small wooden table where the pink plastic bath stood among food and kitchen pots,
and picked up the bundle from the snugly blanketed grocer's box where it lay. The
infant was asleep; she revealed the closed, pale, plump tiny face, with a bubble of spit
at the corner of the mouth, the spidery pink hands stirring. She took off the woollen cap 145
and the straight fine hair flew up after it in static electricity, showing gilded strands here
and there. He said nothing. She was watching him as she had done when they were
little, and the gang of children had trodden down a crop in their games or transgressed
in some other way for which he, as the farmer's son, the white one among them, must
intercede with the farmer. She disturbed the sleeping face by scratching or tickling 150
gently at a cheek with one finger, and slowly the eyes opened, saw nothing, were still
asleep, and then, awake, no longer narrowed, looked out at them, grey with yellowish
flecks, his own hazel eyes.

He struggled for a moment with a grimace of tears, anger and self-pity. She could not
put out her hand to him. He said, 'You haven't been near the house with it?' 155

She shook her head.

'Never?'

Again she shook her head.

'Don't take it out. Stay inside. Can't you take it away somewhere. You must give it to
someone –' 160

She moved to the door with him.

He said, 'I'll see what I will do. I don't know.' And then he said: 'I feel like killing
myself.'

Her eyes began to glow, to thicken with tears. For a moment there was the feeling
between them that used to come when they were alone down at the river-bed. 165

He walked out.

Two days later, when his mother and father had left the farm for the day, he appeared
again. The women were away on the lands, weeding, as they were employed to do as
casual labour in the summer; only the very old remained, propped up on the ground
outside the huts in the flies and the sun. Thebedi did not ask him in. The child had not 170
been well; it had diarrhoea. He asked where its food was. She said, 'The milk comes
from me.' He went into Njabulo's house, where the child lay; she did not follow but
stayed outside the door and watched without seeing an old crone who had lost her
mind, talking to herself, talking to the fowls who ignored her.

She thought she heard small grunts from the hut, the kind of infant grunt that indicates 175
a full stomach, a deep sleep. After a time, long or short she did not know, he came out
and walked away with plodding stride (his father's gait) out of sight, towards his father's
house.

The baby was not fed during the night and although she kept telling Njabulo it was
sleeping, he saw for himself in the morning that it was dead. He comforted her with 180
words and caresses. She did not cry but simply sat, staring at the door. Her hands were
cold as dead chickens' feet to his touch.

Njabulo buried the little baby where farm workers were buried, in the place in the veld
the farmer had given them. Some of the mounds had been left to weather away
unmarked, others were covered with stones and a few had fallen wooden crosses. He 185
was going to make a cross but before it was finished the police came and dug up the
grave and took away the dead baby: someone – one of the other labourers? their

women? – had reported that the baby was almost white, that, strong and healthy, it had died suddenly after a visit by the farmer's son. Pathological tests on the infant corpse showed intestinal damage not always consistent with death by natural causes.

Thebedi went for the first time to the country town where Paulus had been to school, to give evidence at the preparatory examination into the charge of murder brought against him. She cried hysterically in the witness box, saying yes, yes (the gilt hoop ear-rings swung in her ears), she saw the accused pouring liquid into the baby's mouth. She said he had threatened to shoot her if she told anyone.

195

More than a year went by before, in that same town, the case was brought to trial. She came to Court with a new-born baby on her back. She wore gilt hoop ear-rings; she was calm; she said she had not seen what the white man did in the house.

Paulus Eysendyck said he had visited the hut but had not poisoned the child.

The Defence did not contest that there had been a love relationship between the accused and the girl, or that intercourse had taken place, but submitted there was no proof that the child was the accused's.

200

The judge told the accused there was strong suspicion against him but not enough proof that he had committed the crime. The Court could not accept the girl's evidence because it was clear she had committed perjury either at this trial or at the preparatory examination. There was the suggestion in the mind of the Court that she might be an accomplice in the crime; but, again, insufficient proof.

205

The judge commended the honourable behaviour of the husband (sitting in the court in a brown-and-yellow quartered golf cap bought for Sundays) who had not rejected his wife and had 'even provided clothes for the unfortunate infant out of his slender means'.

210

The verdict on the accused was 'not guilty'.

The young white man refused to accept the congratulations of press and public and left the Court with his mother's raincoat shielding his face from photographers. His father said to the press, 'I will try and carry on as best I can to hold up my head in the district'.

215

Interviewed by the Sunday papers, who spelled her name in a variety of ways, the black girl, speaking in her own language, was quoted beneath her photograph: 'It was a thing of our childhood, we don't see each other any more.'

> ⟨•⟩ ⚬ ⟨•⟩ <

Role writing

The purpose of this activity is to consider the story's ending in relation to the narrative as a whole. Your insight into the novels that you are studying for A level will be deepened by trying out this technique on them.

Freeze-frame Paulus Eysendyck's trial. As you re-read it (from 'More than a year went by …', line 196), think of the episode as the final scene in a film.

Draw on your knowledge of the whole story to write in role an account of your *real* feelings as if you are (a) Paulus, (b) Thebedi, and (c) Paulus's father. All three are in a public situation where, for various reasons, they cannot say what is actually in their minds. Your own response to the story as a whole will allow you to do so. The accounts need only be brief; concentrate more on their content than on the 'accuracy' of their grammar, punctuation, spelling and so on.

well, and everything suggests he will, one day he will inherit everything we own. If we do by chance have children, he would share equally with them. But if he does not make the most of his opportunities, we will give him the sum of twenty thousand francs when he comes of age, this sum to be deposited as of now in his name with a lawyer. And because we have also been thinking of you, you will receive a hundred francs a month for as long as you live. Do you understand?'

The farmer's wife rose to her feet like a fury: 'You want us to sell you our Charlot? No. Never! It's a thing nobody's got no right asking a mother to do. I won't have it! It'd be sinful and wicked!'

Her husband, looking grave and thoughtful, said nothing. But he indicated his approval of what his wife said by nodding his head all the time she spoke.

It was all too much for Madame d'Hubières who burst into tears and, turning to her husband, stammered in the tear-choked voice of a little girl who always got her way: 'They don't want to, Henri, they don't want to!'

They made one last attempt: 'Listen. Think about your son's future, about his happiness, about …'

Losing patience, the wife interrupted. 'We've heard you out, we've understood, and we've made up our minds … Now just go and don't ever let me see you round this way again. Never heard the like! The very idea! Wanting to take away a baby just like that!'

As she was leaving, Madame d'Hubières recalled that there were two little boys and asked, through her tears, and with the persistence of a headstrong, spoilt woman who is not prepared to wait: 'The other little boy isn't yours, is he?'

Monsieur Tuvache answered, 'No. He's next door's. You can go and see them if you like.' And he went back into his house where his wife could be heard complaining indignantly.

The Vallins were sitting round their table, with a plate between them, slowly eating slices of bread thinly spread with rancid butter.

Monsieur d'Hubières restated his proposal to them, but this time he was more subtle, shrewder, and he put honey in his voice.

The man and his wife shook their heads to indicate their unwillingness. But when they learned that they would get a hundred francs a month, they looked at each other, exchanged enquiring glances, and seemed to hesitate.

Torn and uncertain, they did not say anything for some time. In the end, the wife asked her husband: 'Well, what have you got to say?'

He replied sententiously: 'What I say is that it's not to be sneezed at.'

Madame d'Hubières, trembling with anguish, then spoke to them about the future their little boy would have, how happy he would be and how much money he would be able to give them later on.

'This business of the twelve hundred francs,' the man asked, 'it'd be all properly settled by a lawyer?'

'Absolutely,' Monsieur d'Hubières replied. 'It could all be arranged tomorrow.'

The wife, who had been thinking, went on:

'A hundred francs a month, well, it don't compensate us nowhere near for not having our boy around. Give him a couple of years and he'll be old enough to be set to work. We'd need a hundred and twenty.'

Madame d'Hubières was so impatient to finalise matters that she agreed immediately. And since she was anxious to take the child away with her at once, she gave them an extra hundred francs as a present while her husband was drawing up a written agreement. The mayor and a neighbour were hurriedly summoned and willingly witnessed the document.

The young woman, radiant, took the screaming child away as others might bear off a coveted bargain from a shop.

The Tuvaches stood on their doorstep and watched him go, saying nothing, grim-faced, and perhaps regretting that they had said no.

That was the last that was heard of little Jean Vallin. Each month his parents collected their one hundred and twenty francs from the lawyer. They quarrelled with their neighbours, because Madame Tuvache said the most awful things about them and went around other people's houses saying that anyone who sells a child for money must be unnatural, that it was a horrible, disgusting, dirty business. And sometimes she would pick up her little Charlot for all to see and say loudly, as though he could understand: 'I din't sell you, my precious, I din't! I don't go round selling my children. I haven't got a lot of money, but I don't go round selling my children!'

It was the same each day for years and years. Each day coarse jeers were bellowed on one doorstep so that they were heard in the house next door. In the end, Madame Tuvache came to believe that she was better than anybody else for miles around because she had refused to sell her little Charlot. And when people talked about her, they said: ''Twas a tempting offer, right enough. But she wasn't interested. She done what a good mother oughter.'

He was held up as a model. Little Charlot, who was now almost 18 and had been brought up having this idea constantly repeated to him, also thought he was a cut above his friends because he had not been sold.

The Vallins pottered along quite comfortably on their pension. Which explains why the fury of the Tuvaches, who remained poor, was so implacable.

Their oldest boy went off to do his military service. The second died and Charlot was left alone to work alongside his old father to support his mother and his two younger sisters.

He was getting on for 21 when, one morning, a gleaming carriage pulled up outside the two cottages. A young gentlemen, wearing a gold watch-chain, got out and helped down an old lady with white hair. The old lady said to him, 'It's there, dear. The second house.'

He walked straight into the Vallins' hovel as though it were his own.

Old Madame Vallin was washing her aprons. Her husband, now infirm, was dozing by the fire. Both looked up and the young man said:

'Good morning, mother. Good morning, father.'

They both stood up in dismay. Madame Vallin was in such a state that she dropped her soap into the water. She stammered: 'Is that you, son? Is it really you?'

He took her in his arms and kissed her, repeating: 'Hello, mother.' Meanwhile the old man, shaking all over, kept saying in the calm tone of voice which never deserted him, 'Here you are back again, Jean,' as though he had seen him only the month before.

When they had got over the shock, the parents said they wanted to take their boy out and show him off everywhere. They took him to see the mayor, the deputy mayor, the village priest, and the schoolmaster.

Charlot watched them go from the doorstep of the cottage next door.

That night, at supper, he said to his parents, 'You can't have been right in the head letting the Vallin kid get took away.'

His mother replied stubbornly, 'I'd never have let a child of ours get took.'

His father said nothing.

The son went on: 'I really missed the boat the day I got made a sacrifice of.'

At this, old Tuvache said angrily: 'You're not blaming us for keeping you?'

The young man replied cruelly: 'O' course I blame you. I blame you for being so soft in the head. Parents like you is the reason why children get held back. It'd serve you right if I upped sticks and off.'

The old woman cried into her dinner. She gave little moans as she swallowed each mouthful of soup, half of which she spilled: 'You kill yourself to bring up your kids and what thanks do you get?'

Then the lad said roughly: 'I'd as soon have never been born than be as I am. When I saw him from next door earlier on, it come right home to me. I said to myself: That's what I could have been like now!' He stood up. 'Listen, I think it'd be best if I didn't stay around the place, because I'd only be throwing it in your faces morning, noon and night. I'd just make your lives a misery. I'll never forgive you. Never.' 170

The two old people sat in silence, utterly crushed and in tears. He continued: 'I couldn't stand the thought of that. I'd rather go off and make a fresh start somewhere else.'

He opened the door. Through it came the sound of voices. The Vallins were celebrating with their boy who had come back. 175

Charlot stamped his feet in rage and, turning to his parents, screamed: 'Know what you are? Stupid, bog-trotting yokels!'

And he vanished into the night.

Moral frames

Writers, particularly novelists, often pose questions about the moral and ethical behaviour of their characters. The activities below on Maupassant's story demonstrate three different ways of framing your own response to the 'moral dimension' in fiction. Try out at least one of them; you will be able to use similar approaches for the novels you are studying for A level.

Hot-seating

Work in a group (the ideal number is four). Elect two people to role-play the mothers in 'Country Living', Madame Tuvache and Madame Vallin.

The local newspaper has learned the history of Charlot and Jean after Charlot walks out on his family at the end of the story. It sounds as if it would make a good front page article. Two reporters or more – the other members of your group – have been assigned to interview the mothers together, in return for a generous fee. (The local paper wants to ensure that it gets an 'exclusive' on this.)

Conduct the interview in role. Bear in mind that the facts of the story are by now well known. The reporters will be interested in getting each mother to justify her actions and to defend the personal attitudes and values that lay behind them.

In order to do justice to the moral issues involved, the interview should last not less than 10–15 minutes. Take longer if you wish.

On trial

Turn your classroom into a court. After Jean returns home at the end of the story, it is discovered that his parents have, in fact, committed a crime in 'selling' him to Monsieur and Madame d'Hubières. The French police have no choice but to bring a retrospective action against the Vallins for serious child neglect.

Role-play their trial. As well as a judge and counsel for the prosecution and defence, you will need as witnesses: the d'Hubières, Madame and Monsieur Tuvache, Jean, Charlot (who has had to respond to being summoned to give evidence) and – if you wish – any neighbours whose testimony may prove important. Other members of your class act as the jury.

Remain faithful to the facts of Maupassant's story. What interpretation those involved in the trial put on them is, of course, the point of this exercise.

When you have reached your verdict, come out of role and discuss whether it is consistent with the 'judgement' you believe Maupassant is making about the Vallins in his story.

Judgement charts

Evaluate the moral/ethical conduct of characters in comparative terms by constructing a judgement chart on which you plot your conclusions about how 'well' or how 'badly' they behave.

The criteria you use for making judgements are all-important: for example, in the case of 'Country Living', a chart based on the criterion of 'moral responsibility' may look very different from one based on the criterion of 'parental love'.

Put it to the test. Below is a bar chart which evaluates the comparative behaviour of different characters according to the criterion of 'moral responsibility'.

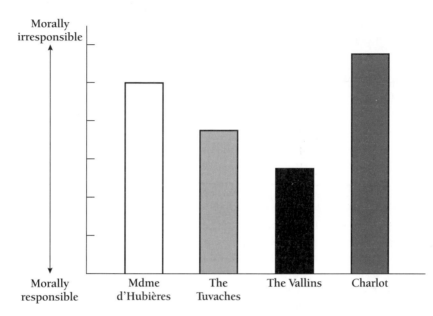

How accurately does the bar chart reflect your own judgements?

Select a different moral/ethical criterion which arises out of the story. In the light of it, construct a chart to express your responses to the conduct of the same characters as those in the bar chart above.

This is a deliberately simple example. When you are trying to arrive at balanced judgements about characters' behaviour in a whole novel, the technique can be particularly useful as a way of clarifying your own ideas and of promoting discussion. (If you know the books in question, speculate about making judgement charts to compare the ethical behaviour of Cathy and Heathcliff and/or of Alec d'Urberville and Angel Clare.) The advantage of 'charting' in this way is that you can keep a clear overall framework at the same time as adding whatever 'refinements' you need in the way of detail: chapter numbers, different settings throughout the novel, main plot/sub-plot, page references and so on.

Networks: selecting material, exploring links

Planning to write

When writing about novels, you will be repeatedly urged (a) to select your material carefully, and (b) to plan to use this material relevantly in a way that 'hangs together' when you write. This can sound like daunting advice when you sit staring at a mass of lesson notes – especially if they have been hastily transcribed 'during discussion' – and wonder: 'How on earth does all this connect up?' It is easy to lose a sense of perspective, and it is often difficult to see a clear shape for the writing task set.

The difficulty is increased when you come to practise exam answers. The selection of 'relevant' material now also depends on the (often unpredictable) kind of question you face, not only on the need to turn your lesson notes into a (usually predictable) essay form.

This section demonstrates that, in order to plan – and therefore to write – effectively, it is important to train yourself to think in particular ways throughout the A level course. The 'thinking for writing' priorities are as follows.

- Above all, aim to make a personal response to the text, whether you are reading it for the first time or revising it immediately before the exam. This is quite different from taking the arrogant view: 'I know best, therefore I'll ignore everyone else.' Common sense tells you that teachers, classmates and academic commentators on novels can extend and deepen your own understanding, which will change as you continue to study the text. But unless, in the end, these understandings are genuinely your own, your ideas will be muddled and your ability to plan a written response will be seriously impaired.

- When planning a line of argument, work through to your *own* conclusions using your own powers of reasoning. It will prove impossible to plan confidently if you merely take over someone else's argument. You will not have 'tuned in' to the thought processes that went into it, something that is always apparent to the reader/teacher/examiner.

- Make yourself stand back from the welter of textual detail facing you and think first in broad terms. This is similar to an artist 'blocking' a painting. It is vital to construct a clear mental picture of the whole composition so that you can get a reliable perspective on whatever topic you are planning to write about. Resist the temptation to 'plunge in' too soon. The details will be much easier to deploy if you are clear about the outline into which they are going to fit. This way of thinking also helps you to be selective in your use of detail and to avoid repetition.

- 'Think in links'. The links may be narrative: 'X happens because of Y, which leads to Z; as a result …'. They may concern the relationships between characters; or the development of a central theme; or some aspect of the author's technique, such as the use of time-shifts, parallel plots etc. The more you train yourself to think of the text as a network of inter-connected strands, not just as a 'straight line', the better your ability to plan a piece of writing on any topic will become.

Two examples

The network plans that follow are the work of Year 12 students. Both demonstrate well the approach described above and show the quite different forms such planning can take on the page. The first was prepared for a lesson in which the student was asked to lead a discussion on the theme of racial conflict in 'Country Lovers' (pages 61–5).

Network Plan 1

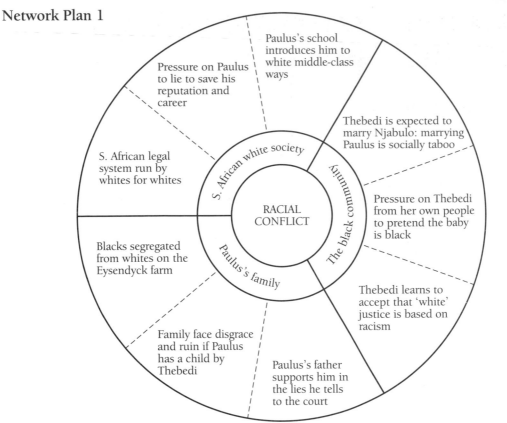

Discuss with your teacher the strengths and/or weaknesses of this approach to planning. Then take some aspect of an A level novel you are currently studying and construct a similar plan for writing on it. The topic is obviously up to you and your teacher to decide.

Now look at the more detailed network plan on pages 74–5. It was produced jointly by three students preparing to write an essay on *Mansfield Park* about the importance to the whole novel of the 'theatricals'. Even if you do not know *Mansfield Park*, examine the structure of this network plan. (The page references are to the Penguin edition.)

Discuss with your teacher your response to this 'work of art'. It looks extremely complicated. In fact, for readers of *Mansfield Park* it's far easier to absorb than a dense jungle of conventionally made notes on the same topic.

What was valuable for the students who produced it was the process of doing so. What do you consider they learned from this process? They didn't just learn about the novel in question, but also:

● how to think about a given essay subject;

● how to make links between different ideas;

● how to pull together the general and the particular.

The best way to test out this method is to take an essay topic about a novel you are currently studying and make your own network plan on it. One of the many benefits of this will be to provide you with confidence-giving revision material when you come to end-of-course (or modular) exams.

Network Plan 2: What importance do the 'theatricals' have in Mansfield Park?

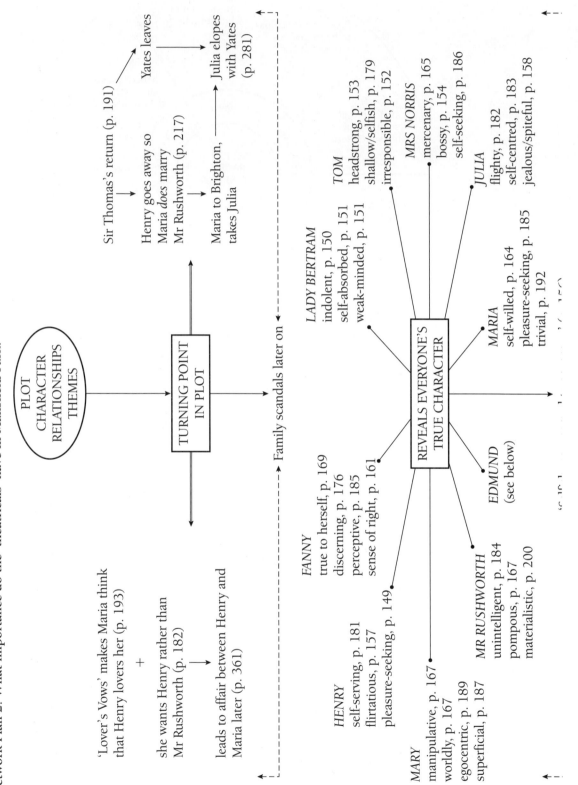

PLOT
CHARACTER
RELATIONSHIPS
THEMES

TURNING POINT
IN PLOT

Sir Thomas's return (p. 191) → Yates leaves

Henry goes away so
Maria *does* marry
Mr Rushworth (p. 217)

Maria to Brighton, → Julia elopes
takes Julia   with Yates
                     (p. 281)

'Lover's Vows' makes Maria think
that Henry lovers her (p. 193)
+
she wants Henry rather than
Mr Rushworth (p. 182)

leads to affair between Henry and
Maria later (p. 361)

← → Family scandals later on →

REVEALS EVERYONE'S
TRUE CHARACTER

LADY BERTRAM
indolent, p. 150
self-absorbed, p. 151
weak-minded, p. 151

TOM
headstrong, p. 153
shallow/selfish, p. 179
irresponsible, p. 152

MRS NORRIS
mercenary, p. 165
bossy, p. 154
self-seeking, p. 186

JULIA
flighty, p. 182
self-centred, p. 183
jealous/spiteful, p. 158

MARIA
self-willed, p. 164
pleasure-seeking, p. 185
trivial, p. 192

FANNY
true to herself, p. 169
discerning, p. 176
perceptive, p. 185
sense of right, p. 161

EDMUND
(see below)

HENRY
self-serving, p. 181
flirtatious, p. 157
pleasure-seeking, p. 149

MR RUSHWORTH
unintelligent, p. 184
pompous, p. 167
materialistic, p. 200

MARY
manipulative, p. 167
worldly, p. 167
egocentric, p. 189
superficial, p. 187

EFFECT ON EDMUND'S RELATIONSHIPS

— with FANNY

E. sees play in same light as Fanny (pp. 155, 161)

F. sees that Mary is flirting with E. (p. 168)

Fanny flattered to be asked her opinion by E. (p. 175)

E. says 'We have all been somewhat to blame ... except Fanny' (p. 203)

F. dismayed by E's decision to act (p. 177)

— with MARY

E. first opposed to the play (pp. 151, 152)

Mary asks his advice about who should play Anhalt (p. 167)

E. agrees to act the part of Mary's lover (p. 187)

E. wavers 'between his theatrical and real selves' (p. 183)

E. approves of Mary's defence of Fanny not acting (p. 170)

'The whole subject of it was love' (p. 187)

DEVELOPS NOVEL'S MAJOR THEMES

'LONDON' VALUES / 'MANSFIELD' VALUES

Chosen play is 'improper' and 'immodest': brings London values into the heart of Mansfield Park and almost destroys them

The 'London' play is modern and urban: its values are opposed to those of tradition and the civilised manners of rural society

Order and restraint only restored at the last moment by Sir Thomas's return: this stops the play

ACTING A PART / BEING TRUE TO YOURSELF

'Lover's Vows' turn out to be deceiving throughout the novel: the theatricals reflect this

Henry and Mary at their truest when acting: their real selves are a façade

Maria and Julia can't distinguish appearance from reality: leads to calamity for both

Theatricals make Edmund appreciate Fanny's 'truth' and recover his real self

Edmund almost taken in by the power of 'acting'

Fanny 'cannot act' and sees through those who *can*

Chapter 4 Approaches to Shakespeare: four plays for the stage

 Seeing things in perspective

Main text: *A Streetcar Named Desire*, Tennessee Williams

 Stage-crafting a scene: shape and rhythm

Main text: *The Merchant of Venice*

 Patterns of language: reading with the ear

Main text: *King Lear*

 The nature of the play: theatrical conventions

Main text: *The Tempest*

Seeing things in perspective

Keep in mind two basic facts about 'doing' Shakespeare at A level. The first is that all examining boards compel you to make a detailed study of his plays. The second is that the plays were not written to be 'studied' but to be seen, heard and experienced in the theatre. This second fact is more important than the first – and is perfectly compatible with it. Approach Shakespeare's plays as theatrical events, written for the stage rather than the page, and your study of them can be both personally and academically rewarding. Confine the plays to the classroom – or, worse still, to the notebook – and you'll kill them.

This chapter demonstrates various methods of working on Shakespeare which will help you strike a balance between fulfilling examination requirements and responding to the plays *as* plays.

Drama text as script

Why must the study of a drama text at A level – a play by Shakespeare or by any other playwright – take a different form from the study of novels, poems and non-fictional prose? The activity that follows will help you to come up with answers of your own which apply directly to the way you tackle Shakespeare.

In groups, read aloud the extract below from Scene 1 of Tennessee Williams's play *A Streetcar Named Desire* as if you were preparing a production of it. Begin with a 'first read-through' – in other words, plunge straight in. Four female characters speak (the Negro Woman has only two lines).

Blanche Dubois has just arrived in New Orleans to visit her younger married sister Stella who occupies a small flat in a run-down apartment building. Her neighbour is Eunice. It is important that one member of your group reads the playwright's stage-directions as expressively as possible: think of them as a 'character' in the play.

>─┤◄►•─○─•◄►├─◄

from A Streetcar Named Desire

by Tennessee Williams

[Blanche comes around the corner, carrying a valise. She looks at a slip of paper, then at the building, then again at the slip and again at the building. Her expression is one of shocked disbelief. Her appearance is incongruous to this setting. She is daintily dressed in a white suit with a fluffy bodice, necklace and ear-rings of pearl, white gloves and hat, looking as if she were arriving at a summer tea or cocktail party in the garden district. She is about five years older than Stella. Her delicate beauty must avoid a strong light. There is something about her uncertain manner, as well as her white clothes, that suggests a moth.]

Eunice [*finally*]:   What's the matter, honey? Are you lost?

Blanche [*with faintly hysterical humour*]:   They told me to take a streetcar named Desire, and then transfer to one called Cemeteries and ride six blocks and get off at – Elysian Fields!

Eunice: That's where you are now.

Blanche: At Elysian Fields?

Eunice: This here is Elysian Fields.

Blanche: They musn't have – understood – what number I wanted …

Eunice: What number you lookin' for?

[Blanche wearily refers to the slip of paper.]

Blanche: Six thirty-two. 10

Eunice: You don't have to look no further.

Blanche [uncomprehendingly]: I'm looking for my sister, Stella Dubois. I mean – Mrs Stanley Kowalski.

Eunice: That's the party. – You just did miss her, though.

Blanche: This – can this be – her home? 15

Eunice: She's got the downstairs here and I got the up.

Blanche: Oh. She's – out?

Eunice: You noticed that bowling alley around the corner?

Blanche: I'm – not sure I did.

Eunice: Well, that's where she's at, watchin' her husband bowl. [There is a pause.] 20
You want to leave your suitcase an' go find her?

Blanche: No.

Negro Woman: I'll go tell her you come.

Blanche: Thanks.

Negro Woman: You welcome. [She goes out.] 25

Eunice: She wasn't expecting you?

Blanche: No. No, not tonight.

Eunice: Well, why don't you just go in and make yourself at home till they get back.

Blanche: How could I – do that?

Eunice: We own this place so I can let you in. 30

[She gets up and opens the downstairs door. A lights goes on behind the blind, turning it light blue. Blanche slowly follows her into the downstairs flat. The surrounding areas dim out as the interior is lighted. Two rooms can be seen, not too clearly defined. The one first entered is primarily a kitchen but contains a folding bed to be used by Blanche. The room beyond this is a bedroom. Off this room is a narrow door to a bathroom.]

Eunice [defensively, noticing Blanche's look]: It's sort of messed up right now but when it's clean it's real sweet.

Blanche: Is it?

Eunice: Uh-huh, I think so. So you're Stella's sister?

Blanche: Yes. [Wanting to get rid of her.] Thanks for letting me in. 35

Eunice: Por nada, as the Mexicans say, por nada! Stella spoke of you.

Blanche: Yes?

Eunice: I think she said you taught school.

Blanche in a scene from the film version of 'A Streetcar Named Desire' with Stella's husband, Stanley

Blanche: Yes.

Eunice: And you're from Mississippi, huh?   40

Blanche: Yes.

Eunice: She showed me a picture of your home-place, the plantation.

Blanche: Belle Reve?

Eunice: A great big place with white columns.

Blanche: Yes …   45

Eunice: A place like that must be awful hard to keep up.

Blanche: If you will excuse me, I'm just about to drop.

Eunice: Sure, honey. Why don't you set down?

Blanche: What I meant was I'd like to be left alone.

Eunice *[offended]:*   Aw, I'll make myself scarce, in that case.   50

Blanche: I didn't mean to be rude, but –

Eunice: I'll drop by the bowling alley an' hustle her up. [*She goes out of the door.*]

> [*Blanche sits in a chair very stiffly with her shoulders slightly hunched and her legs pressed closed together and her hands tightly clutching her purse as if she were quite cold. After a while the blind look goes out of her eyes and she begins to looks slowly around. A cat screeches. She catches her breath with a startled gesture. Suddenly she notices something in a half-opened closet. She springs up and crosses to it, and removes a whisky bottle. She pours a half tumbler of whisky and tosses it down. She carefully replaces the bottle and washes out the tumbler at the sink. Then she resumes her seat in front of the table.*]

Blanche [*faintly to herself*]:   I've got to keep hold of myself!

[*Stella comes quickly around the corner of the building and runs to the door of the downstairs flat.*]

Stella [*calling out joyfully*]:   Blanche!

[*For a moment they stare at each other. Then Blanche springs up and runs to her with a wild cry.*]

Blanche: Stella, oh, Stella, Stella! Stella for Star!   55

[*She begins to speak with feverish vivacity as if she feared for either of them to stop and think. They catch each other in a spasmodic embrace.*]

Blanche: Now, then, let me look at you. But don't you look at me, Stella, no, no, no, not till later, not till I've bathed and rested! And turn that over-light off! Turn that off! I won't be looked at in this merciless glare! [*Stella laughs and complies.*] Come back here now! Oh, my baby! Stella! Stella for Star! [*She embraces her again.*] I thought you would never come back to his horrible   60
place! What am I saying! I didn't mean to say that. I meant to be nice about it and say – Oh, what a convenient location and such – Ha-a-ha! Precious lamb! You haven't said a *word* to me.

Stella: You haven't given me a chance to, honey! [*She laughs but her glance at Blanche is a little anxious.*]

Blanche: Well, now you talk. Open you pretty mouth and talk while I look around for   65
some liquor! I know you must have some liquor on the place! Where could it be, I wonder? Oh, I spy, I spy!

[*She rushes to the closet and removes the bottle; she is shaking all over and panting for breath as she tries to laugh. The bottle nearly slips from her grasp.*]

Stella [*noticing*]:   Blanche, you sit down and let me pour the drinks. I don't know what we've got to mix with. Maybe a coke's in the icebox. Look'n see, honey, while I'm –   70

Blanche: No coke, honey, not with my nerves tonight! Where – where is – ?

Stella: Stanley? Bowling! He loves it. They're having a – found some soda – tournament …

Blanche: Just water, baby, to chase it! Now don't get worried, your sister hasn't turned into a drunkard, she's just all shaken up and hot and tired and dirty! You sit   75
down, now, and explain this place to me! What are you doing in a place like this?

Stella: Now, Blanche –

Blanche: Oh, I'm not going to be hypocritical, I'm going to be honestly critical about it! Never, never, never in my worst dreams could I picture – Only Poe! Only   80
Mr Edgar Allan Poe! – could do it justice! Out there I suppose is the ghoul-haunted woodland of Weir! [*She laughs.*]

Stella: No, honey, those are the L & N tracks.

Blanche: No, now seriously, putting joking aside. Why didn't you tell me, why didn't you write me, honey, why didn't you let me know?   85

Stella [*carefully, pouring herself a drink*]: Tell you what, Blanche?

Blanche: Why, that you had to live in these conditions!

Stella: Aren't you being a little intense about it? It's not that bad at all! New Orleans isn't like other cities.

Blanche: This has got nothing to do with New Orleans. You might as well say – forgive   90
             me, blessed baby! [*She suddenly stops short.*] The subject is closed!

Stella [*a little drily*]:   Thanks.

             [*During the pause, Blanche stares at her. She smiles at Blanche.*]

Blanche [*looking down at her glass, which shakes in her hand*]: You're all I've got in the
             world, and you're not
             glad to see me!

Immediately after your read-through, the people who have played Eunice, Blanche and Stella should write on their own for 10–15 minutes about the kind of characters they think they are. This is best done in note form and in role ('I …'). Whoever has read the stage-directions should jot notes about all three characters, referring only to the stage-directions, not to the dialogue.

● Now take turns to describe 'yourself' to each other verbally. Do so as if you are the character you have played, quoting your lines to justify the account you give. The other characters should add to what you say by developing your ideas further, questioning and/or challenging you, saying how they see you from the point of view of 'their' character, and so on.

● Next, the stage-directions reader should comment on the relationships the playwright is building up between Eunice and Blanche and, in particular, between Blanche and Stella. S/he should suggest ways in which these relationships might be made clear on stage by means of movement, gesture, tone of voice, use of props and so on. Again, the three readers should join in, still speaking from the viewpoint of 'their' character and adding their own perspectives to the discussion. (Don't be afraid to disagree!)

● Finally, the whole group should form themselves into a production team. Discuss how to play the scene as a whole and how best to convey your understanding of it to an audience. In particular:
  • Agree on two or three **keynote lines** for each character which you want to emphasise in order to shape the audience's response to Eunice, Stella and Blanche.
  • Consider the **rhythm** of the scene. Where is the pace of the dialogue at its fastest, and why? Where is the pace of the dialogue at its slowest, and why?
  • Identify the points in the scene where there is the strongest degree of **tension and conflict**. How could these be highlighted in performance?

By now you have moved well beyond your first read-through. Draw on the understandings you have achieved in discussion to perform a rehearsed reading of the scene, playing the same parts as you did before. If you feel confident enough, do your reading onto audio-tape: this will be of great benefit in comparing your version with those of other groups.

What has all this to do with studying Shakespeare?

Almost everything. You have established a theatrical perspective on a play text which you've worked on as a script to be performed rather than as a museum piece to be gazed on in frightened reverence. The 'difficulty' of Shakespeare's language apart (and it is often greatly over-stated: any decent edition has adequate footnotes), you've confronted some of the principal elements in all drama. Above all, you've played an active part in making your own meanings by exploring the text collaboratively, not by listening to a lecture.

Discuss as a class your feelings about working in this way as a means of 'getting inside' a drama text the first time you encounter it. What do you think might be the advantages and disadvantages of this approach as you open your brand new copy of *Othello*, *Richard III*, *The Winter's Tale* or whatever

– knowing that, at the end of the day, you will have to answer questions on them in an external exam? It's of the utmost importance to decide with your teacher how best to proceed before you begin work on a 'set' Shakespeare play: there is nothing to be gained by either of you grousing that 'it's not going well' when you're thirty lessons into *Hamlet*.

The Globe Theatre: Shakespeare's wooden 'O'

This section ends with the most important 'perspective' of all: the nature of the theatre for which Shakespeare's plays were written. Use the illustrations of two Globe Theatres on pages 82–3 to consider with your teacher how Shakespeare must have 'seen' his plays on stage as he was writing them – both in his mind's eye and as a performer himself. Focus in particular on:

● What you can deduce about how a play written in the late 1590s must have been staged.

● The differences between Shakespeare's Globe and a typical modern theatre. What can you learn from these about how a production of (say) *Macbeth* would have been mounted in about 1605? Think about both the staging of particular scenes you may know – such as the opening Witches' scene, the Banquet scene, Lady Macbeth's sleepwalking, the battle scenes in Act V – and other aspects of production such as verse-speaking and the relationship between actors and audience.

A scene from a performance of 'Henry V' at the reconstructed Globe Theatre in London (1997)

An artist's impression of a performance of 'Henry IV' at the original Globe Theatre (about 1597)

Stage-crafting a scene: shape and rhythm

Shakespeare was an actor who became a playwright (which means a maker or crafter, not a 'writer', of plays). The best way of getting to grips with the writing is to respond to the way the plays are 'made' from an actor's standpoint. This section uses an extract from *The Merchant of Venice* to show how such an approach can illuminate the crafting of the drama more usefully than a line-by-line 'analysis' of the text.

As with *A Streetcar Named Desire*, form groups and do a first read-through of the following extract as if you were preparing a performance of it.

>-|-<>-·-O-·-<>-|-<

from The Merchant of Venice

> Shylock, a Jew, makes his living by money-lending in Venice. Antonio is a merchant trader who has borrowed a large sum from Shylock to help his friend Bassanio achieve his dearest wish: to journey to Belmont and win the beautiful Portia for his wife. This Bassanio has done.
>
> When Antonio is unable to repay Shylock the loan – he loses all his capital after his merchant ships sink in a sea-storm – Shylock takes him to court to claim his 'bond'. This is the forfeit Antonio has agreed to pay if he fails to honour the debt: Shylock is to be allowed a pound of Antonio's flesh, cut from 'nearest his heart'.
>
> In Belmont, Portia has heard of the predicament her husband's friend is in. Secretly, she disguises herself as a male doctor of law and arranges with Bellario, the appointed judge, to be allowed to judge the case Shylock has brought against Antonio. No one else in Venice knows of this arrangement: Bellario pleads sickness and sends Portia in his place with a strong letter of recommendation for the Duke of Venice, who presides over the court.
>
> This, then, is the trial scene. Shylock, the petitioner, is the only Jew present. Everyone else is a Christian, including Gratiano, a close friend of Antonio and Bassanio. In Venice there is an on-going history of hatred between Christians and Jews.

[*The Court. Enter Portia, dressed like a Doctor of Laws.*]

Duke: Come you from old Bellario?

Portia: I did, my lord.

Duke: You are welcome; take your place.
Are you acquainted with the difference
That holds this present question in the court?

Portia: I am informèd thoroughly of the cause.
Which is the merchant here, and which the Jew?

Duke: Antonio and old Shylock, both stand forth.

Portia: Is your name Shylock?

Shylock: Shylock is my name.

5

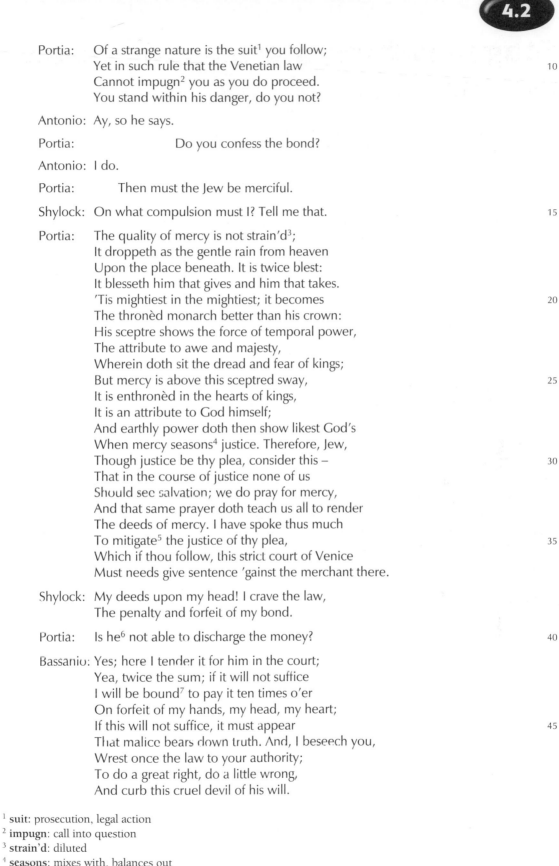

Portia: Of a strange nature is the suit[1] you follow;
Yet in such rule that the Venetian law 10
Cannot impugn[2] you as you do proceed.
You stand within his danger, do you not?

Antonio: Ay, so he says.

Portia: Do you confess the bond?

Antonio: I do.

Portia: Then must the Jew be merciful.

Shylock: On what compulsion must I? Tell me that. 15

Portia: The quality of mercy is not strain'd[3];
It droppeth as the gentle rain from heaven
Upon the place beneath. It is twice blest:
It blesseth him that gives and him that takes.
'Tis mightiest in the mightiest; it becomes 20
The thronèd monarch better than his crown:
His sceptre shows the force of temporal power,
The attribute to awe and majesty,
Wherein doth sit the dread and fear of kings;
But mercy is above this sceptred sway, 25
It is enthronèd in the hearts of kings,
It is an attribute to God himself;
And earthly power doth then show likest God's
When mercy seasons[4] justice. Therefore, Jew,
Though justice be thy plea, consider this – 30
That in the course of justice none of us
Should see salvation; we do pray for mercy,
And that same prayer doth teach us all to render
The deeds of mercy. I have spoke thus much
To mitigate[5] the justice of thy plea, 35
Which if thou follow, this strict court of Venice
Must needs give sentence 'gainst the merchant there.

Shylock: My deeds upon my head! I crave the law,
The penalty and forfeit of my bond.

Portia: Is he[6] not able to discharge the money? 40

Bassanio: Yes; here I tender it for him in the court;
Yea, twice the sum; if it will not suffice
I will be bound[7] to pay it ten times o'er
On forfeit of my hands, my head, my heart;
If this will not suffice, it must appear 45
That malice bears down truth. And, I beseech you,
Wrest once the law to your authority;
To do a great right, do a little wrong,
And curb this cruel devil of his will.

[1] **suit**: prosecution, legal action
[2] **impugn**: call into question
[3] **strain'd**: diluted
[4] **seasons**: mixes with, balances out
[5] **mitigate**: moderate the harshness
[6] **he**: i.e. Antonio
[7] **bound**: liable in law

Portia: It must not be; there is no power in Venice   50
          Can alter a decree establishèd;
          'Twill be recorded for a precedent,
          And many an error, by the same example,
          Will rush into the state; it cannot be.

Shylock: A Daniel[1] come to judgement! Yea, a Daniel!   55
          O wise young judge, how I do honour thee!

Portia: I pray you, let me look upon the bond.

Shylock: Here 'tis, most reverend Doctor; here it is.

Portia: Shylock, there's thrice thy money offer'd thee.

Shylock: An oath, an oath! I have an oath in heaven.   60
          Shall I lay perjury upon my soul?
          No, not for Venice.

Portia: Why, this bond is forfeit[2];
          And lawfully by this the Jew may claim
          A pound of flesh, to be by him cut off
          Nearest the merchant's heart. Be merciful.   65
          Take thrice thy money; bid me tear the bond.

Shylock: When it is paid according to the tenour[3].
          It doth appear you are a worthy judge;
          You know the law; your exposition
          Hath been most sound; I charge you by the law,   70
          Whereof you are a well-deserving pillar,
          Proceed to judgement. By my soul I swear
          There is no power in the tongue of man
          To alter me. I stay here on my bond.

Antonio: Most heartily I do beseech the court   75
          To give the judgement.

Portia: Why then, thus it is:
          You must prepare your bosom for his knife.

Shylock: O noble judge! O excellent young man!

Portia: For the intent and purpose of the law
          Hath full relation[4] to the penalty,   80
          Which here appeareth due upon the bond.

Shylock: 'Tis very true. O wise and upright judge,
          How much more elder art thou than thy looks!

Portia: Therefore, lay bare your bosom.

Shylock: Ay, his breast –
          So says the bond; doth it not, noble judge?   85
          'Nearest his heart', those are the very words.

---

[1] **Daniel**: the name means 'God is my Judge' (Old Testament)
[2] **forfeit**: payable
[3] **tenour**: the exact reading of the legal document
[4] **relation**: application

Portia: It is so. Are there balance[1] here to weigh
            The flesh?

Shylock: I have them ready.

Portia: Have by[2] some surgeon, Shylock, on your charge,
            To stop his wounds, lest he do bleed to death.   90

Shylock: Is it so nominated in the bond?

Portia: It is not so express'd, but what of that?
            'Twere good you do so much for charity.

Shylock: I cannot find it; 'tis not in the bond.

Portia: You, merchant, have you anything to say?   95

Antonio: But little: I am arm'd[3] and well prepar'd.
            Give me your hand Bassanio; fare you well.
            Grieve not that I am fall'n to this for you,
            For herein Fortune shows herself more kind
            Than is her custom. It is still her use   100
            To let the wretched man outlive his wealth,
            To view with hollow eye and wrinkled brow
            An age of poverty; from which ling'ring penance
            Of such misery doth she cut me off.
            Commend me to your honourable wife;   105
            Tell her the process of Antonio's end;
            Say how I lov'd you; speak me fair in death;
            And, when the tale is told, bid her be judge
            Whether Bassanio had not once a love.
            Repent not that you shall lose your friend,   110
            And he repents not that he pays your debt;
            For if the Jew do cut but deep enough,
            I'll pay it instantly with all my heart.

Bassanio: Antonio, I am married to a wife
            Which is as dear to me as life itself;   115
            But life itself, my wife, and all the world,
            Are not with me esteem'd above thy life;
            I would lose all, ay, sacrifice them all
            Here to this devil, to deliver you …

Shylock [Aside]: These be the Christian husbands! I have a daughter[4] –   120
            Would any of the stock of Barrabas[5]
            Had been her husband, rather than a Christian! –
            We trifle time; I pray thee pursue sentence.

Portia: A pound of that same merchant's flesh is thine.
            The court awards it and the law doth give it.   125

Shylock: Most rightful judge!

Portia: And you must cut this flesh from off his breast.
            The law allows it and the court awards it.

Shylock: Most learned judge! A sentence! Come, prepare.

[1] **balance**: weighing-scales
[2] **by**: i.e. close at hand
[3] **arm'd**: fortified mentally
[4] **daughter**: Shylock's daughter, Jessica, has eloped to marry a Christian
[5] **Barrabas**: proverbial name of Jews

Portia:	Tarry a little; there is something else.	130
	This bond doth give thee here no jot of blood:	
	The words expressly are 'a pound of flesh'.	
	Take then thy bond, take thou thy pound of flesh;	
	But, in the cutting it, if thou dost shed	
	One drop of Christian blood, thy lands and goods	135
	Are, by the laws of Venice, confiscate	
	Unto the state of Venice.	

Portia: Tarry a little; there is something else.   130
        This bond doth give thee here no jot of blood:
        The words expressly are 'a pound of flesh'.
        Take then thy bond, take thou thy pound of flesh;
        But, in the cutting it, if thou dost shed
        One drop of Christian blood, thy lands and goods   135
        Are, by the laws of Venice, confiscate
        Unto the state of Venice.

Gratiano: O upright judge!
        Mark, Jew. O learned judge!

Shylock: Is that the law?

Portia: Thyself shall see the act;
        For, as thou urgest justice, be assur'd
        Thou shalt have justice, more than thou desir'st.   140

Gratiano: O learned judge! Mark, Jew. A learned judge!

Shylock: I take this offer then: pay the bond thrice
        And let the Christian go.

Bassanio: Here is the money.

Portia: Soft![1]
        The Jew shall have all justice. Soft! No haste.   145
        He shall have nothing but the penalty.

Gratiano: O Jew! An upright judge, a learned judge!

---

[1] **Soft**: not so fast

Shylock prepares to cut his 'pound of flesh' from Antonio's body

Portia: Therefore, prepare thee to cut off the flesh.
           Shed thou no blood, nor cut thou less nor more
           But just a pound of flesh; if thou tak'st more   150
           Or less than a just pound – be it but so much
           As makes it light or heavy in the substance,
           Or the division of the twentieth part
           Of one poor scruple; nay, if the scale do turn
           But in the estimation[1] of a hair –   155
           Thou diest, and all thy goods are confiscate[2].

Gratiano: A second Daniel, a Daniel, Jew!
          Now infidel, I have thee on the hip.

Portia: Why doth the Jew pause? Take thy forfeiture.

Shylock: Give me my principal[3] and let me go.   160

Bassanio: I have it ready for thee; here it is.

Portia: He hath refus'd it in the open court;
           He shall have merely justice, and his bond.

Gratiano: A Daniel still say I, a second Daniel!
          I thank thee, Jew, for teaching me that word.   165

Shylock: Shall I not have barely my principal?

Portia: Thou shalt have nothing but the forfeiture
           To be so taken at thy peril, Jew.

Shylock: Why, then the devil give him good of it!
          I'll stay no longer question.

Portia: Tarry, Jew.   170
           The law hath yet another hold on you.
           It is enacted in the laws of Venice,
           If it be proved against an alien[4]
           That by direct or indirect attempts
           He seek the life of any citizen,   175
           The party 'gainst the which he doth contrive
           Shall seize one half his goods; the other half
           Come to the privy coffer of the state;
           And the offender's life lies in the mercy
           Of the Duke only, 'gainst all other voice.   180
           In which predicament, I say, thou stand'st;
           For it appears by manifest proceeding
           That indirectly, and directly too,
           Thou hast contrived against the very life
           Of the defendant; and thou hast incurr'd   185
           The danger formerly by me rehears'd.
           Down, therefore, and beg mercy of the Duke.

Gratiano: Beg that thou mayst have leave to hang thyself;
          And yet, thy wealth being forfeit to the state,
          Thou hast not left the value of a cord;   190
          Therefore thou must be hang'd at the state's charge.

[1] **estimation**: smallest weight, fraction
[2] **confiscate**: seized from you
[3] **principal**: the value of the original loan
[4] **alien**: a Jewish immigrant

Duke: That thou shalt see the difference of our spirit[1],
           I pardon thee thy life before thou ask it.
           For half thy wealth, it is Antonio's;
           The other half comes to the general state,   195
           Which humbleness may drive unto a fine.

Portia: Ay, for the state; not for Antonio.

Shylock: Nay, take my life and all, pardon not that.
           You take my house when you do take the prop
           That doth sustain my house; you take my life   200
           When you do take the means whereby I live.

Portia: What mercy can you render him, Antonio?

Gratiano: A halter gratis[2]; nothing else, for God's sake!

Antonio: So please my lord the Duke and all the court
           To quit[3] the fine for one half of his goods;   205
           I am content, so he will let me have
           The other half in use, to render it
           Upon his death unto the gentleman
           That lately stole his daughter –
           Two things provided more[4]: that, for this favour,   210
           He presently become a Christian;
           The other, that he do record a gift,
           Here in the court, of all he dies possess'd
           Unto his son[5] Lorenzo and his daughter.

Duke: He shall do this, or else I do recant   215
           The pardon that I late pronouncèd here.

Portia: Art thou contented, Jew? What dost thou say?

Shylock: I am content.

Portia: Clerk, draw a deed of gift.

Shylock: I pray you, give me leave to go from hence;
           I am not well; send the deed after me   220
           And I will sign it.

Duke: Get thee gone, but do it.

        [*Exit Shylock.*]

---

[1] **spirit**: attitude, state of mind
[2] **halter gratis**: a noose free-of-charge to hang himself with
[3] **quit**: remit, reduce
[4] **Two … more**: depending on the further conditions
[5] **son**: i.e. his daughter's Christian husband, Lorenzo, Shylock's son-in-law

Inserting stage-directions

Look back to the Tennessee Williams extract in Section 4.1, where the stage-directions are frequent and very explicit. Find examples of their various functions which can be listed under these ten headings:

① Entrances and exits

② Details of set

③ Costume and props

④ Lighting effects

⑤ Physical movements across stage

⑥ Gestures/body language

⑦ Pauses/pace of dialogue

⑧ Tone of voice

⑨ Descriptions of characters' moods and feelings

⑩ Comments on personality

In the *Merchant of Venice* trial scene, Shakespeare's stage-directions are extremely sparse: they are confined to fixing the location, specifying entrances and exits, and indicating one 'aside'. Help yourself to see and hear the scene from the audience's standpoint by (a) imagining the stage-directions Shakespeare might have included to correspond with ② ③ and ④ above; and (b) inserting anywhere in the scene at least *two* stage-directions you think are appropriate for each of ⑤ ⑥ ⑦ ⑧ ⑨ and ⑩ above. For example:

● line 42, ⑤ – Bassanio moves slightly forward towards the Duke, holding out money-bags.

● line 130, ⑥ and ⑦ – Portia makes a long pause after ' … there is something else'. She reads the bond to herself, scanning it closely. A tense silence in the court. Shylock, impatient, freezes with his hand clasped around his knife, giving her a half-puzzled, half-suspicious stare.

● lines 219–21, ⑥ ⑧ and ⑨ – Shylock's words are barely audible. He is crushed, defeated. He turns from looking at the Duke and walks slowly and unsteadily towards the courtroom door, as if in another world.

If you use this technique as a starting point for your class discussion of any Shakespearean scene, you should be better equipped to consider plot development, character, theme and so on at a later stage. Adding the theatrical dimensions in this way will become automatic with practice. It is far less laborious, and far more illuminating, than spending all your mental energy on summarising 'what the words mean'.

Plotting the trial scene

To actors, the term 'plotting' applies to the movements they make and their positions on stage at specific points during the scene. These are obviously worked out with the producer or director, for whom 'plotting' has a broader meaning. S/he will come to rehearsals with a sense of the overall shape and rhythm of the scene – which will, in turn, reflect the way s/he wants the audience to respond as they watch and listen.

For the trial scene, a director's rehearsal notes might begin like this:

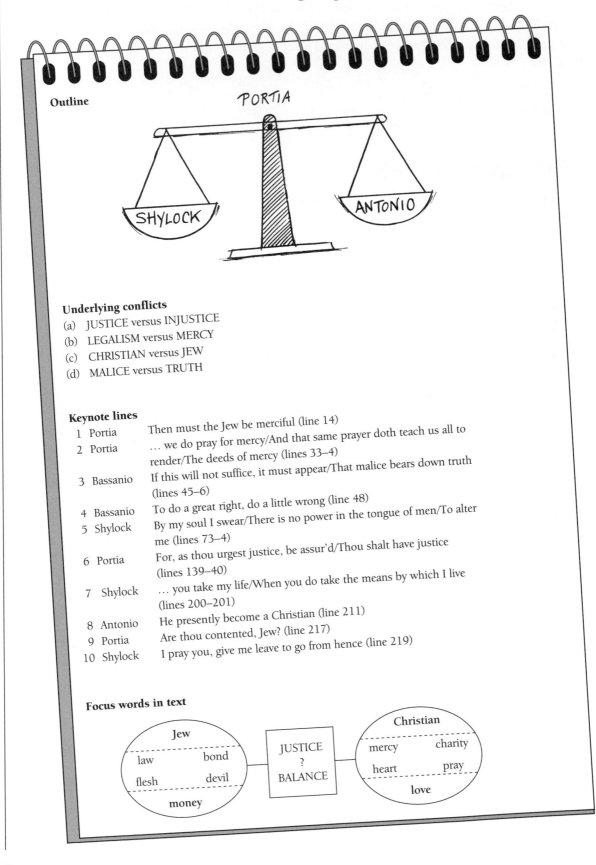

Outline

PORTIA

SHYLOCK — ANTONIO

Underlying conflicts

(a) JUSTICE versus INJUSTICE

(b) LEGALISM versus MERCY

(c) CHRISTIAN versus JEW

(d) MALICE versus TRUTH

Keynote lines

1	Portia	Then must the Jew be merciful (line 14)
2	Portia	… we do pray for mercy/And that same prayer doth teach us all to render/The deeds of mercy (lines 33–4)
3	Bassanio	If this will not suffice, it must appear/That malice bears down truth (lines 45–6)
4	Bassanio	To do a great right, do a little wrong (line 48)
5	Shylock	By my soul I swear/There is no power in the tongue of men/To alter me (lines 73–4)
6	Portia	For, as thou urgest justice, be assur'd/Thou shalt have justice (lines 139–40)
7	Shylock	… you take my life/When you do take the means by which I live (lines 200–201)
8	Antonio	He presently become a Christian (line 211)
9	Portia	Are thou contented, Jew? (line 217)
10	Shylock	I pray you, give me leave to go from hence (line 219)

Focus words in text

Jew
law   bond
flesh   devil
money

JUSTICE
?
BALANCE

Christian
mercy   charity
heart   pray
love

In a group, or as a class, now discuss how you would direct a performance of this scene. Draw on all the approaches covered so far in this chapter, and any others you consider important. Keep constantly in mind the fact that the play can only be brought fully into being on the stage: drama is a dialogue between playwright and audience (who are not 'reading the book' but responding to what they see and hear as a form of experience).

If you wish, use the work you have done in this section to mount your own performance of the trial scene. The extent to which you include a degree of action and movement is, of course, up to you. What is more important is that your reading of the text is informed by the understanding you have gained of the scene as a piece of theatre.

Exam preparation?

Discuss with your teacher your reactions to exploring the trial scene in this way. Does it differ significantly from the way you 'did' Shakespeare for GCSE? If so, how far has this approach assisted – or failed to assist – your appreciation and enjoyment of a Shakespearean text?

Finally, consider how adequate such an approach might be in preparing a Shakespeare set play for the A level exam. A recent question on *The Merchant of Venice* was:

> *'Shylock may be portrayed in a critical light, but the Christians in the play emerge with little more credit.' Consider this view of* The Merchant of Venice, *making clear where your own sympathies lie.*

Unless you know the whole play already, you only have the trial scene to go on. How much relevant material for answering this question could you draw from the work you have just done?

Patterns of language: reading with the ear

Section 4.1 reminds you that Shakespeare's theatre was almost entirely bare of scenery and other stage devices familiar to us, such as lighting effects. The Globe was not a theatre of visual illusion but, as one Shakespearean director has termed it, an 'empty space'. In this space, the actors' voices were of paramount importance; it is worth recalling that the literal meaning of audience is 'a collection of listeners'.

When Shakespeare the actor became Shakespeare the dramatist, he wrote his plays largely in blank verse. Like all forms of poetry, blank verse is patterned language. Learn to recognise and respond to this verbal patterning and you will get nearer to the heart of the plays than by any other means. In order to do so, you need to hear, rather than just read, the text – as you would, of course, in the theatre.

The extract below from *King Lear* begins twenty lines into the play. It is used in this section to help you discover for yourself how the language patterns in Shakespeare not only create the drama but also convey to an audience plot, character and theme – those aspects of your set plays on which A level examiners most frequently ask questions.

By yourself, read through the extract, noting carefully the glosses at the foot of the page. Then read it aloud as a class or in a group.

from King Lear

> The elderly King Lear has decided to abdicate from the throne of Britain. He has three daughters: Goneril, the eldest, who has married the Duke of Albany; Regan, wife to the Duke of Cornwall; and Cordelia, the youngest, for whose hand in marriage the King of France and the Duke of Burgundy are competing.
>
> Lear's plan is to divide the control of his kingdom between the three daughters. His decision will be based on the extent to which they say they love him.
>
> This scene, in which the 'love test' and the formal division of the kingdom are due to take place, begins the play. Also present are the Earl of Gloucester, an elder statesman, and the Earl of Kent, who has served Lear devotedly throughout his life.

[*Lear's palace. Enter one bearing a coronet, then King Lear, then the Dukes of Cornwall and Albany, next Goneril, Regan, Cordelia, and Attendants.*]

Lear:	Attend the lords of France and Burgundy, Gloucester.
Gloucester:	I shall, my lord. [*Exit*]
Lear:	Meantime we[1] shall express our darker purpose[2].
	Give me the map there. Know that we have divided
	In three our kingdom; and 'tis our fast[3] intent 5

---

[1] **we**: I (Lear uses the 'royal plural')
[2] **darker purpose**: hidden intention
[3] **fast**: fixed

To shake all cares and business from our age,
Conferring them on younger strengths, while we
Unburdened crawl toward death. Our son[1] of Cornwall,
And you our no less loving son of Albany,
We have this hour a constant will to publish   10
Our daughters' several dowers[2], that future strife
May be prevented now. The Princes, France and Burgundy,
Great rivals in our youngest daughter's love,
Long in our court have made their amorous sojourn,
And here are to be answered. Tell me, my daughters   15
(Since now we will divest us both of rule,
Interest[3] of territory, cares of state),
Which of you shall we say doth love us most,
That we our largest bounty may extend
Where nature doth with merit challenge[4]. Goneril,   20
Our eldest-born, speak first.

Goneril: Sir, I love you more than word can wield[5] the matter;
                Dearer than eyesight, space[6] and liberty;
                Beyond what can be valued, rich or rare;
                No less than life, with grace, health, beauty, honour;   25
                As much as child e'er loved, or father found;
                A love that makes breath[7] poor, and speech unable;
                Beyond all manner of so much I love you.

Cordelia [aside]: What shall Cordelia speak? Love, and be silent.

Lear: Of all these bounds, even from this line to this,   30
                With shadowy forests, and with champains riched[8],
                With plenteous rivers, and wide-skirted meads,
                We make thee lady. To thine and Albany's issues[9]
                By this perpetual. What says our second daughter,
                Our dearest Regan, wife to Cornwall? Speak.   35

Regan: I am made of that self mettle[10] as my sister,
                And prize me at her worth[11]. In my true heart
                I find she names my very deed of love;
                Only she comes too short, that[12] I profess
                Myself an enemy to all other joys   40
                Which the most precious square of sense professes,
                And find I am alone felicitate[13]
                In your dear Highness' love.

[1] **son**: i.e. son-in-law
[2] **several dowers**: separate dowries
[3] **Interest**: legal right
[4] **nature … challenge**: love contends with desert
[5] **wield**: deal with
[6] **space**: scope
[7] **breath**: language
[8] **champains riched**: fertile plains
[9] **issues**: descendants
[10] **mettle**: temperament
[11] **worth**: the same value
[12] **that**: i.e. in that
[13] **felicitate**: made happy

Cordelia [*aside*]:   Then poor Cordelia!
                  And yet not so, since I am sure my love's
                  More ponderous[1] than my tongue.   45

Lear: To thee and thine hereditary ever
                  Remain this ample third of our fair kingdom,
                  No less in space, validity[2], and pleasure
                  Than that conferred on Goneril. Now, our joy,
                  Although the last and least[3]; to whose young love   50
                  The vines of France and milk[4] of Burgundy
                  Strive to be interessed[5]; what can you say to draw
                  A third more opulent than your sisters? Speak.

Cordelia: Nothing, my lord.

Lear: Nothing?   55

Cordelia: Nothing.

Lear: Nothing will come of nothing. Speak again.

Cordelia: Unhappy that I am, I cannot heave
                  My heart into my mouth. I love your Majesty
                  According to my bond[6], no more nor less.   60

Lear: How, now, Cordelia? Mend your speech a little,
                  Lest you may mar your fortunes.

Cordelia: Good my lord,
                  You have begot me, bred me, loved me. I
                  Return those duties back as are right fit[7],
                  Obey you, love you, and most honour you.   65
                  Why have my sisters husbands if they say
                  They love you all? Haply[8], when I shall wed,
                  That lord whose hand must take my plight[9] shall carry
                  Half my love with him, half my care and duty.
                  Sure I shall never marry like my sisters   70
                  To love my father all.

Lear: But goes thy heart with this?

Cordelia: Ay, good my lord.

Lear: So young, and so untender?

Cordelia: So young, my lord, and true.

Lear: Let it be so. Thy truth then be thy dower!   75
                  For, by the sacred radiance of the sun,
                  The mysteries of Hecate[10] and the night,

[1] **ponderous**: weighty
[2] **validity**: value
[3] **least**: youngest
[4] **milk**: i.e. pastures
[5] **interessed**: connected
[6] **bond**: natural duty as a daughter
[7] **right fit**: correspondingly dutiful
[8] **Haply**: perhaps
[9] **plight**: duty as a wife
[10] **Hecate**: goddess of witchcraft

By all the operations of the orbs[1]
From whom we do exist and cease to be,
Here I disclaim all my paternal care, 80
Propinquity and property of blood[2],
And as a stranger to my heart and me
Hold thee from this for ever. The barbarous Scythian[3],
And he that makes his generations messes[4]
To gorge his appetite, shall to my bosom 85
Be as well neighboured, pitied, and relieved,
As thou my sometime[5] daughter.

Kent: Good my liege –

Lear: Peace, Kent!
Come not between the Dragon[6] and his wrath.
I loved her most, and thought to set my rest 90
On her kind nursery[7]. Hence and avoid my sight!
So be my grave my peace, as here I give
Her father's heart from her! Call France. Who stirs?
Call Burgundy. Cornwall and Albany,
With my two daughters' dowers digest[8] the third; 95
Let pride, which she call plainness, marry her[9].
I do invest you jointly with my power,
Pre-eminence, and all the large effects
That troop with majesty[10]. Ourself, by monthly course,
With reservation of a hundred knights, 100
By you to be sustained, shall our abode
Make with you by due turn. Only we shall retain
The name, and all th'addition[11] to a king. The sway,
Revenue, execution of the rest,
Beloved sons, be yours; which to confirm, 105
This coronet[12] part between you.

Kent: Royal Lear,
Whom I have ever honoured as my king,
Loved as my father, as my master followed,
As my great patron thought on in my prayers –

Lear: The bow is bent and drawn; make from the shaft[13]. 110

---

[1] **orbs**: stars (as in astrology)
[2] **Propinquity … blood**: relationship and parental bond
[3] **Scythian**: type of savage
[4] **makes his generations messes**: eats his own offspring
[5] **sometime**: former
[6] **Dragon**: symbol of (a) British kingship (b) ferocity
[7] **nursery**: care and comfort
[8] **digest**: divide up, aborb
[9] **marry her**: find her a husband
[10] **troop with majesty**: befit a king
[11] **th'addition**: titles and honours
[12] **coronet**: the crown Lear intended for Cordelia
[13] **make from the shaft**: avoid the arrow

Lear superintends the 'love test'

Kent: Let it fall[1] rather, though the fork[2] invade
The region of my heart. Be Kent unmannerly
When Lear is mad. What wouldst thou do, old man?
Think'st thou that duty shall have dread to speak
When power to flattery bows? To plainness honour's bound   115
When majesty stoops to folly. Reserve thy state[3],
And in thy best consideration check
This hideous rashness. Answer my life my judgement[4],
Thy youngest daughter does not love thee least,
Nor are those empty-hearted whose low sounds   120
Reverb no hollowness[5].

Lear: Kent, on thy life, no more!

Kent: My life I never held but as a pawn
To wage[6] against thine enemies; nor fear to lose it,
They safety being motive[7].

Lear: Out of my sight!

Kent: See better, Lear, and let me still remain   125
The true blank[8] of thine eye.

Lear: Now by Apollo –

Kent: Now by Apollo, King,
Thou swear'st thy gods in vain.

Lear: O vassal! Miscreant![9] [*lays his hand
on his sword*]

[1] **fall:** strike
[2] **fork:** point
[3] **Reserve thy state:** retain your kingship
[4] **Answer … judgement:** I stake my life on my opinion
[5] **Reverb no hollowness:** do not sound hollow
[6] **wage:** fight
[7] **thy safety being motive:** your life being the cause
[8] **blank:** centre
[9] **vassal! Miscreant!:** wretch! Traitor!

Language contrasts, dramatic conflicts

1 It has become something of a cliché to say that 'drama is conflict'. Like most clichés, however, it embodies a truism. There are three strong and specific conflict-points in the mere 128 lines that comprise this extract:

- between Goneril and Regan, on the one hand, and Cordelia on the other;
- between Lear and Cordelia;
- between Lear and Kent.

Scan the extract and note down all the reasons you can find to explain why these conflicts occur.

2 As a class, examine how the conflict between the three sisters is dramatised through contrasts between the kinds of language they speak. Look first at the speeches made by Goneril (lines 22–8) and Regan (lines 36–43). Read them aloud.

- How are these two speeches alike in their tone?

- Each of the seven lines in Goneril's speech (lines 22–8) has a similar form. Describe it. What impression is conveyed by this in terms of the structure of the speech as a whole?

- In protesting against Lear's outburst against Cordelia, Kent condemns the older sisters' speeches as hollow 'flattery' of Lear (line 115). On the evidence of Regan's speech, is he right?

- Later on in the scene, Cordelia says she 'lacks that glib and oily art / To speak and purpose not' (i.e. the ability to be hypocritical and say things she doesn't mean). Do you think her implicit criticism of her sisters' speeches as exercises in artifice is justified?

- Now look at Cordelia's two asides (line 29 and lines 43–5), her exchange with Lear (lines 54–60) and her longer speech at lines 62–71. In how many ways does her language differ from her sisters'? What do these contrasts in language indicate about their differences in character?

3 Look next at how verbal patterning serves to highlight the conflict between Lear and Cordelia.

- On the evidence of lines 49–53, how does Lear want Cordelia to reply to his question, 'what can you say to draw / A third more opulent than your sisters'?

- How does the language pattern of the whole scene suddenly change at this point (lines 54–7):

  Cordelia: Nothing, my lord.
  Lear: Nothing?
  Cordelia: Nothing.
  Lear: Nothing will come of nothing. Speak again.

  What should be the effect in the theatre of this short passage? Direct the two actors in how to speak the lines here, adding instructions on other relevant matters such as pauses, facial expressions, gestures, body language and so on.

- Look at Lear's condemnation of Cordelia in his speech running from line 75 to line 86. Read it aloud until you are satisfied that you have established a suitable tone, pace and rhythm. Then contrast these elements in the speech with Lear's language at the start of the scene, from line 3 to line 21. What do the very different kinds of language patterning tell you about the change in Lear's feelings as the scene progresses?

4 Finally, contrast the language used by Lear and Kent in their confrontation at the end of the extract.

- Comment on the tone and choice of language in which Kent first addresses Lear (lines 106–9). In another context, Kent's phraseology – 'Royal Lear', 'my king', 'my father', 'my master', 'my great patron' – might be construed as flattery. Why do you think he chooses these terms?

- In his next speech, Kent uses a very different vocabulary: 'Lear is mad', 'What would'st thou do, old man', 'folly', 'hideous rashness'. What do you think Kent's intention is here in adopting this changed mode of speech?

- From line 111 onwards, Kent speaks nine sentences (as opposed to lines). Read them in turn around the class, one after the other, ignoring Lear's interruptions. How are Kent's sentences alike in their form – and how are they reminiscent of the form of Cordelia's sentences? What does this suggest about the similarities between Kent and Cordelia?

- Contrast the form and tone of the six sentences Lear speaks to Kent with those you have just examined. What do they indicate about Lear's state of mind towards the end of the extract? How do they differ from the way in which Lear spoke at the start of this scene?

- Think of the language pattern of Kent's dialogue with Lear as a verbal contest. Which of the two achieves the upper hand? How do you know?

- What do you deduce from the way Lear's capacity for language collapses altogether by the end of the extract – [*lays his hand on his sword*]?

Rehearsed reading

As always, your study of a Shakespeare scene should end, as well as begin, with reading aloud. Use the insights you have gained into the verbal patterning of the extract from *King Lear* to rehearse and produce an informed reading of it. Your preparations should concentrate, as this whole section has done, on (a) tone, (b) pace (including pauses), (c) rhythm and (d) emphasis.

The nature of the play: theatrical conventions

In the theatre, your response to Shakespeare – as to any other dramatist – depends upon the sort of play you are watching. It seems almost too obvious to say that not all of Shakespeare's plays are of the same kind. You will have little trouble in identifying *Twelfth Night* as a comedy and *Romeo and Juliet*, on the other hand, as a tragedy – although such trite labels sometimes turn out to obscure as much as they enlighten.

Far more important is to recognise that, in preparing his plays for performance, Shakespeare used theatrical conventions ('ways of crafting') less familiar to us than they were to audiences in the early 1600s. This is particularly true of a group of plays from which A level examiners are fond of selecting 'set' texts: the cluster of so-called last plays or romances which include *The Winter's Tale*, *Cymbeline* and *The Tempest*; and the 'problem plays' – notably *Measure for Measure*, *Troilus and Cressida* and *Coriolanus*. They need to be approached in certain ways which take account of the fact that they were (a) written for a theatre at the furthest end of the spectrum from contemporary slice-of-life television, and (b) written according to conventions which make sense only if you read them quite differently from a typical modern novel, story or magazine serial.

Understanding the medium for which they were written and within which they were performed will allow you to get your bearings on works like *The Tempest*, which is used in this section to illustrate that the theatrical conventions of a Shakespeare play are an essential part of 'what it means'.

Read the extract from *The Tempest* below, this time first to yourself.

>-·-◄>-·-◯-·-◄>-·-◄

from The Tempest

Twelve years ago Prospero, the Duke of Milan, was overthrown by a conspiracy between Alonso, the King of Naples, and two other lords: Antonio, Prospero's own brother, and Sebastian. These three cast Prospero and his infant daughter Miranda adrift in an open boat, expecting them to be drowned. Everyone in Milan believes that they were.

In fact, Providence decreed that Prospero and Miranda would live. They reached the safety of an island, where Prospero found two non-human inhabitants: Caliban, a savage monster, and Ariel, an 'airy spirit' (similar to Puck in *A Midsummer Night's Dream*). Prospero's loyal elder statesman Gonzalo hid Prospero's books about magic in the boat. Through studying them, Prospero has now perfected his magic powers to the extent that they are god-like.

With the help of Ariel, Prospero uses magic to raise a tempest which brings all those involved in his overthrow to the island. (They were making a sea voyage to celebrate the marriage of an African king and were shipwrecked in the storm.) Travelling with them was Alonso's son Ferdinand, whom Prospero has picked out to be the future husband of Miranda: under his influence they have fallen in love. Alonso and Ferdinand each believes the other to have been drowned in the shipwreck.

The extract below is from the play's final scene. Prospero's enemies, and Gonzalo, have wandered the island for three hours, aware only that they are 'lost' geographically and emotionally. Prospero plans to gather them all together and call them to account for their former actions. At this point, he has induced in them a collective trance. The audience knows of Prospero's plans and the power he has to carry them out; the play's human characters do not.

[*Solemn music. Enter Ariel before: then Alonso, with a frantic[1] gesture, attended by Gonzalo; Sebastian and Antonio in like manner. They all enter the circle which Prospero has made, and there stand charm'd; which Prospero observing, speaks.*]

Prospero:	A solemn air[2], and the best comforter
	To an unsettled fancy[3], cure thy brains,
	Now useless, boil'd within thy skull! There stand,
	For you are spell-stopp'd.
	Holy Gonzalo, honourable man,
	Mine eyes, even sociable[4] to the show of thine,
	Fall fellowly drops. Thy charm dissolves apace,
	And as the morning steals upon the night,
	Melting the darkness, so their rising senses
	Begin to chase the ignorant fumes that mantle[5]
	Their clearer reason. O good Gonzalo,
	My true preserver, and a loyal sir
	To him thou follow'st! I will pay thy graces
	Home both in word and deed. Most cruelly
	Didst thou, Alonso, use me and my daughter;
	Thy brother was a furtherer in the act.
	Thou art pinch'd[6] for't now, Sebastian. Flesh and blood,
	You, brother mine, that entertain'd ambition,
	Expell'd remorse and nature, who, with Sebastian –
	Whose inward pinches therefore art most strong –
	Would here have kill'd your king, I do forgive thee,
	Unnatural though thou art. Their understanding
	Begins to swell[7], and the approaching tide
	Will shortly fill the reasonable shore
	That now lies foul and muddy. Not one of them
	That yet looks on me, or would know me. Ariel,
	Fetch me the hat and rapier in my cell;
	I will discase[8] me, and myself present
	As I was sometime Milan. Quickly, spirit;
	Thou shalt ere long be free.

Line numbers: 5, 10, 15, 20, 25, 30

[*Ariel, on returning, sings and helps to attire him.*]

Ariel:	Where the bee sucks, there suck I;
	In a cowslip's bell I lie;
	There I couch when owls do cry.
	On the bat's back I do fly
	After summer merrily.
	Merrily, merrily, shall I live now
	Under the blossom that hangs on the bough.

Line numbers: 35

Prospero:	Why, that's my dainty Ariel! I shall miss thee;
	But yet thou shalt have thy freedom. So, so, so.
	To the king's ship, invisible as thou art;

Line number: 40

[1] **frantic**: distressed
[2] **air**: tune
[3] **unsettled fancy**: disturbed mind
[4] **sociable**: sensitive, sympathetic to
[5] **mantle**: obscure
[6] **pinch'd**: suffering
[7] **swell**: increase
[8] **discase**: take off my magician's robe

	There thou shalt find the mariners asleep
	Under the hatches; the master and the boatswain
	Being awake, enforce them to this place;
	And presently, I prithee.

Ariel: I drink the air before me, and return 45
Or ere your pulse beat twice.   [*Exit*]

Gonzalo [*waking*]: All torment, trouble, wonder and amazement
Inhabits here. Some heavenly power guide us
Out of this fearful country!

Prospero [*to Alonso*]:   Behold, Sir King,
The wrongèd Duke of Milan, Prospero. 50
For more assurance that a living prince
Does now speak to thee, I embrace thy body;
And to thee and thy company I bid
A hearty welcome.

Alonso: Whe'er[1] thou be'st he or no,
Or some enchanted trifle to abuse me, 55
As late I have been, I not know. Thy pulse
Beats, as of flesh and blood; and, since I saw thee,
Th'affliction of my mind[2] amends, with which,
I fear, a madness held me. This must crave –
An if this be at all – a most strange story. 60
Thy dukedom I resign[3], and do entreat
Thou pardon me my wrongs. But how should Prospero
Be living and be here?

Prospero [*to Gonzalo*]:   First, noble friend,
Let me embrace thine age, whose honour cannot
Be measur'd or confin'd.

Gonzalo: Whether this be 65
Or be not, I'll not swear.

Prospero: You do yet taste
Some subtleties[4] of th'isle, that will not let you
Believe things certain. Welcome, my friends all!
[*Aside to Sebastian and Antonio*]
But you, my brace[5] of lords, were I so minded,
I here could pluck his Highness' frown upon you, 70
And justify[6] you traitors; at this time
I will tell no tales.

Sebastian [*aside*]:   The devil speaks in him.

Prospero: No.
[*to Antonio*] For you, most wicked sir, whom to call brother
Would even infect my mouth, I do forgive

[1] **whe'er**: whether
[2] **affliction … mind**: i.e. grief for the 'death' of his son
[3] **resign**: restore to you
[4] **subtleties**: magical qualities
[5] **brace**: pair
[6] **justify**: prove you to be

	Thy rankest fault – all of them; and require	75
	My dukedom of thee, which perforce I know	
	Thou must restore.	

Alonso: If thou beest Prospero,
Give us particulars of thy preservation;
How thou hast met us here, whom three hours since
Were wreck'd upon this shore; where I have lost –   80
How sharp the point of this remembrance is! –
My dear son Ferdinand

Prospero: I am woe[1] for't, sir.

Alonso: Irreperable is the loss; and patience
Says it is past her cure.

Prospero: I rather think
You have not sought her help, of whose soft grace   85
For the like loss I have her sovereign aid,
And rest myself content.

Alonso: You the like loss!

Prospero: As great to me, as late; and, supportable
To make the dear loss, have I means much weaker
Than you may call to comfort you, for I   90
Have lost my daughter.

Alonso: A daughter!
O heavens, that they were living both in Naples,
The King and Queen there! That they were[2], I wish
Myself were muddied in that oozy bed
Where my son lies. When did you lose your daughter?   95

Prospero: In this last tempest. I perceive these lords
At this encounter[3] do so much admire[4]
That they devour their reason, and scarce think
Their eyes do offices of truth, their words
Are natural breath; but, howsoe'er you have   100
Been justled[5] from your senses, know for certain
That I am Prospero, and that very duke
Which was thrust forth of Milan; who most strangely
Upon this shore, where you were wreck'd, was landed
To be the lord on't. No more yet of this;   105
For 'tis a chronicle of day by day,
Not a relation for a breakfast, nor
Befitting this first meeting. Welcome, Sir;
This cell's[6] my court; here have I few attendants,
And subjects none abroad; pray you, look in.   110
My dukedom since you have given me again,

---

[1] **woe**: sorry
[2] **That they were**: so that they could be
[3] **encounter**: revelation
[4] **admire**: feel amazement
[5] **justled**: wrenched, separated
[6] **cell**: cave

I will requite[1] you with as good a thing;
At least bring forth a wonder, to content ye
As much as my dukedom.

[*Here Prospero discovers[2] Ferdinand and Miranda, playing at chess.*]

Miranda: Sweet lord, you play me false.

Ferdinand: No, my dearest love,   115
I would not for the world.

Miranda: Yes, for a score of kingdoms you should wrangle[3],
And I would call it fair play.

Alonso: If this prove
A vision of the island[4], one dear son
Shall I twice lose.

Sebastian: A most high miracle!   120

Ferdinand: Though the seas threaten, they are merciful;
I have curs'd them without cause[5].   [*Kneels.*]

Alonso: Now all the blessings
Of a glad father compass thee about!
Arise, and say how thou cam'st here.

Miranda: O, wonder!
How many goodly creatures are there here!   125
How beauteous mankind is! O brave[6] new world
That has such people in't!

Prospero: 'Tis new to thee.

Alonso: What is this maid with whom thou wast at play?
Your eld'st acquaintance cannot be three hours;
Is she the goddess that hath sever'd us,   130
And brought us thus together?

Ferdinand: Sir, she is mortal;
But by immortal Providence she's mine.
I chose her when I could not ask my father
For his advice, not thought I had one. She
Is daughter to this famous Duke of Milan,   135
Of whom so often I have heard renown
But never saw before; of whom I have
Receiv'd a second life; and second father
This lady makes him to me.

Alonso: I am hers.
But O, how oddly will it sound that I   140
Must ask my child forgiveness!

[1] **requite**: repay, reward
[2] **discovers**: reveals
[3] **wrangle**: win by cheating
[4] **vision of the island**: one of the island's illusions
[5] **without cause**: i.e. because his father isn't drowned
[6] **brave**: magnificent

Prospero: There, sir, stop;
            Let us not burden our remembrances with
            A heaviness that's gone.

Gonzalo: I have inly wept,
            Or should have spoke ere this. Look down, you gods,
            And on this blessed couple drop a blessed crown;   145
            For it is you[1] that have chalk'd forth[2] the way
            Which brought us hither.

Alonso: I say, Amen, Gonzalo.

---

[1] **you**: i.e. the gods
[2] **chalk'd forth**: mapped out, guided

Plot: 'not natural events'

Further on in this scene, Alonso comments:

> These are not natural events; they strengthen
> From strange to stranger.

Using his words as your cue, stand back from this extract (including the introduction) for a moment. What kind of play are you dealing with here?

Try defining it by negatives. List as many elements as you can which suggest that, whatever else *The Tempest* is, it is not – by contrast with, say, *A Streetcar Named Desire* in Section 4.1 – a 'realistic' play concerned to reflect 'life as it actually is', at least on its surface.

When your list is complete, use it to discuss as a class how you think Shakespeare intended his audience to respond to *The Tempest* from what you now know about it. Include at some point in your discussion a consideration of: (a) fable; (b) allegory; and (c) myth. These are all words that a good dictionary will define, and that your teacher will be able to illuminate further.

Character as type-figure

Imagine yourself directing the actor playing Gonzalo in this extract. Look first at the language Prospero uses about him in his opening speech and in lines 63–5. The focus words (see page 92 above) would be something like:

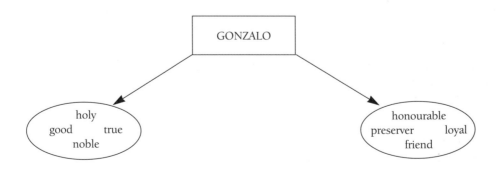

Now look at Gonzalo's three speeches in the course of the extract. Discuss how far they bear out Prospero's descriptions of him.

How much information about Gonzalo as an individual do the focus words and his speeches give? The answer is: virtually none. Strikingly, the words Prospero uses to describe him are all abstract. In other words, he is a type-figure, more important for what he represents than for what he is. Rather than any depth or subtlety of personality, it is Gonzalo's function that is the most important fact about him.

Is the same true of other characters in the scene? Look at Ferdinand and Miranda (lines 115–27). In 'real time', they have known each other for less than three hours, as Alonso reminds us on line 129. With this in mind, consider the following facts about their relationship which the extract reveals:

- they are so deeply in love that they are, at first, oblivious to the other characters;
- Ferdinand says their love has been guided by 'immortal Providence';
- their marriage is imminent.

If Ferdinand and Miranda are, like Gonzalo, type-figures, what qualities in human life do you think Shakespeare intends them to represent? Discuss this question, and include a consideration of their first appearance in the scene:

[*Here Prospero discovers Ferdinand and Miranda, playing at chess.*]

What do you think Shakespeare wants to suggest about them by this carefully placed picture?

Stage imagery

The symbolic 'picture' of Ferdinand and Miranda playing chess is contained within a larger frame of stage imagery: Prospero's magic circle (see the opening stage-direction). In a scene principally concerned with *revelation* – for example, Prospero: 'I will discase me' (line 28); Miranda: 'O brave new world / That hath such people in't! (lines 126–7) – and *reconciliation*, discuss Shakespeare's theatrical purposes in staging this scene within a circle.

Language: 'a most high miracle'

Throughout this extract, the verbal patterning contributes to one dominant impression: a semi-religious sense of wonder, amazement and divine mystery. Collectively, the characters' language is chorus-like in creating this effect. List all the words and phrases you can find which help evoke it. What might Shakespeare's intention be in emphasising this language pattern here?

Summing up: stages of meaning

All your work in this chapter has been based on a single premise: a play's 'meaning' begins to be clear when you consider how to see and hear it on the stage. During your study of Shakespeare, this approach will serve you much better than scribbling page after page of plot summaries, character studies, background notes on historical sources and the like.

Put it to the test. Now read the extract from *The Tempest* aloud as a class, drawing on what you know from this chapter about Shakespeare's theatrical art. Hear and see it from the viewpoint of director and audience. Then, as a class, put forward your ideas about the main themes of the whole of *The Tempest* on the basis of this 147-line extract.

Your teacher may be surprised.

Chapter 5 Seeing into the unseen

 5.1 **Unseen – or unknown?**

> Main text: 'The Flowers', Alice Walker

 5.2 **Planning and writing to task**

> Main text: 'The Horses', Edwin Muir

 5.3 **One-offs: single passages, single poems**

> Main texts: 'Rising Five', Norman Nicholson
> *The Way of all Flesh*, Samuel Butler
> 'I Live on Your Visits', Dorothy Parker

 5.4 **Starting out: what to say about 'openings'**

> Main texts: *A Gun for Sale*, Graham Greene
> *Huckleberry Finn*, Mark Twain
> *Hotel du Lac*, Anita Brookner

 5.5 **Cross-overs: comparing linked texts**

> Main texts: *Hard Times*, Charles Dickens
> *The Road to Wigan Pier*, George Orwell
> 'The Darkling Thrush', Thomas Hardy
> 'A Blackbird Singing', R.S. Thomas

Unseen – or unknown?

Many A level candidates approach unseen exams with a good deal of trepidation. Understandably. Although you can prepare for an unseen, there is an obvious sense in which your preparation can't be the same as for a set text paper. Nothing induces more panic than the prospect of simply not seeing 'what there is to say' about an unfamiliar poem, prose extract or chunk of drama – except being told by examiners to 'comment' on it in a way that completely mystifies you. For an hour!

This chapter demonstrates several methods of taking the unknown out of the unseen. As a starting-point, hold on to the fact that, statistically speaking, A level candidates score as well on the unseen as they do in any other part of the exam. Often they do significantly better. You may wish to discuss with your teacher why this should be so.

Clean sheet, open mind

One of the things about the unseen that makes it different is, of course, that you are alone with the text. Learn to see this as an advantage, not as a liability, and you are half-way to success. What examiners reward most when marking unseens is your own individual response to the task set, uncluttered by other people's ideas or by half-remembered lesson notes.

Try making such a response to 'The Flowers', the short story reproduced below. It was written in 1984 by Alice Walker (author of *The Color Purple*).

Read it at least twice, disregarding for the moment the instructions that follow. Respond to it entirely in your own way.

>–‹◆›–◯–‹▶–‹

The Flowers

by Alice Walker

It seemed to Myop as she skipped lightly from hen house to pigpen to smokehouse that the days had never been as beautiful as these. The air held a keenness that made her nose twitch. The harvesting of the corn and cotton, peanuts and squash, made each day a golden surprise that caused excited little tremors to run up her jaws.

Myop carried a short, knobbly stick. She struck out at random at chickens she liked, and worked out the beat of a song on the fence around the pigpen. She felt light and good in the warm sun. She was ten, and nothing existed for her but her song, the stick clutched in her dark brown hand, and the tat-de-ta-ta-ta of accompaniment.

Turning her back on the rusty boards of her family's share-cropper cabin, Myop walked along the fence till it ran into the stream made by the spring. Around the spring, where the family got drinking water, silver ferns and wild-flowers grew. Along the shallow banks pigs rooted. Myop watched the tiny white bubbles disrupt the thin black scale of soil and the water that silently rose and slid away down the stream.

She had explored the woods behind the house many times. Often, in late autumn, her mother took her to gather nuts among the fallen leaves. Today she made her own path, bouncing this way and that way, vaguely keeping an eye out for snakes. She found, in addition to various common but pretty ferns and leaves, an armful of strange blue flowers with velvety ridges and a sweetsuds bush full of the brown, fragrant buds.

5

10

15

By twelve o'clock, her arms were laden with sprigs of her findings, she was a mile or more from home. She had often been as far before, but the strangeness of the land made it not as pleasant as her usual haunts. It seemed gloomy in the little cove in which she found herself. The air was damp, the silence close and deep. 20

Myop began to circle back to the house, back to the peacefulness of the morning. It was then she stepped smack into his eyes. Her heel became lodged in the broken ridge between brow and nose, and she reached down quickly, unafraid, to free herself. It was 25 only when she saw his naked grin that she gave a little yelp of surprise.

He had been a tall man. From feet to neck covered a long space. His head lay beside him. When she pushed back the leaves and layers of earth and debris Myop saw that he'd had large white teeth, all of them cracked or broken, long fingers, and very big bones. All his clothes had rotted away except some threads of blue denim from his 30 overalls. The buckles of the overalls had turned green.

Myop gazed around the spot with interest. Very near where she'd stepped into the head was a wild pink rose. As she picked it to add to her bundle she noticed a raised mound, a ring, around the rose's root. It was the rotted remains of a noose, a bit of shredding plowline, now blending benignly into the soil. 35

Around an overhanging limb of a great spreading oak clung another piece. Frayed, rotted, bleached, and frazzled – barely there – but spinning restlessly in the breeze. Myop laid down her flowers.

And the summer was over.

Now 'free write' for about thirty minutes in response to the story. Free writing means spilling out your thoughts and feelings on to a clean sheet of paper without being concerned about any of the usual A level writing conventions (organisation, 'critical' vocabulary, paragraphs, quotation-to-illustrate-points and so on). You can make statements, ask questions, use sentences or jottings or both. No one will 'mark' this. Its purpose is to catch your thoughts on paper before they vanish out of sight and mind.

Spend at least a further thirty minutes sharing your thoughts with a partner, in a small group, or as a class. If you have made different comments from others, celebrate the fact. The purpose of unseens is not for everyone to spot exactly the same points. Examiners give credit for what is written; they do not have expectations of a single 'right' answer.

Especially in the early stages of your course, this method of 'attacking' unseens without filtering your response through specific set questions will serve you well. As the next section shows, free writing followed by a sharing of ideas will actually equip you with the raw material you need to tackle any task examiners choose to set.

The range of possible exam tasks

Glance through a selection of past unseen papers and you will, at first, be struck by the apparent diversity of instructions about 'what to do'. Here are three typical tasks which you could expect to find set on 'The Flowers':

● Comment on what interests you about the subject matter of this story and the way in which it is written.

- Explain how Alice Walker engages the reader's interest. You should comment particularly on the structure of the story, on the development of feeling within it and on the author's powers of description.

- How is atmosphere created in this story? Examine the way in which Alice Walker directs the reader's response, paying particular attention to the use she makes of the setting and to specific uses of language.

Discuss with your teacher (a) how far these tasks make different demands on you, and (b) which of them you would prefer to tackle, and why.

Finally, look back to your free writing; then recall the discussion that followed it. Given that you will judge both of these to be 'rambling', 'disorganised', 'messy' and so on, consider how much of your commentary could be used to respond relevantly to the three tasks listed above. Unless you got virtually nothing out of 'The Flowers', you'll find that, however sketchily, you have covered enough ground to answer all of the tasks to an acceptable A level standard.

Planning and writing to task

Unseen questions look very 'open'. Even the 'prompts' that examiners often use to trigger your responses can seem, at a casual glance, to be distinctly lacking in focus, such as 'Comment on the movement of the verse in this poem ...', or 'Examine the way in which tension is built up throughout this passage ...', and so on.

In devising such instructions, examiners are not giving you just enough rope with which to hang yourself. They are helping you guard against writing irrelevantly, and/or in an unstructured way, by offering you a basic 'frame' for your answer – without predetermining exactly what you put into it. As long as your answer addresses what you are directed to write about, they will reward any and every intelligent point you make.

Key wording

A recent examiners' report on the work of candidates in unseens ends with this salutary statement:

> What examiners would dearly like to see in the scripts next year is more careful examination of the tasks and their key words.
>
> Most candidates who score low marks in this part of the exam do so not because they write nonsense but because they disregard what they are asked to write about.

Get your teacher to compile a set of up to ten instructions on unseen poems and prose passages taken from past papers. The poems and passages to which they refer are not important. Go through them together, agreeing on what the 'key words' actually are. Build up and keep a class list of these as you practise throughout the course. The golden rule is this: *Even if you are doubtful about what to write in response to a 'key word' instruction, you will gain far more credit for attempting to do so than you will by ignoring it.*

Paraphrase versus comment

The most frequently used key word in unseen instructions is 'Comment'. This does not mean 'put the poem or passage into your own words': that is *paraphrase*, which is, by itself, never given credit in an A level answer of any kind.

The activity that follows is designed to give you practice in differentiating between paraphrase and comment. Especially early on in your course, it is one of the most important skills you need to acquire.

Read the poem below at least twice. Respond to it entirely in your own way.

>―+―◂▸―◦―◂▸―+―◃

The Horses

Barely a twelvemonth after
The seven days war that put the world to sleep,
Late in the evening the strange horses came.
By then we had made our covenant with silence,
But in the first few days it was so still
We listened to our breathing and were afraid.
On the second day

5

The radios failed; we turned the knobs; no answer.
On the third day a warship passed us, heading north,
Dead bodies piled on the deck. On the sixth day   10
A plane plunged over us into the sea. Thereafter
Nothing. The radios dumb;
And still they stand in corners of our kitchens,
And stand, perhaps, turned on, in a million rooms
All over the world. But now if they should speak,   15
If on a sudden they should speak again,
If on the stroke of noon a voice should speak,
We would not listen, we would not let it bring
That old bad world that swallowed its children quick
At one great gulp. We would not have it again.   20
Sometimes we think of the nations lying asleep,
Curled blindly in impenetrable sorrow,
And then the thought confounds us with its strangeness.
The tractors lie about our fields; at evening
They look like dank sea-monsters couched and waiting.   25
We leave them where they are and let them rust:
'They'll moulder away and be like other loam'.
We make our oxen drag our rusty ploughs,
Long laid aside. We have gone back
Far past our father's land.
               And then, that evening   30
Late in the summer the strange horses came.
We heard a distant tapping on the road,
A deepening drumming; it stopped, went on again
And at the corner changed to hollow thunder.
We saw the heads   35
Like a wild wave charging and were afraid.
We had sold our horses in our fathers' time
To buy new tractors. Now they were strange to us
As fabulous steeds set on an ancient shield
Or illustrations in a book of knights.   40
We did not dare go near them. Yet they waited,
Stubborn and shy, as if they had been sent
By an old command to find our whereabouts
And that long-lost archaic companionship.
In the first moment we had never a thought   45
That they were creatures to be owned and used.
Among them were some half dozen colts
Dropped in some wilderness of the broken world,
Yet new as if they had come from their own Eden.
Since then they have pulled our ploughs and borne our loads   50
But that free servitude still can pierce our hearts.
Our life is changed; their coming our beginning.

Edwin Muir

><-><-·O·-<><-<

As with 'The Flowers' in section 5.1 above, free write your thoughts and feelings about this poem for thirty minutes or so. Then spend another thirty minutes sharing your responses in discussion with a partner, in a small group or as a class.

Now copy out the table below and draw on your free writing and your discussion to fill in the three columns. The entries already made offer a starting-point; there is a good deal more to add.

1 PARAPHRASE factual information conveyed by the poet	2 COMMENT (A) attitudes and feelings expressed by the poet	3 COMMENT (B) the poet's form, style and language
a) War (nuclear?) occurs at some future time b) Horses suddenly arrive, seemingly of their own accord	a) Horror at the barbarity resulting from modern technology b) A blessing in disguise for the survivors: new start, new way of life	a) Shifting time-scale: past/present, past/present b) Parallels with the Bible: creation story, biblical language, a form of parable

Consider your completed columns, preferably by comparing them with other people's. All the material in Column 1 expresses your literal understanding of what the poet is writing about: in other words, your comprehension. Imagine that your entire response to the poem were made up from Column 1 entries alone. You would have done nothing more than paraphrase. As a result, an examiner could award you only a very low 'token' mark.

The material in columns 2 and 3 is what an examiner *would* reward you for. It provides a valid basis for comment because (a) it identifies the poem's themes: that is, Edwin Muir's thoughts and feelings on the subject he has chosen, and (b) it focuses on the way in which 'The Horses' is written: that is, it describes aspects of the poem's form, style and language and relates these to its themes.

Until you feel confident enough to distinguish automatically between paraphrase and comment in writing about unseen poems and passages, it will prove helpful to use this 'columns' approach with every new exercise you attempt.

Sample commentary

Printed below is an A level student's commentary on 'The Horses' written in response to this instruction:

> *What interests you about the subject matter of Muir's poem and the way it is expressed? Among other things you should comment on: imagery; the use of language; tone; and structure.*

Read and discuss the commentary together with your teacher. Compare the points it contains with the ones you came up with in compiling your columns. Then put yourself in the role of an A level examiner and try to agree on a mark out of twenty for it. (Your teacher will advise you on points that a 'real' examiner would reward, and on the equivalence between the mark you arrive at and an A level grade.)

>─┤◄├─•─O─•─┤►├─◄

In 'The Horses', Edwin Muir contrasts two alternative ways of life: the world of modern technology and a more old-fashioned, primitive and simple world. The central theme of the poem is that the former is a 'bad world' which brings about death and destruction, whereas the latter is preferable because it enriches life and leads to people living in harmony with each other. The poem asks us to reject the world of modern science and return to a life-style 'back / Far past our father's land' where 'that long-lost archaic companionship' with Nature can be recreated in the form of 'the good life'.

5

Muir relies a great deal on symbolism to convey his themes. The poem seems more like a modern parable than realistic description. It begins by imagining that the modern-day world has destroyed itself by its own technology: 'The seven days war that put the world to sleep'. This suggests that there has been a global war, probably a nuclear one. Only a small number of people in some remote area have survived. It would take a nuclear war on a world-wide scale to 'swallow its children quick / At one great gulp.' The 'war' has lasted seven days, which is significant because according to the Bible it took seven days to create the world and now it has been 'uncreated', not by God but by man himself. Man has destroyed the world that was created for him.

The survivors have made a choice to remain isolated from the death and destruction they see evidence of ('a warship passed us, heading north … A plane plunged over us into the sea'). Their radios, which might put them back in contact with other survivors, are 'dumb' – deliberately so:

> 'But now if they should speak again …
> If on the stroke of noon a voice should speak,
> We would not listen, we would not let it bring
> That old bad world.'

They have few resources for living, but they make the most of them: 'oxen' and 'rusty ploughs'. They could use tractors for farming, but they think of these now as being in the same league as the more sophisticated machinery that caused the war, so: 'We leave them where they are and let them rust.' The war has given them a dread of all forms of machinery, which is why they see their tractors as being a threat to them, 'like dank sea-monsters couched and waiting'. They prefer to work the land with animals and primitive equipment 'long laid aside'.

The first thirty lines of the poem deliberately raise questions in the reader's mind. Who is speaking in the poem? What has caused the 'seven days war'? Above all, who are the 'strange horses': why, and from where, have they come? The effect of this technique is partly to create an atmosphere of strangeness, centred on the horses. Muir does not want us to think of the poem as realistic but more as a fable. The horses are symbolic, not natural, and what they represent is something timeless.

This impression is heightened in several ways. The time-scale of the poem is made to shift from the past to the present and back to the past, then finally to look to the future: 'Our life is changed: their coming our beginning.' Technological society, in Muir's view, is a passing phase, whereas man's relationship with Nature is both enduring and eternal. References to the Bible reinforce this theme. For instance, the horses are 'new as if they came from their own Eden'. After man's self-inflicted destruction of the world he has made comes a new creation – a new 'beginning', equivalent to paradise.

The question the poem leaves us with is this: unlike Adam and Eve, will humanity keep this paradise unspoiled? It seems to depend on how the survivors respond to the horses. At first they are afraid: 'We did not dare go near them.' However, as time passes they start to realise that what the horses offer is not a threat but 'free servitude'. They are 'creatures to be owned and used', asking nothing in return except a restoration of 'that long-lost archaic companionship' between man and Nature. The poem seems to end on an optimistic note. Having accepted what the horses bring to them, the survivors' lives are 'changed' for the better. It is noticeable that the last word of the poem is 'beginning'. We are made to feel that, out of the rubble of a destroyed modern world, it really will be possible for humanity to make a 'new start' – by reverting to a way of life as old as 'fabulous steeds set on an ancient shield'.

10

15

20

25

30

35

40

45

50

55

One-offs: single passages, single poems

Common to all unseen papers is the option to write about a single poem and/or a free-standing passage of prose fiction. The instructions for commenting on them may sound rather general, but they are, in fact, carefully constructed around the key words examined in Section 5.2. Typical examples from recent examinations include:

- Read the following poem carefully and then write about it as fully as you can. It may help you to consider the poet's tone and style as well as form and subject matter.

- Write a critical appreciation of the following poem. Among other things you might like to consider are: the mood and meanings of the poem; the poet's use of imagery; and the effects of verse form and punctuation.

- Read the passage below carefully and then write a critical analysis of it. You may wish to comment on such matters as: the impression given of the society depicted; the personalities and attitudes of the two characters (showing how these are revealed); the attitude of the writer (explaining how you reached your conclusion); and the language.

The phrase 'You may wish to comment on …' is in effect not an invitation but a requirement; decide not to 'wish to' at your peril! Particularly in the case of a single poem, look very carefully at the elements highlighted, for example 'the effects of verse form and punctuation'. Examiners do not draw your attention to these arbitrarily: when you come to study the poem in question, you should find good reason why they are given prominence in the instructions.

Launching out: poetry

The best way to get 'inside' a one-off task is simply to roll up your sleeves and try it. Like all A level students, you will find this difficult. The task below offers you a measure of help and support by demonstrating a way (but only one way) of sorting out 'what to say' in note form. If you find it helpful, use it.

Before you begin, it will be useful to look back to Chapter 2 (especially Sections 2.3 to 2.5 inclusive) and ahead to Chapter 9 (especially Section 9.3).

Take as much time as you need for this task. By all means use the free writing approach demonstrated in Section 5.1 as a starting-point if you find it gives you confidence.

Read the poem printed below and then write a critical interpretation of it, paying attention to such things as: the content, mood and tone; imagery; use of language; and structure. Offer further comment on any aspects of the poem that interest you. Illustrate your answer by reference to specific details of the poem.

Rising Five

'I'm rising five', he said
'Not four', and little coils of hair
Un-clicked themselves upon his head.
His spectacles, brimful of eyes to stare
At me and the meadow, reflected cones of light   5
Above his toffee-buckled cheeks. He'd been alive
Fifty-six months or perhaps a week more:
                              not four,
But rising five.

Around him in the field the cells of spring
Bubbled and doubled; buds unbuttoned; shoot   10
And stem shook out the creases from their frills,
And every tree was swilled with green.
It was the season after blossoming,
Before the forming of the fruit:
                         not May,
But rising June.

                    And in the sky   15
The dust dissected in the tangential light:
                              not day,
But rising night;
               not now,
But rising soon.

The new buds push the old leaves from the bough.
We drop our youth behind us like a boy   20
Throwing away his toffee-wrappers. We never see the flower,
But only the fruit in the flower; never the fruit,
But only the rot in the fruit. We look for the marriage bed
In the baby's cradle, we look for the grave in the bed:
                              not living,
But rising dead.   25

Norman Nicholson

Graffiti notes

Try preparing for your analysis by spending fifteen minutes after you have 'absorbed' the poem engaging in what one A level group christened 'creative graffiti'. This means that you jot on, around, over and under the poem – always bearing in mind the instruction you have been given for what your final draft should contain.

There are several good reasons for making graffiti notes as a 'first step'. You ought to find:

- you start to make the poem your own by 'trespassing' on the virgin territory of an unsullied page;

- the more you graffiti, the more you will find to graffiti;

- you keep panic at bay and start thinking more clearly/logically;

- the shape of your answer will start to emerge, giving you confidence.

Part of this process is demonstrated below (page 119). Complete it – or, if you prefer, start graffiti-noting from scratch with a clean photocopy of the poem.

Shaping your final draft – and how not to write it

Look back to the sample commentary on 'The Horses' in Section 5.2. Then straight after doing so, read or re-read Wilfred Owen's poem 'The Send-Off', together with the analysis of it and the 'points arising' in Chapter 2 (pages 35–40). The way you plan and write your final draft about 'Rising Five' will benefit from these examples and the advice accompanying them.

Aim to complete the task in no more than $1\frac{1}{2}$ hours at one sitting, to a length of between three and four sides of A4 paper.

Before you begin, take careful note of the 'Don't' list below. Even with good notes, it is all too easy to write a commentary which earns you less credit than you deserve by constructing your answer in a 'play-it-safe' way. So:

- Don't trawl 'chronologically' through the poem as if it is a story, starting your analysis with the first line and ending with the last.

- Don't spend most of your time paraphrasing the literal meaning of the poem (see Section 5.2 above).

- Don't feel you have to comment on everything that could possibly be said about the poem.

- Don't take each of the examiners' prompts in turn ('the content; mood and tone; imagery' and so on) and devote a separate paragraph to each.

- Don't say anything that disregards the poet's intentions, as you understand them, in writing the poem.

- Don't commit yourself to commenting on rhythm, sound and verse form unless you are confident about what you are saying: if you aren't, it is far better to remain silent than to make desperate stabs in the dark.

- Don't shy away from making personal response comments, as long as you can support them from the text.

- Don't forget to 'illustrate your answer by reference to specific details of the poem': examiners really do mean this.

- Don't write paragraphs which are mini-essays in themselves and which fail to link up with what comes immediately before and after them.

- Don't write any one-sentence paragraphs.

Before handing in your commentary on 'Rising Five', work through the ten points in this list and check that you are not guilty of any of them!

Rising Five

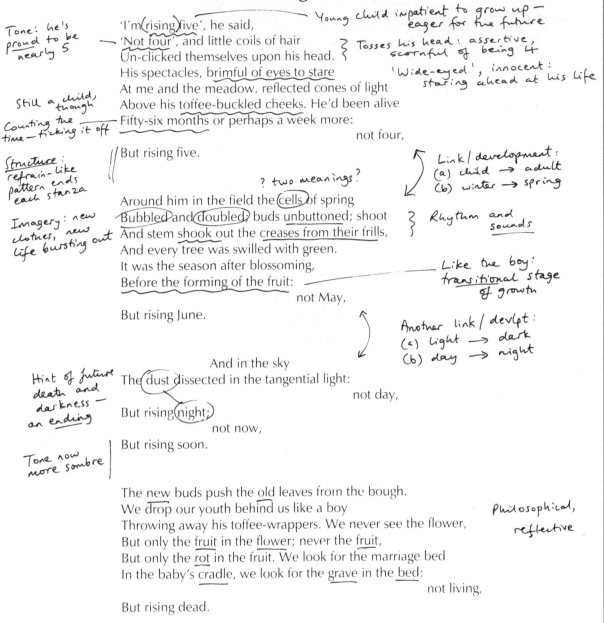

Tone: he's proud to be nearly 5

'I'm rising five', he said,
'Not four', and little coils of hair
Un-clicked themselves upon his head.
His spectacles, brimful of eyes to stare
At me and the meadow, reflected cones of light
Above his toffee-buckled cheeks. He'd been alive
Fifty-six months or perhaps a week more:
                                    not four,

But rising five.

Around him in the field the cells of spring
Bubbled and doubled, buds unbuttoned; shoot
And stem shook out the creases from their frills,
And every tree was swilled with green.
It was the season after blossoming,
Before the forming of the fruit:
                        not May,

But rising June.

                    And in the sky
The dust dissected in the tangential light:
                                not day,

But rising night;
                not now,

But rising soon.

The new buds push the old leaves from the bough.
We drop our youth behind us like a boy
Throwing away his toffee-wrappers. We never see the flower,
But only the fruit in the flower; never the fruit,
But only the rot in the fruit. We look for the marriage bed
In the baby's cradle, we look for the grave in the bed:
                                        not living,

But rising dead.

Norman Nicholson

Annotations:
- Young child impatient to grow up — eager for the future
- Tosses his head: assertive, scornful of being 4
- 'Wide-eyed', innocent: staring ahead at his life
- Still a child, though. Counting the time — ticking it off
- Structure: refrain-like pattern ends each stanza
- Imagery: new clothes, new life bursting out
- ? two meanings?
- Link/development: (a) child → adult (b) winter → spring
- Rhythm and sounds
- Like the boy: transitional stage of growth
- Another link/devlpt: (a) light → dark (b) day → night
- Hint of future death and darkness — an ending
- Tone now more sombre
- Philosophical, reflective

Commenting on a single passage of prose

Every year, A level examiners bemoan the fact that students perform less well on the unseen prose passage than they do on unseen poetry. The main reason is simple: large numbers of candidates treat the prose as if it were a GCSE English comprehension question. The purpose of this section is to suggest ways in which you can avoid falling into this trap.

Read the extract overleaf from a novel written about 100 years ago. For the moment concentrate only on building up in your mind an impression of the character of Dr Skinner.

from **The Way of All Flesh**

by Samuel Butler

When Dr Skinner was a very young man, hardly more than five-and-twenty, the head-mastership of Roughborough Grammar School had fallen vacant, and he had been unhesitatingly appointed. The result justified the selection. Dr Skinner's pupils distinguished themselves at whichever University they went to. He moulded their minds after the manner of his own, and stamped an impression upon them which was indelible in after-life. Some boys, of course, were incapable of appreciating the beauty and loftiness of Dr Skinner's nature. Some such boys, alas! there will be in every school: upon them Dr Skinner's hand was very properly a heavy one.

I once had the honour of playing a game of chess with this great man. It was during the Christmas holidays, and I had come down to Roughborough for a few days on business. It was very gracious of him to take notice of me, for if I was a light of literature at all it was of the very lightest kind.

The game had been a long one, and at half-past nine, when supper came in, we had each of us a few pieces remaining. 'What will you take for supper, Dr Skinner?' said Mrs. Skinner in a silvery voice.

He made no answer for some time, but at last in a tone of almost superhuman solemnity, he said, first, 'Nothing,' and then, 'Nothing whatever.'

By and by, however, I had a sense come over me as though I were nearer the consummation of all things than I had ever yet been. The room seemed to grow dark, as an expression came over Dr Skinner's face, which showed that he was about to speak. The expression gathered force, the room grew darker and darker. 'Stay,' he at length added, and I felt that here at any rate was an end to a suspense which was rapidly becoming unbearable. 'Stay – I may presently take a glass of cold water – and a small piece of bread and butter.'

As he said the word 'butter' his voice sank to a hardly audible whisper; then there was sigh as though of relief when the sentence was concluded, and the universe this time was safe.

Another ten minutes of solemn silence finished the game. The Doctor rose briskly from his seat and placed himself at the supper table. 'Mrs Skinner,' he exclaimed jauntily, 'what are those mysterious-looking objects surrounded by potatoes?'

'Those are oysters, Dr Skinner.

'Give me some, and give Overton some.'

And so on till he had eaten a good plate of oysters, a scallop shell of minced veal nicely browned, some apple tart, and a hunk of bread and cheese. This was the small piece of bread and butter.

The cloth was now removed and tumblers with teaspoons in them, a lemon or two and a jug of boiling water were placed upon the table. Then the great man unbent. His face beamed.

'And what shall it be to drink?' he exclaimed persuasively. 'Shall it be brandy and water? No. It shall be gin and water. Gin is the more wholesome liquor.'

So gin it was, hot and stiff too.

Who can wonder at him or do anything but pity him? Was he not head-master of Roughborough School? To whom had he owed money at any time? Whose ox had he taken, whose ass had he taken, or whom had he defrauded? What whisper had ever been breathed against his moral character? If he had become rich it was by the most honourable of all means – his literary attainments; over and above his great works of scholarship, his 'Meditations upon the Epistle and Character of St Jude' had placed him among the most popular of English theologians; it was so exhaustive that no one who bought it need ever meditate upon the subject again – indeed it exhausted all who had anything to do with it. He had made £5000 by this work alone, and would very likely make another £5000 before he died. A man who had done all this and wanted a piece of bread and butter had a right to announce the fact with some pomp and circumstance. Nor should his words be taken without searching for what he used to call a 'deeper and more hidden meaning'. Those who searched for this even in his lighter utterances would not be without their reward. They would find that 'bread and butter' was Skinnerese for oyster-patties and apple tart, and 'gin hot' the true translation of water.

45

50

55

Characterisation, not 'character study'

If this passage were set as a GCSE assignment, most of the marks would be given for describing the character of Dr Skinner – 'in your own words', of course. At A level, you will be asked about *characterisation* rather than about character. This means being able to comment on two things:

● the author's use of various writing techniques to present/portray a character;

● the way in which these techniques shape and direct the reader's attitude towards the character (or characters) in question.

Look again at lines 13–17 of the passage. Then, on the evidence of these lines alone, think of one word of your own which most accurately describes Dr Skinner's character.

Now read the following extract from an A level commentary on Butler's characterisation of Dr Skinner:

> Dr Skinner has such a high opinion of himself that he requires everyone to defer to him, including his wife. This is indicated by the way she addresses him by his formal title 'Dr' Skinner, despite the domestic setting and the informal situation. Her 'silvery voice' further reinforces the impression of a servility which 'this great man' demands – and gets – from all who know him. Utterly wrapped up in his own pomposity, he is clearly incapable of naturalness and human warmth.
>
> His reply to Mrs Skinner's intellectually undemanding question is entirely typical of him. The author's use of irony is particularly marked here. It is absurdly incongruous that Dr Skinner gives the question of what to eat such prolonged and serious consideration that he answers it in a tone of 'almost superhuman solemnity'. Butler is using ironic exaggeration to make his point: not only is Dr Skinner totally humourless, he is also a pretentious egotist, incapable of seeing himself as such. This is highlighted by the long pause he makes before saying, in a profoundly anti-climactic manner, 'Nothing'. Ironically again, even when he has 'nothing' to say, he cannot resist repeating himself: 'Nothing whatever'. By this Butler shows that, like all vain and self-regarding men, Dr Skinner relishes the sound of his own voice – even more than the four-course meal which he goes on greedily to devour.

List the words and phrases in the above commentary that are concerned with Butler's techniques of portraying Dr Skinner and with building up your attitude towards him.

Together with your teacher, continue from this starting-point and comment on the characterisation of Dr Skinner in the passage as a whole. Pay particular attention to Butler's tone and his use of irony. Either follow your own agenda for discussion or use the prompts below to help you explore the text further:

- What impression does Butler give of Dr Skinner's teaching methods in paragraph 1? In particular, comment on the phrasing of '[He] stamped an impression upon them which was indelible in after-life' and 'Some boys, of course, were incapable of appreciating the beauty and loftiness of Dr Skinner's nature.'

- What is the tone of Butler's observations in the paragraph beginning 'By and by, however, I had a sense come over me …' (lines 18–24)? Comment on the language of 'the universe this time was safe' (lines 26–7).

- What might Butler's purpose be in drawing our attention to the difference between what Dr Skinner orders for supper and what he actually eats and drinks?

- Look closely at lines 39–41. In what ways does this short paragraph confirm our impressions of Dr Skinner as they have built up during the passage to this point?

- How does Butler's method of presenting Dr Skinner change in the last paragraph (lines 42–56)? Comment on the ways in which this concluding part of the passage is much more openly satirical than what has preceded it.

A note on irony

Single prose passages in the A level unseen are often partly or wholly ironic in tone and effect – as *The Way of All Flesh* extract is intended to show. It will pay you to be absolutely clear in your mind about (a) the various ways in which authors use irony, and (b) the effects they achieve by it. At A level, it is never adequate merely to say 'The author has his tongue in his cheek here.'

Think of irony as an aspect of satire: that is, a technique by which the author holds up to ridicule and/or criticism a character's foolishness (and, quite commonly, his/her moral nature). Irony often 'works' in one or more of the following ways:

- The author will write, with a 'straight face', the opposite of what s/he really means; for example, 'A man who had done all this and wanted a piece of bread and butter had a right to announce the fact with some pomp and circumstance.' The effect is normally to expose either the character's hypocrisy or the character's blindness to his or her real self.

- The author will use deliberate incongruity: that is, a striking mis-match between two things; for example, Butler's statement that such an obviously dull and unreadable book as 'Meditations upon the Epistle and Character of St Jude' is 'a great work of scholarship'. The effect is normally to mock the pretentiousness of the character in question.

- The author will use comic exaggeration (at A level, examiners will be pleased to see you calling this *hyperbole*); for example, 'I had a sense come over me as though I were nearer the consummation of all things than I had ever yet been.' The effects of this depend upon context and the author's intentions. Hyperbole, by its very nature, makes possible a further ironic technique which is invariably linked with it: anti-climax (which A level examiners will be pleased to see you calling *bathos*); for example, 'in a tone of almost superhuman solemnity, he said, first, "Nothing".' The effect of this is normally to point up the extent to which the character's value system is seriously distorted.

- The author will use rhetorical questions, the 'true' answers to which are the opposite of those that the character in question would give; for example, 'Whose ox had he taken, whose ass had he taken, or whom had he defrauded? What whisper had ever been breathed against his moral character?' The effect is normally similar to that of the first example cited above.

Bear in mind that this is a very partial and selective list. Irony is an enormously subtle technique which authors use in many ways to achieve a wide variety of effects. As you progress through your A level course, consciously 'collect' examples to deepen your understanding of ironic technique. (If you know Jane Austen's *Pride and Prejudice*, consider the weight of irony behind the novel's opening sentence: 'It is a truth universally acknowledged that a single man in possession of a good fortune must be in want of a wife.')

In practice

Depending on your degree of confidence, undertake one of the following tasks.

Either

Write a commentary on the extract from *The Way of All Flesh*, examining the ways in which Samuel Butler conducts his characterisation of Dr Skinner.

Or

Read the following extract from a story written in 1928 by the American author Dorothy Parker. Then write a commentary on it, considering in particular:

● the techniques Parker uses to portray the mother;

● how the relationship between mother and son is conveyed to us;

● the overall mood and tone of the passage.

from I Live on Your Visits

by Dorothy Parker

The boy came into the hotel room and immediately it seemed even smaller.

'Hey, it's cool in here,' he said. This was not meant as a comment on the temperature. 'Cool,' for reasons possibly known in some department of Heaven, was a term then in use among many of those of his age to express approbation.

It was indeed cool in the room, after the hard grey rain in the streets. It was warm, and it was so bright. The many-watted electric bulbs his mother insisted upon were undimmed by the thin frilled shades she had set on the hotel lamps, and there were shiny things everywhere: sheets of mirror along the walls; a square of mirror backing the mirror-plated knob on the door that led to the bedroom; cigarette boxes made of tiny bits of mirror and matchboxes slipped into little mirror jackets placed all about; and, on consoles and desk and table, photographs of himself at two and a half and five and seven and nine framed in broad mirror bands. Whenever his mother settled in a new domicile, and she removed often, those photographs were the first things out of the luggage. The boy hated them. He had had to pass his fifteenth birthday before his body had caught up with his head; there was that head, in those presentments of his former selves, that pale, enormous blob. Once he had asked his mother to put the pictures somewhere else – preferably some small, dark place that could be locked. But he had had the bad fortune to make his request on one of the occasions when she was given to weeping suddenly and long. So the photographs stood out on parade, with their frames twinkling away.

There were twinklings, too, from the silver top of the fat crystal cocktail shaker, but the liquid low within the crystal was pale and dull. There was no shine, either, to the glass his mother held. It was cloudy from the clutch of her hand, and on the inside there were oily dribbles of what it had contained.

5

10

15

20

25

His mother shut the door by which she had admitted him, and followed him into the room. She looked at him with her head tilted to the side.

'Well, aren't you going to kiss me?' she said in a charming, wheedling voice, the voice of a little, little girl. 'Aren't you, you beautiful big ox, you?'

'Sure,' he said. He bent down toward her, but she stepped suddenly away. A sharp change came over her. She drew herself tall, with her shoulders back and her head flung high. Her upper lip lifted over her teeth, and her gaze came cold beneath lowered lids. So does one who has refused the white handkerchief regard the firing squad.

'Of course,' she said in a deep, iced voice that gave each word its full due, 'if you do not wish to kiss me, let it be recognized that there is no need for you to do so. I had not meant to overstep. I apologize. *Je vous demande pardon*. I had no desire to force you. I have never forced you. There is none to say I have.'

'Ah, Mom,' he said. He went to her, bent again, and this time kissed her cheek.

There was no change in her, save in the slow, somehow offended lifting of her eyelids. The brows arched as if they drew the lids up with them. 'Thank you,' she said. 'That was gracious of you. I value graciousness. I rank it high. *Mille grazie*.'

'Ah, Mom,' he said.

For the past week, up at his school, he had hoped – and coming down in the train he had hoped so hard that it became prayer – that his mother would not be what he thought of only as 'like that.' His prayer had gone unanswered. He knew by the two voices, by the head first tilted then held high, by the eyelids lowered in disdain then raised in outrage, by the little lisped words and then the elegant enunciation and the lofty diction. He knew.

He stood there and said, 'Ah, Mom.'

'Perhaps,' she said, 'you will award yourself the privilege of meeting a friend of mine. She is a true friend. I am proud that I may say it.'

There was someone else in the room. It was preposterous that he had not seen her, for she was so big. Perhaps his eyes had been dazzled, after the dim-lit hotel corridor; perhaps his attention had been all for his mother. At any rate, there she sat, the true friend, on the sofa covered with embossed cotton fabric of the sickened green that is peculiar to hotel upholsteries. There she sat, at one end of the sofa, and it seemed as if the other end must fly up into the air.

'I can give you but little,' his mother said, 'yet life is still kind enough to let me give you something you will always remember. Through me, you will meet a human being.'

Yes, oh, yes. The voices, the stances, the eyelids – those were the signs. But when his mother divided the race into people and human beings – that was the certainty.

He followed her the little way across the room, trying not to tread on the train of her velvet tea gown that slid along the floor after her and slapped at the heels of her gilt slippers. Fog seemed to rise from his raincoat and his shoes cheeped. He turned out to avoid the coffee table in front of the sofa, came in again too sharply and bumped it.

'Mme Marah,' his mother said, 'may I present my son?'

'Christ, he's a big bastard, isn't he?' the true friend said.

Starting out: what to say about 'openings'

Unseen papers include – or may include – an option to comment on the opening section of a novel. A typical instruction is:

Give your opinion on the passage below as the opening to a novel. How far, and in what ways, does the writer succeed in maintaining your interest?

Examiners' reports note that candidates are often reluctant to take up this option – and, year after year, express the wish that they would. This section offers suggestions on how to tackle a 'novel opening' unseen question. The principal purpose is to help you decide whether it is a task with which you would feel confident in the exam, and to assist you in preparing for it if you do.

Brainstorming beginnings

Select six novels from the library which you haven't read and which look to be of A level standard. At least two of them must pre-date 1900. Read carefully the first two or three pages of each. Then put them in a rank order which reflects your honest response to what you have read (for example, 1 = 'Looks good'; 6 = 'Three pages is enough').

Jot down brief reasons for placing each 'opening' where you have in the rank order, however subjective or vague the reasons may seem. Form a group with fellow students who have done the same with six different novels. Exchange explanations for the rank orders you have produced.

Establishing your own criteria

With your teacher, discuss your personal yardsticks, or criteria, from commenting on the way a novel begins. Whatever else you decide, they should touch on – but not necessarily be limited to – the following aspects:

● the nature of the subject matter and its intrinsic interest to you;

● the links between subject matter and style/language;

● the presentation of character, or characters in relation to each other;

● narrative techniques such as building up suspense/tension, the use of first or third person narrative, the way in which the setting is established, the purpose (if relevant) of a humorous or ironic tone.

Following this discussion, make your own list of what to look for when responding to, and judging, the opening section of a novel. Note that *judging* is important. You will be asked to do it in the exam. Don't shy away from making criticisms as long as you can produce clear reasons for doing so: examiners are impressed by independent thinking.

Interrogating the text

Commenting on 'openings' – commenting, in fact, on any passage set in an unseen – depends on asking yourself the kind of questions about it that will produce a relevant response. Seeing 'what there is to say' is never a matter of just staring at the passage and waiting for inspiration to strike. You need to train yourself to read the passage in a questioning way: in other words, to interrogate the text.

The activity below will help you get used to doing this.

Read the passage that follows. It is the opening of Graham Greene's novel *A Gun for Sale* (1936), in which a hired assassin is sent to shoot a political enemy of the organisation that employs him.

>―◀▷―∘―◁▶―◁

from **A Gun for Sale**

by Graham Greene

Murder didn't mean much to Raven. It was just a new job. You had to be careful. You had to use your brains. It was not a question of hatred. He had only seen the Minister once: he had been pointed out to Raven as he walked down the new housing estate between the little lit Christmas trees, an old, rather grubby man without any friends, who was said to love humanity. 5

The cold wind cut his face in the wide continental street. It was a good excuse for turning the collar of his coat well up above his mouth. A hare-lip was a serious handicap in his profession; it had been badly sewn in infancy, so that now the upper lip was twisted and scarred. When you carried about you so easy an identification you couldn't help becoming ruthless in your methods. It had always, from the first, been necessary for 10 Raven to eliminate the evidence.

He carried an attaché case. He looked like any other youngish man going home after his work; his dark overcoat had a clerical air. He moved steadily up the street like hundreds of his kind. A tram went by, lit up in the early dusk: he didn't take it. An economical young man, you might have thought, saving money for his home. Perhaps even now he 15 was on his way to meet his girl.

But Raven had never had a girl. The hare-lip prevented that. He had learnt, when he was very young, how repulsive it was. He turned into one of the tall grey houses and climbed the stairs, a sour bitter screwed-up figure.

Outside the top flat he put down his attaché case and put on gloves. He took a pair of 20 clippers out of his pocket and cut through the telephone wire where it ran out from above the door to the lift shaft. Then he rang the bell.

He hoped to find the Minister alone. This little top-floor flat was the socialist's home; he lived in a poor bare solitary way and Raven had been told that his secretary always left him at half past six; he was very considerate with his employees. But Raven was a 25 minute too early and the Minister half an hour too late. A woman opened the door, an elderly woman with pince-nez and several gold teeth. She had her hat on and her coat was over her arm. She had been on the point of leaving and she was furious at being caught. She didn't allow him to speak, but snapped at him in German: 'The Minister is engaged.' 30

He wanted to spare her, not because he minded a killing but because his employers might prefer him not to exceed his instructions. He held the letter of introduction out to her silently; as long as she didn't hear his foreign voice or see his hare-lip she was safe. She took the letter primly and held it up close to her pince-nez. Good, he thought, she's short-sighted. 'Stay where you are,' she said, and walked back up the passage. He could 35 hear her disapproving governess voice, then she was back in the passage saying: 'The Minister will see you. Follow me, please.' He couldn't understand the foreign speech, but he knew what she meant from her behaviour.

His eyes, like little concealed cameras, photographed the room instantaneously: the desk, the easy chair, the map on the wall, the door to the bedroom behind, the wide window above the bright cold Christmas street. A little oil-stove was all the heating, and the Minister was using it now to boil a saucepan. A kitchen alarm-clock on the desk marked seven o'clock. A voice said: 'Emma, put another egg in the saucepan.' The Minister came out from the bedroom. He had tried to tidy himself, but he had forgotten the cigarette ash on his trousers. He was old and small and rather dirty. The secretary took an egg out of one of the drawers in the desk: 'And the salt. Don't forget the salt,' the Minister said. He explained in slow English, 'It prevents the shell cracking. Sit down, my friend. Make yourself at home. Emma, you can go.'

Raven sat down and fixed his eyes on the Minister's chest. He thought: I'll give her three minutes by the alarm-clock to get well away: he kept his eyes on the Minister's chest: just there I'll shoot. He let his coat collar fall and saw with bitter rage how the old man turned away from the sight of his hare-lip.

The Minister said: 'It's years since I heard from him. But I've never forgotten him, never. I can show you his photograph in the other room. It's good of him to think of an old friend. So rich and powerful too. You must ask him when you go back if he remembers the time –'. A bell began to ring furiously.

Raven thought: the telephone. I cut the wire. It shook his nerve. But it was only the alarm-clock drumming on the desk. The Minister turned it off. 'One egg's boiled,' he said, and stooped for the saucepan. Raven opened his attaché case: in the lid he had fixed his automatic fitted with a silencer. The Minister said: 'I'm sorry the bell made you jump. You see I like my egg just four minutes.'

Feet ran along the passage. The door opened. Raven turned furiously in his seat, his hare-lip flushed and raw. It was the secretary. He thought: my God, what a household. They won't let a man do things tidily. He forgot his lip, he was angry, he had a grievance. She came in flashing her gold teeth, prim and ingratiating. She said: 'I was just going out when I heard the telephone,' then she winced slightly, looked the other way, showed a clumsy delicacy before his deformity which he couldn't help noticing. It condemned her. He snatched the automatic out of the case and shot the Minister twice in the back.

Below is a list of 'sub-questions' or 'interrogations' you might draw up before commenting on the passage as the opening to a novel. Discuss your responses to them with a partner or in a small group.

Plot

- What methods does Greene use to draw the reader into the story? How far do you find these methods to be successful?

- Greene holds back a lot of information that we might expect to be given at the start of a novel, for example, who are Raven's 'employers'? Why do they want the Minister 'eliminated'? (Think of other matters of fact or context that the author withholds.) Why do you think he gives us only 'selective' information? Does this add to, or detract from, the effectiveness of the passage?

- At what points in the passage is there a strong degree of suspense? Is it, in your view, effectively created?

- Why do you think Greene makes so much of the Minister's boiled egg? Does this hold up the story or add to the drama of the situation?

- If this episode were to be adapted into either a stage play or a film, which medium would be the more suitable? For what reasons?

Character

- What are the main elements of Raven's character? In what ways are they conveyed to us (for example, through what he does and how he does it? Through what he thinks? Through what the author tells us about him?)?

- Raven never speaks throughout the passage. Why do you think Greene chooses to represent him as an entirely 'silent' figure?

- How important to your understanding of Raven is his hare-lip? Does this help to direct your view of him?

- What impressions have you formed of the Minister? Does the way in which Greene presents him affect your attitude towards his murder?

- Why do you think Greene introduces the Minister's secretary, Emma, as a central figure in this episode?

Style and structure

- Look again at the first two paragraphs. It would have been quite possible for Greene to begin his novel with paragraph 2. What do you think is gained (if anything) by the inclusion of paragraph 1?

- There is considerable emphasis on the physical appearance of all three characters – and on their reactions to each other's appearance. Find examples. Why do you think Greene chooses to highlight this aspect?

- Throughout the passage, there is a significant number of short – or fairly short – sentences. What effects do you think Greene achieves by using this device?

- Several times in the course of the passage Greene departs from a purely narrative description of events and takes us inside Raven's mind. Find examples. Why do you think he interweaves these two modes of writing?

- On the evidence of this opening passage, what kind of novel would you expect *A Gun for Sale* to be; for example, a crime 'thriller'? A psychological study of Raven and his relationships with others? A book whose central theme is strongly political? And so on. State your reasons, clearly, referring (as always) to details in the text.

General

- What interests you most about this passage? If you had the whole novel in front of you, would you want to carry on reading it? Give your reasons.

In practice

Below are the opening sections of two novels. Passage A was written in 1885, Passage B in 1984. Read both passages. Then decide which one you prefer to comment on (see page 131).

(A) *from* **Huckleberry Finn**

by Mark Twain

You don't know about me, without you have read a book by the name of *The Adventures of Tom Sawyer*, but that ain't no matter. That book was made by Mr Mark Twain, and he told the truth, mainly. There was things which he stretched, but mainly he told the truth. That is nothing. I never seen anybody but lied, one time or another, without it was Aunt Polly, or the widow, or maybe Mary. Aunt Polly – Tom's Aunt Polly, she is – and Mary, and the Widow Douglas, is all told about in that book – which is mostly a true book; with some stretchers, as I said before.

Now the way that the book winds up, is this: Tom and me found the money that the robbers hid in the cave, and it made us rich. We got six thousand dollars apiece – all gold. It was an awful sight of money when it was piled up. Well, Judge Thatcher, he took it and put it out at interest, and it fetched us a dollar a day apiece, all the year round – more than a body could tell what to do with. The Widow Douglas, she took me for her son, and allowed she would sivilize me; but it was rough living in the house all the time, considering how dismal regular and decent the widow was in all her ways; and so when I couldn't stand it no longer, I lit out. I got into my old rags, and my sugar-hogshead again, and was free and satisfied. But Tom Sawyer, he hunted me up and said he was going to start a band of robbers, and I might join if I would go back to the widow and be respectable. So I went back.

The widow she cried over me, and called me a poor lost lamb, and she called me a lot of other names, too, but she never meant no harm by it. She put me in them new clothes again, and I couldn't do nothing but sweat and sweat, and feel all cramped up. Well, then, the old thing commenced again. The widow rung a bell for supper, and you had to come to time. When you got to the table you couldn't go right to eating, but you had to wait for the widow to tuck down her head and grumble a little over the victuals, though there warn't really anything the matter with them. That is, nothing only everything was cooked by itself. In a barrel of odds and ends it is different; things get mixed up, and the juice kind of swaps around, and the things go better.

After supper she got out her book and learned me about Moses and the Bulrushes; and I was in a sweat to find out all about him; but by-and-by she let it out that Moses had been dead a considerable long time; so then I didn't care no more about him; because I don't take no stock in dead people.

Pretty soon I wanted to smoke, and asked the widow to let me. But she wouldn't. She said it was a mean practice and wasn't clean, and I must try not to do it any more. That is just the way with some people. They get down on a thing when they don't know nothing about it. Here she was a bothering about Moses, which was no kin to her, and no use to anybody, being gone, you see, yet finding a power of fault with me for doing a thing that had some good in it. And she took snuff too; of course that was all right, because she done it herself.

Her sister, Miss Watson, a tolerable slim old maid, with goggles on, had just come to live with her, and took a set at me now, with a spelling-book. She worked me middling hard for about an hour, and then the widow made her ease up. I couldn't stand it much longer. Then for an hour it was deadly dull, and I was fidgety. Miss Watson would say, 'Don't put your feet up there, Huckleberry'; and 'don't scrunch up like that, Huckleberry – set up straight'; and pretty soon she would say, 'Don't gap and stretch like that, Huckleberry – why don't you try to behave?' Then she told me all about the bad place, and I said I wished I was there. She got mad, then, but I didn't mean no harm. All I wanted was to go somewheres; all I wanted was a change, I warn't particular. She said it was wicked to say what I said; said she wouldn't say it for the whole world; *she* was going to live so as to go to the good place. Well, I couldn't see no advantage in going where she was going, so I made up my mind I wouldn't try for it. But I never said so, because it would only make trouble, and wouldn't do no good.

B   *from* **Hotel du Lac**

by Anita Brookner

From the window all that could be seen was a receding area of grey. It was to be supposed that beyond the grey garden, which seemed to sprout nothing but the stiffish leaves of some unfamiliar plant, lay the vast grey lake, spreading like an anaesthetic towards the invisible further shore, and beyond that, in imagination only, yet verified by the brochure, the peak of the Dent d'Oche, on which snow might already be slightly and silently falling. For it was late September, out of season; the tourists had gone, the rates were reduced, and there were few inducements for visitors in this small town at the water's edge, whose inhabitants, uncommunicative to begin with, were frequently rendered taciturn by the dense cloud that descended for days at a time and then vanished without warning to reveal a new landscape, full of colour and incident: boats skimming on the lake, passengers at the landing stage, an open air market, the outline of the gaunt remains of a thirteenth-century castle, seams of white on the far mountains, and on the cheerful uplands to the south a rising backdrop of apple trees, the fruit sparkling with emblematic significance. For this was a land of prudently harvested plenty, a land which had conquered human accidents, leaving only the weather distressingly beyond control.

Edith Hope, a writer of romantic fiction under a more thrusting name, remained standing at the window, as if an access of good will could pierce the mysterious opacity with which she had been presented, although she had been promised a tonic cheerfulness, a climate devoid of illusions, an utterly commonsensical, not to say pragmatic, set of circumstances – quiet hotel, excellent cuisine, long walks, lack of excitement, early nights – in which she could be counted upon to retrieve her serious and hard-working personality and to forget the unfortunate lapse which had led to this brief exile, in this apparently unpopulated place, at this slowly darkening time of the year, when she should have been at home … But it was home, or, rather, 'home', which had become inimical all at once, so that she had acquiesced, rather frightened at what was happening to her, when her friends had suggested a short break, and had allowed herself to be driven to the airport by her friend and neighbour, Penelope Milne, who, tight-lipped, was prepared to forgive her only on condition that she disappeared for a decent length of time and came back older, wiser, and properly apologetic. For I am not to be allowed my lapse, as if I were an artless girl, she thought; and why should I be? I am a serious woman who should know better and am judged by my friends to be past the age of indiscretion; several people have remarked upon my physical resemblance to Virginia Woolf; I am a householder, a ratepayer, a good plain cook, and a deliverer of typescripts well before the deadline; I sign anything that is put in front of me; I never telephone my publisher; and I make no claims for my particular sort of writing, although I understand that it is doing quite well. I have held this rather dim and trusting personality together for a considerable length of time, and although I have certainly bored others I was not to be allowed to bore myself. My profile was deemed to be low and it was agreed by those who thought they knew me that it should stay that way. And no doubt after a curative stay in this grey solitude (and I notice that the leaves of that plant are quite immobile) I shall be allowed back, to resume my peaceable existence, and to revert to what I was before I did that apparently dreadful thing, although, frankly, once I had done it I didn't give it another thought. But I do now. Yes.

Turning her back on the toneless expanse beyond the window, she contemplated the room, which was the colour of over-cooked veal; veal-coloured carpet and curtains, high, narrow bed with a veal-coloured counterpane, small austere table with a correct chair placed tightly underneath it, a narrow, costive wardrobe, and, at a very great height above her head, a tiny brass chandelier, which, she knew, would eventually

twinkle drearily with eight weak bulbs. Stiff white lace curtains, providing even more 50
protection against the sparse daylight, could be parted to allow access, through long
windows, to a narrow strip of balcony on which were placed a green metal table and
chair. I shall be able to write there when the weather is fine, she thought.

Prepare for writing your commentary by putting into practice the method you have tried out on *A
Gun for Sale*, this time setting and answering your own 'sub-questions'.

If you choose Passage A, write to this instruction:

*How effective do you consider this passage to be as the opening to a novel? In the course of your answer,
you should consider:*

- *the narrative style;*

- *characterisation;*

- *the use of humour;*

- *the form and structure of the passage.*

If you choose Passage B, write to this instruction:

*Comment on the presentation of character and the writer's description of landscape in the passage. What
qualities in the writing do you find to recommend it as the opening of a novel?*

Take as much time as you need. Aim to produce a final draft of three or four sides of A4 paper.

It will be highly beneficial if you make a first draft and then exchange it with at least one other
person working on the same passage. Share in discussion both the reasons for your comments and,
in particular, the difficulties you encountered in deciding what to write.

Cross-overs: comparing linked texts

Unseen papers also invite comment on poems and prose passages which are similar in their subject matter. This final section offers you advice about, and practice in, writing a comparative analysis of related texts. Some students fight shy of this exercise, often because a single poem or passage seems to be a 'safer bet' and to involve less text-searching. In fact, this is almost never the case. Comparing linked texts in the unseen will pay handsome dividends, as long as you use a bit of common sense and develop through practice a reliable method for dealing with them.

Planning and structuring your answer

The specific techniques of analysing two linked poems or passages are exactly the same as those dealt with in Sections 5.1 to 5.4 above. What you need to keep in the forefront of your mind when conducting comparisons is the way you shape and construct your commentary. During planning and writing, refer to the following checklist of Do's and Don't's until you are able to put them into practice automatically.

- Do pay particular attention to the examiner's instructions. They are likely to be more directed and less 'open-ended' than those for other types of unseen and will guide you into writing relevantly. Don't – as always – make up your own instructions.

- Do be selective; don't try to 'tell all'. Comparative analysis is at its best when you identify a limited number of key points and draw them out in some details. Go for the heart of the matter and by-pass 'fringe' points. Thus you will gain credit for demonstrating that, in two poems about winter, poet X sees it as a season of death and decay whereas poet Y sees it as the prelude to a resurgence of new life and growth. Conversely, you will gain no credit for noting that there is twice as much description of snow in poem A as there is in poem B.

- Do use each paragraph you write to compare specific elements in both poems or passages. Don't spend the first half of your answers writing exclusively about one poem/passage and the second half writing exclusively about the other – with a short paragraph at the end which starts 'Thus the two poems/passages are similar because …'. Bring out comparative points all the way through your answer: make this the central principle for organising the whole of your commentary and every paragraph within it.

- Do, when planning, establish an order of priority for your points of comparison. If you pin-point the really fundamental similarity or difference between two poems/passages only in the middle of side 3 of your answer, an examiner will be less impressed than if you do so at the outset. By the same token, don't start off by discussing a relatively minor comparison – it may be 'easy to spot', but it is just as likely to be a fairly superficial point.

- Do combine points about subject matter with points about style as you progress; don't deal with these in separate sections of your answer. (Remind yourself of the reason why by referring back to page 40.)

In practice

Below are two typical unseen questions requiring comparison. It may be fruitful to use one for class or group discussion, planning together an answer with your eye on the checklist above, and one for 'timed' exam practice on your own. However you proceed, draw on the methods of tackling unseens that you personally have found most helpful during your work on this chapter.

Prose

The following passages describe industrial landscapes and the people who inhabit them. Compare the impressions of both given by each writer, taking into account, among other things:

- the particular nature of the writer's interest in his subject matter;

- the viewpoint established by each writer and the way he directs the reader's response to what he describes;

- any uses of language you find especially interesting and effective.

(A) from **Hard Times** (1854)

by Charles Dickens

It was a town of red brick, or of brick that would have been red if the smoke and ashes had allowed it; but as matters stood it was a town of unnatural red and black like the painted face of a savage. It was a town of machinery and tall chimneys, out of which interminable serpents of smoke trailed themselves for ever and ever, and never got uncoiled. It had a black canal in it, and a river that ran purple with ill-smelling dye, and 5 vast piles of building full of windows where there was a rattling and a trembling all day long, and where the piston of the steam-engine worked monotonously up and down like the head of an elephant in a state of melancholy madness. It contained several large streets all very like one another, and many small streets still more like one another, inhabited by people equally like one another, who all went in and out at the same 10 hours, with the same sound upon the same pavements, to do the same work, and to whom every day was the same as yesterday and to-morrow, and every year the counterpart of the last and the next.

You saw nothing in Coketown but what was severely workful. If the members of a religious persuasion built a chapel there – as the members of eighteen religious 15 persuasions had done – they made it a pious warehouse of red brick, with sometimes (but this is only in highly ornamental examples) a bell in a birdcage on the top of it. The solitary exception was the New Church; a stuccoed edifice with a square steeple over the door, terminating in four short pinnacles like florid wooden legs. All the public inscriptions in the town were painted alike, in severe characters of black and white. The 20 jail might have been the infirmary, the infirmary might have been the jail, the town-hall might have been either, or both, or anything else, for anything that appeared to the contrary in the graces of their construction. Fact, fact, fact everywhere in the material aspect of the town; fact, fact, fact, everywhere in the immaterial. The M'Choakumchild school was all fact, and the school of design was all fact, and the relations between 25 master and man were all fact, and everything was fact between the lying-in hospital and the cemetery, and what you couldn't state in figures, or show to be purchasable in the cheapest market and saleable in the dearest, was not, and never should be, world without end, Amen.

A town so sacred to fact, and so triumphant in its assertion, of course got on well? Why 30 no, not quite well. No? Dear me!

No. Coketown did not come out of its own furnaces, in all respects like gold that had stood the fire. First, the perplexing mystery of the place was, Who belonged to the eighteen denominations? Because, whoever did, the labouring people did not. It was

very strange to walk through the streets on a Sunday morning, and note how few of 35
them the barbarous jangling of bells that was driving the sick and nervous mad, called
away from their own quarter, from their own close rooms, from the corners of their own
streets, where they lounged listlessly, gazing at all the church and chapel going, as at a
thing with which they had no manner of concern. Nor was it merely the stranger who
noticed this, because there was a native organization in Coketown itself, whose 40
members were to be heard of in the House of Commons every session, indignantly
petitioning for acts of parliament that should make these people religious by main force.
Then came the Teetotal Society, who complained that these same people *would* get
drunk, and showed in tabular statements that they did get drunk, and proved at tea
parties that no inducement, human or Divine (except a medal), would induce them to 45
forego their custom of getting drunk. Then came the chemist and druggist, with other
tabular statements, showing that when they didn't get drunk, they took opium. Then
came the experienced chaplain of the jail, with more tabular statements, outdoing all
the previous tabular statements, and showing that the same people *would* resort to low
haunts, hidden from the public eye, where they heard low singing and saw low dancing, 50
and mayhap joined in it; and where A. B., aged twenty-four next birthday, and
committed for eighteen months' solitary, had himself said (not that he had ever shown
himself particularly worthy of belief) his ruin began, as he was perfectly sure and
confident that otherwise he would have been a tip-top moral specimen. Then came Mr
Gradgrind and Mr Bounderby, the two gentlemen at this present moment walking 55
though Coketown, and both eminently practical, who could, on occasion, furnish more
tabular statements derived from their own personal experience, and illustrated by cases
they had known and seen, from which it clearly appeared – in short, it was the only
clear thing in the case – that these same people were a bad lot altogether, gentlemen;
that do what you would for them they were never thankful for it, gentlemen; that they 60
were restless, gentlemen; that they never knew what they wanted; that they lived upon
the best, and bought fresh butter; and insisted on Mocha coffee, and rejected all but
prime parts of meat, and yet were eternally dissatisfied and unmanageable. In short, it
was the moral of the old nursery fable:

> There was an old woman, and what do you think? 65
> She lived upon nothing but victuals and drink;
> Victuals and drink were the whole of her diet,
> And yet this old woman would NEVER be quiet.

(B) *from* **The Road to Wigan Pier** (1937)

by George Orwell

As you walk through the industrial towns you lose yourself in labyrinths of little brick
houses blackened by smoke, festering in planless chaos round miry alleys and little
cindered yards where there are stinking dust-bins and lines of grimy washing and half-
ruinous WCs. The interiors of these houses are always very much the same, though the
number of rooms varies between two or five. All have an almost exactly similar living- 5
room, ten or fifteen feet square, with an open kitchen range; in the larger ones there is
a scullery as well, in the smaller ones the sink and copper are in the living-room. At the
back there is the yard, or part of a yard shared by a number of houses, just big enough
for the dustbin and the WC. Not a single one has hot water laid on. You might walk, I
suppose, through literally hundreds of miles of streets inhabited by miners, every one of 10
whom, when he is in work, gets black from head to foot every day, without ever passing
a house in which one could have a bath. It would have been very simple to install a hot-
water system working from the kitchen range, but the builder saved perhaps ten pounds
on each house by not doing so, and at the time when these houses were built no one
imagined that miners wanted baths. 15

For it is to be noted that the majority of these houses are old, fifty or sixty years old at least, and great numbers of them are by any ordinary standard not fit for human habitation. They go on being tenanted simply because there are no others to be had. And that is the central fact about housing in the industrial areas: not that the houses are poky and ugly, and insanitary and comfortless, or that they are distributed in incredibly filthy slums round belching foundries and stinking canals and slag-heaps that deluge them with sulphurous smoke – though all this is perfectly true – but simply that there are not enough houses to go round.

The train bore me away, through the monstrous scenery of slag-heaps, chimneys, piled scrap-iron, foul canals, paths of cidery mud criss-crossed by the prints of clogs. This was March, but the weather had been horribly cold and everywhere there were mounds of blackened snow. As we moved slowly through the outskirts of the town we passed row after row of little grey slum houses running at right angles to the embankment. At the back of one of the houses a young woman was kneeling on the stones, poking a stick up the leaden waste-pipe which ran from the sink inside and which I suppose was blocked. I had time to see everything about her – her sacking apron, her clumsy clogs, her arms reddened by the cold. She looked up as the train passed, and I was almost near enough to catch her eye. She had a round pale face, the usual exhausted face of the slum girl who is twenty-five and looks forty, thanks to miscarriages and drudgery; and it wore, for the second in which I saw it, the most desolate, hopeless expression I have ever seen. It struck me then that we are mistaken when we say that 'It isn't the same for them as it would be for us', and that people bred in the slums can imagine nothing but the slums. For what I saw in her face was not the ignorant suffering of an animal. She knew well enough what was happening to her – understood as well as I did how dreadful a destiny it was to be kneeling there in the bitter cold, on the slimy stones of a slum backyard, poking a stick up a foul drain pipe.

But quite soon the train drew away into open country, and that seemed quite strange, almost unnatural, as though the open country had been a kind of park; for in the industrial areas one always feels that the smoke and filth must go on for ever and that no part of the earth's surface can escape them. In a crowded, dirty little country like ours one takes defilement almost for granted. Slag-heaps and chimneys seem a more normal, probable landscape than grass and trees, and even in the depths of the country when you drive your fork into the ground you can half expect to lever up a broken bottle or a rusty can. But out here the snow was untrodden and lay so deep that only the tops of the stone boundary-walls were showing, winding over the hills like black paths. I remembered that D.H. Lawrence, writing of this same landscape or another near by, said that the snow-covered hills rippled away into the distance 'like muscle'. It was not the simile that would have occurred to me. To my eye the snow and the black walls were more like a white dress with black piping running through it.

The whole of the industrial districts are really one enormous town, of about the same population as Greater London but, fortunately, of much larger area; so that even in the middle of them there is still room for patches of cleanness and decency. That is an encouraging thought. In spite of hard trying, man has not yet succeeded in doing his dirt everywhere. The earth is so vast and still so empty that even in the filthy heart of civilization you find fields where the grass is green instead of grey; perhaps another twenty minutes, the train was rolling through open country before the villa-civilization began to close in upon us again, and then the outer slums, and then the slag-heaps, belching chimneys, blast-furnaces, canals, and gasometers of another industrial town.

Poetry

In the following poems, two writers describe their responses to hearing birdsong. Compare these responses, including in your answer a consideration of:

- the circumstances in which the birds are singing;

- the thoughts and feelings provoked in each poet by the bird's song;

- the form and structure of the poems;

- the poets' use of language and imagery.

The Darkling Thrush

I leant upon a coppice gate
    When Frost was spectre-grey,
And Winter's dregs made desolate
    The weakening eye of day.
The tangled bine-stems scored the sky   5
    Like strings of broken lyres,
And all mankind that haunted nigh
    Had sought their household fires.

The land's sharp features seemed to be
    The Century's corpse outleant,   10
His crypt the cloudy canopy,
    The wind his death-lament;
The ancient pulse of germ and birth
    Was shrunken hard and dry,
And every spirit upon earth   15
    Seemed fervourless as I.

At once a voice arose among
    The bleak twigs overhead
In a full-hearted evensong
    Of joy illimited;   20
An aged thrush, frail, gaunt, and small,
    In blast-beruffled plume,
Had chosen thus to fling his soul
    Upon the growing gloom.

So little cause for carollings   25
    Of such ecstatic sound
Was written on terrestrial things
    Afar or nigh around,
That I could think there trembled through
    His happy good-night air   30
Some blessed Hope, whereof he knew
    And I was unaware.

Thomas Hardy
31 December 1900

A Blackbird Singing

It seems wrong that out of this bird,
Black, bold, a suggestion of dark
Places about it, there yet should come
Such rich music, as though the notes'
Ore were changed to a rare metal   5
At one touch of that bright bill.

You have heard it often, alone at your desk
In a green April, your mind drawn
Away from its work by sweet disturbance
Of the mild evening outside your room.   10

A slower singer, but loading each phrase
With history's overtones, love, joy
And grief learned by his dark tribe
In other orchards and passed on
Instinctively as they are now,   15
But fresh always with new tears.

R.S. Thomas

Chapter 6 Non-fiction texts: materials and methods of working

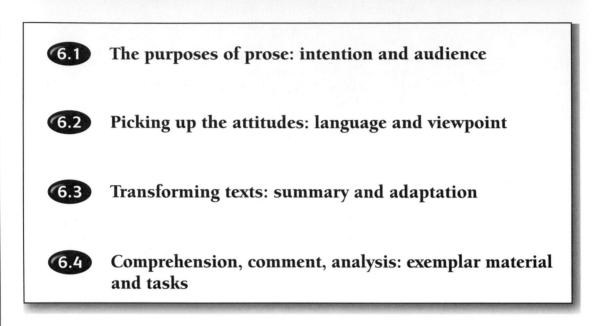

6.1   The purposes of prose: intention and audience

6.2   Picking up the attitudes: language and viewpoint

6.3   Transforming texts: summary and adaptation

6.4   Comprehension, comment, analysis: exemplar material and tasks

The fourteen text items in this chapter are drawn from a range of non-fictional genres, from both contemporary and historical sources. These have been chosen to reflect the kind of material typically used on current A level syllabus for English and English Language and Literature.

Introduction

Many A level English syllabuses go well beyond an exclusively literature-based course and include non-fiction texts in their programmes of study. They are becoming increasingly popular with both students and teachers who wish to combine work on literary texts with a broader appreciation of writing as a medium which can be used to inform, persuade, conduct argument, express opinion and so on.

Hence the purposes of this chapter are:

- to provide a range of non-fictional material for students already working on combined English and English Literature courses to practise the skills that their syllabuses require;

- to demonstrate strategies for responding to non-literary texts in terms of their genre (that is, text-type), purpose, intended readership and stylistic features;

- to help you draw on your appreciation of literature in order to examine the ways in which 'practical prose' uses language to achieve particular effects.

This chapter does not attempt to give guidance on theoretical knowledge about language. Stylistics, sociolinguistics, language acquisition, the history of language change and so on comprise a quite distinct field of study – normally, if loosely, termed Linguistics – which is beyond the scope of this book and for which published resources already exist to support work undertaken in school.*

---

* For example, *An Introduction to Stylistics*, Urszula Clark, 1996 (Stanley Thornes); *The Nature and Functions of Language*, Howard Jackson and Peter Stockwell, 1996 (Stanley Thornes)

The purposes of prose: intention and audience

The nineteenth-century Romantic poet John Keats, living in an age before mass communication and the information superhighway, spoke disparagingly of 'poetry which has a palpable design on us'. As modern readers, we may or may not agree with him about poetry. It is, however, quite clear that much of what we read nowadays does make specific 'designs' upon us. Advertisements attempt to persuade us to buy; political writing influences us to think in certain ways and/or to change our existing opinions; journalism goes far beyond providing us with news, often seeking to impose on us a particular point of view; reviews of books, new cars, plays and music set out to shape our attitudes even before we have had a chance to adopt them in the first place.

If we are not to be mere ciphers for the noisy clamour of public voices which assail us on all sides, it is important to understand how the written word seeks to influence us by appealing to our intellect, to our emotions and to our literacy. By understanding how the 'voices' of what we might call *purposive writing* work on us, we can find our own voice so as to enter into an informed dialogue with what we read. This understanding must begin with an examination of the purposes of non-fiction and of the audience (or readership) for which it is intended – and of how the two are linked.

With this in mind, read Items 1, 2 and 3 on the following pages.

>─┼─◀▶─•─○─•─◀▶─┼─◀

① *Adapted from* **Little Girls in Pretty Boxes:**
The Making and Breaking of Elite Athletes

by Joan Ryan

In the summer of 1993 thirteen-year-old Michelle Kwan became the youngest skater to win a gold medal in US Olympic Festival history, prompting a flurry of excitement about the emergence of a new skating princess. A year later Kwan was 5 inches taller and 1 stone 6 pounds heavier. She struggled with the triple jumps she once landed so easily. She was no longer the 4-foot-9-inch slip of a girl who had captivated the festival crowd   5
with her child-princess looks and delicate grace. Puberty had arrived.

As if off an assembly line, another pixie star promptly rolled onto the scene.

Three weeks after her twelfth birthday, a 4 stone 12 pound girl named Tara Lipinski skated onto the ice at the 1994 US Olympic Festival, a showcase for America's rising Olympic stars. She was so new to competitive skating that the United States Figure   10
Skating Association had barely heard of her. Yet she already had given up school in favour of private tutors. She and her mother had left her father in Texas, so she could train at the University of Delaware's ice arena. Expenses for housing, coaching, ice time, travel, equipment and costumes ran about US$50,000 a year, which her parents paid, in part, by remortgaging their house. By their interviews in the *New York Times*, Tara's   15
parents seemed to know the risks and sacrifices of elite child sports: the stunted social skills, the blurry education, the fractured family, the lost friends, the potentially crushing disappointment. But ultimately the lure of Olympic gold proved too seductive.

'I'd give my daughter anything,' Tara's mother, Pat, told a *Times* reporter, echoing so many parents before her. 'She loves it. And we're seeing results. I can't just demand that   20
she stop. For the rest of my life, I'd have to sit around and think, "What if, what if?"'

By 1994, the US gymnast Shannon Miller, like Michelle Kwan, was falling victim to the ephemeral nature of her sport. Her body was widening and rounding out, growing more womanly. And though only seventeen, she was beginning to lose ground to those younger and smaller. In the spring of 1994 at a gymnastics meet in Atlanta, Shannon's coach Steve Nunno was asked about a gymnast he trained named Jennie Thompson.

'Jennie is Shannon Miller and Kim Zmeskal wrapped up in one,' he gushed. He said she had the most remarkable combination of qualities he had ever seen in a gymnast and that she had the added advantage of learning from Shannon in the gym every day. He declared her one of America's best hopes for a medal at the 1996 Olympics in Atlanta. Jennie barely topped 4 feet and weighed just 4 stone 2 pounds. She was twelve years old.

In the autumn of 1994, Bela Karolyi* emerged from retirement with a startling announcement. 'People are [saying] this is a kid sport, [saying] that the girls are anorexic, that their childhoods are being taken away,' he told the *New York Times*, 'so let's bring back grace and maturity. Maybe it will change the face of gymnastics.' The article dropped jaws across America. Had Karolyi undergone some sort of transformation during his self-imposed exile?

Karolyi said his re-evaluation was brought into sharper focus as he watched twenty-seven-year-old Katarine Witt enchant the crowd – if not the judges – during the 1994 Winter Games. He said he wanted to bring that same grace and maturity back to gymnastics, a direction already endorsed by the International Gymnastics Federation: after the 1996 Summer Games in Atlanta, Olympic gymnasts will be required to be at least sixteen years old instead of fifteen.

Back in the gym, Karolyi was putting in eight, nine, ten hours a day training his two fading champions. He also took on board two other gymnasts, who didn't figure as prominently in Karolyi's manifesto on the changing face of gymnastics. One was the 1994 junior national champion, thirteen-year-old Dominique Moceanu, a tiny, gifted girl who had been training with Karolyi's wife. The other was little Jennie Thompson, who Karolyi had quickly wooed back from Nunno's to his own gym.

Ever the player, Karolyi was moving the chess pieces with both hands. He deftly rode the political wind by denouncing the sad state of the sport, while behind the gym doors he was vigorously training two of the smallest, youngest stars in the country. Zmeskal and Boginskaya could get him good press. But, now as always, the super-tiny, super-young girls could get him the medals.

Tara Lipinski and Jennie Thompson embody the unspoken imperative of elite figure skating and gymnastics: keep them coming, and keep them young, small and more dazzling than the ones we already have. The national appetite for new stars is insatiable. Deep down, we know that our consumption and disposal of these young athletes are tantamount to child exploitation and, in too many cases, child abuse. But we rarely ask what becomes of them when they disappear from view. We don't want to see them parade past us with their broken bodies and mangled spirits, because then we would have to change forever the way we look at our Olympic darlings. They are the pink ballerinas inside a child's jewellery box, always perfectly positioned, perfectly coiffed. They spin on demand without complaint. When one breaks, another pops up from the next box. To close the lid is to close down that part of our soul that still wants to believe in beautiful princesses and happy endings.

25

30

35

40

45

50

55

60

65

* An East European gymnastics coach who had retired in protest against the 'exploitation' of young female gymnasts

(2) *Advertisement for Accelerated Learning Systems Ltd*

New learning method benefits careers, boosts school results.

Learn more in less time

"Knowledge is the key to the 21st Century." "Earning more means learning more." "The information explosion has just begun."

Business leaders, parents and educators are uniting in one belief. In today's fast changing and competitive world, to be able to learn faster and more effectively and to acquire new skills rapidly is no longer desirable, it's essential.

Perhaps you're seeking to improve your employability through new skills. Or your current job is about to change and you need to re-train.

Maybe you have a son or daughter at school or college. They will need the best possible grades.

Or you're far-sighted enough to want your children (or grandchildren) to have a solid foundation of reading, writing, number skill, and creativity, even before they go to school.

There's a new approach to learning that matches today's needs. It's called Accelerated Learning. It's based on Nobel Prize winning research, and it's producing impressive results and reviews:

"Radically different with so many features that recommend it to the learner." **(Education News)** "Children using Accelerated Learning are racing ahead – the results are spectacular." **(Daily Mail)** "Spectacular." **(Mensa)**. Hundreds of the world's most successful companies are using it from Avon Cosmetics to Zurich Insurance.

The basic premise of Accelerated Learning is that we all have untapped potential. Intelligence is **not** fixed, as recent work at Harvard University has now shown. The ability to absorb and retain information can be significantly boosted. Now there is a range of products for all ages based on these new discoveries.

A flying start for pre-schoolers

Did you know that some 50% of your child's brain capacity is developed in the first five or six years of life? Whether that capacity develops to the full depends largely on a stimulating, thought provoking, early home environment.

The pre-school years are critical. Never again will you have a chance to influence your child so profoundly or so positively.

A recent university study showed that " early learning can boost I.Q. by 30 points".

That's the inspiration behind a new programme called *FUNdamentals*. Its aim is a happy, well-rounded child able to read, write and do elementary maths – even before going to school. Plus a child who's acquired other essential attributes – social skills, self-esteem, creativity, a rich vocabulary, memory skills, values and the ability to think clearly.

FUNdamentals contains hundreds of games and activities, word cards, number rods and dot cards, writing templates, a video and a guidebook.

For busy parents it's a treasure chest of the best ideas from child development experts from around the world. You'll certainly never be stuck for something fun and worthwhile to do!

There's a *First FUNdamentals* for 0-18 months and the the full *FUNdamentals* programme for 2-6 years old.

FUNdamentals – Years of fun, purposeful play.

"An amazing array of games and activities. FUNdamentals provides the best building blocks I've seen for raising a brighter, happier child". *John Abbott, Director of Education 2000 and an international advisor on education."*

Its a gift that really does last a lifetime.

Higher grades for students

*What you learn can become out of date, but learning **how** to learn faster and more efficiently is a skill for life. But schools don't teach it.*

Secondary school students can boost their exam results (and motivation) with a programme called *Accelerate Your Learning*. A video, audio tape and Action Handbooks teaches them how to read and absorb information faster, improve memory and writing skills and generally study more effectively.

The programme enables each student uncover his or her preferred way of learning and acquire the learning techniques that best match that learning style.

The programme is a winner. It can help almost anyone of any age to improve their learning." David Bradshaw, Assoc. for Further and Higher Education.

Documented results from a London Educational authority show very significant improvements in

accelerated learning

ACCELERATED LEARNING SYSTEMS LTD, 50 Aylesbury Rd., Aston Clinton, Aylesbury, Bucks HP22 5AH
Telephone Enquiries (01296) 631177   Fax: (01296) 631074   Email: colinrose@globalnet.co.uk

exam results when this programme was introduced. "An excellent programme well worth parents buying" says the National Confederation of Parent Teachers Associations.

It's not enough to urge teenagers to get better results, you need to give them the practical techniques to make that success possible. That's what *Accelerate Your Learning* achieves.

New job skills

Learning faster than the competition is a core skill for both individuals and organisations. This is the aim of the *Accelerated Learning Techniques* Programme. It teaches people in business how to learn any subject or skill in the way that best suits their individual learning style. The result is working smarter, not harder – learning more in less time.

A foreign language in 3 ½ weeks?

You can buy in any language – but you can only sell in your customer's language! Mastering a foreign language is a major career and school advantage and definitely enhances travel.

Accelerated Learning Foreign Language Courses can accomplish in weeks what might have taken years. They use a multi-sensory immersion approach with lots of games and activities to cater to your preferred way of learning.

"Every single student passed GCSE Italian after only two terms of study – 63% at A Grade." Recent report from a London school.

The basic language is learned from a series of entertaining radio plays with real life situations on twelve **audio** cassettes. Unique 'Memory Maps' illustrate the main phrases very vividly and, when you recall the **images**, you recall the words. A video gets you **physically** acting out key words and phrases, and another unique feature, the Name Game builds vocabulary in an astonishingly short time. There are parts you can practice in the car and some sequences are even repeated to music. The words become as easy to remember as a song.

The combination of auditory, visual and physical learning is unique - but is 3 ½ weeks realistic?

Well, the record so far was just 31 hours of study to pass the Institute of Linguists Preliminary certificate. Both BBC and ITV news have featured a school where **ten times** more students using Accelerated Learning got top marks compared with conventional courses. Others have compressed two years work into three months.

Combining seeing, listening, speaking and physical action, is why the Accelerated Learning Language method works faster.

Hundreds of corporate clients like IBM, Glaxo, Rover Cars, and Banks world wide can also testify to the success of this language method.

You can draw!

Ask most people if they can draw and the reply is a rueful "no". Maybe that's why a consistently good seller for us has been our book/video programme "Yes, You Can Draw". After just a morning with the step-by-step course, most people are able to produce portraits they are proud to show.

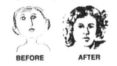

BEFORE   AFTER

From babies to bankers, schoolchildren to corporations, Accelerated Learning is proving that we all have more potential to learn than we have thought. That's why Psychology Today has called it "a key to the 21st century."

If you want more information please use the Freephone or Coupon now. Better still use our risk free trial offer. Order any product and we will not process your credit card or cheque for at least 15 days after you have received it. If you are not **completely** satisfied that it will live up to your fullest expectations, just return it and you'll have paid nothing.

(3) *Transcript of the address by Earl Spencer at the funeral of his sister, Diana, Princess of Wales, September 1997*

I stand before you today the representative of a family in grief, in a country in mourning, before a world in shock. We are all united not only in our desire to pay our respects to Diana, but rather in our need to do so.

For such was her extraordinary appeal that the tens of millions of people taking part in this service all over the world via television and radio who never actually met her feel that they too lost someone close to them in the early hours of Sunday morning. It is a more remarkable tribute to Diana than I can ever hope to offer her today.

Diana was the very essence of compassion, of duty, of style, of beauty. All over the world she was a symbol of selfless humanity. All over the world, a standard bearer for the rights of the truly downtrodden, a very British girl who transcended nationality. Someone with a natural nobility who was classless and who proved in the last year that she needed no royal title to continue to generate her particular brand of magic.

Today is our chance to say thank you for the way you brightened our lives, even though God granted you but half a life. We will all feel cheated always that you were taken from us so young and yet we must learn to be grateful that you came along at all. Only now that you are gone do we truly appreciate what we are now without, and we want you to know that life without you is very, very difficult.

We have all despaired at our loss over the past week, and only the strength of the message you gave us through your years of giving has afforded us the strength to move forward.

There is a temptation to rush to canonise your memory; there is no need to do so. You stand tall enough as a human being of unique qualities not to need to be seen as a saint. Indeed, to sanctify your memory would be to miss out on the very core of your being, your wonderfully mischievous sense of humour with a laugh that bent you double.

Your joy for life transmitted wherever you took your smile and the sparkle in those unforgettable eyes. Your boundless energy which you could barely contain.

But your greatest gift was your intuition, and it was a gift you used wisely. This is what underpinned all your other wonderful attributes, and if we look to analyse what it was about you that had such a wide appeal we find it in your instinctive feel for what was really important in all our lives.

Without your God-given sensitivity we would be immersed in greater ignorance at the anguish of Aids and HIV sufferers, the plight of the homeless, the isolation of lepers, the random destruction of landmines.

Diana explained to me once that it was her innermost feelings of suffering that made it possible for her to connect with her constituency of the rejected.

And here we come to another truth about her. For all the status, the glamour, the applause, Diana remained throughout a very insecure person at heart, almost childlike in her desire to do good for others so she could release herself from deep feelings of unworthiness of which her eating disorders were merely a symptom. The world sensed this part of her character and cherished her for her vulnerability whilst admiring her for her honesty.

The last time I saw Diana was on July the 1st, her birthday, in London, when, typically, she was not taking time to celebrate her special day with friends but was guest of honour at a fundraising charity evening. She sparkled, of course, but I would rather cherish the days I spent with her in March when she came to visit me and my children at our home in South Africa. I am proud of the fact that, apart from when she was on public display meeting President Mandela, we managed to contrive to stop the ever-present paparazzi from getting a single picture of her. That meant a lot to her.

These were days I will always treasure. It was as if we had been transported back to our childhood when we spent such an enormous amount of time together, the two youngest in the family. Fundamentally, she hadn't changed at all from the big sister who mothered me as a baby, fought with me at school and endured those long train journeys between our parents' homes with me at weekends.

It is a tribute to her level-headedness and strength that, despite the most bizarre life imaginable after her childhood, she remained intact, true to herself.

There is no doubt that she was looking for a new direction in her life. She talked endlessly of getting away from England, mainly because of the treatment that she received at the hands of the newspapers. I don't think she ever understood why her genuinely good intentions were sneered at by the media, why there appeared to be a permanent quest on their behalf to bring her down. It is baffling.

My own, and only, explanation is that genuine goodness is threatening to those at the opposite end of the moral spectrum. It is a point to remember that, of all the ironies about Diana, perhaps the greatest was this: a girl given the name of the ancient goddess of hunting was, in the end, the most hunted person of the modern age.

She would want us today to pledge ourselves to protecting her beloved boys, William and Harry, from a similar fate, and I do this here, Diana, on your behalf. We will not allow them to suffer the anguish that used regularly to drive you to tearful despair.

And beyond that, on behalf of your mother and sisters, I pledge that we, your blood family, will do all we can to continue the imaginative and loving way in which you were steering these two exceptional young men so that their souls are not simply immersed by duty and tradition, but can sing openly as you planned. We fully respect the heritage into which they have both been born, and will always respect and encourage them in their royal role, but we, like you, recognise the need for them to experience as many different aspects of life as possible to arm them spiritually and emotionally for the years ahead. I know you would have expected nothing less from us.

William and Harry, we all care desperately for you today. We are all chewed up for sadness at the loss of a woman who wasn't even our mother. How great your suffering is, we cannot ever imagine.

I would like to end by thanking God for the small mercies he has shown us at this dreadful time; for taking Diana at her most beautiful and radiant, and when she had joy in her private life. Above all, we give thanks for the life of a woman I am so proud to call my sister – the unique, the complex, the extraordinary and irreplaceable Diana, whose beauty, both internal and external, will never be extinguished from our minds.

Suggested task

Discuss in groups, or as a class, the following aspects of one or more of Items 1, 2 and 3.

- What does the item in question set out to achieve, precisely?

- What exactly is the intended audience for the item in question? How do you know?

- By what means does the item attempt to achieve its purposes? Among other things, you may wish to consider:
  - the way in which the reader is addressed;
  - choice of vocabulary;
  - sentence structure and grammar;
  - overall structure;
  - language, presentation and graphic images.

- How effective do you judge the item in question to be?

Methods of working: a demonstration

Item 4 is a review of a 'conversation' between Melvyn Bragg, the TV presenter, and Norman Mailer, the American novelist and former boxer, who published in 1997 a version of the New Testament written from the viewpoint of Jesus: *The Gospel According to the Son*. The 'conversation' took place in front of a theatre audience.

(4)

REVIEWS

And the word was with Norman

Normal Mailer in Conversation

Curzon, Shaftesbury Avenue, London

Each and every one of us is seeking out a saviour. Some look for him in churches, others in converted cinemas. On Monday night, the designated spot was the Curzon, Shaftesbury Avenue.

Things had started promisingly enough: the audience had entered the auditorium to a blast from a gospel choir, and Melvyn Bragg, interceding toothsomely on our behalf with Stormin' Norman Mailer, that Grand Old Pugilist of American Letters, had reminded us of his interviewee's impeccable credentials: 'You were hoping to bring about a revolution in people's consciousness when you started writing,' said Melvyn. 'But what exactly drove you to write?'

The word, when it came, was endearingly human. 'It used to be a desire to meet beautiful women,' said Norman, knocking over the microphone for the second time, 'but in the last few years I've paid the price for being happily married. I've turned to blubber.' He clearly wasn't referring to his intellect.

Mailer had set things going with a couple of readings at the lectern, a mock-obituary of himself in which Truman Capote called him 'so butch', and 'After Death Comes Limbo'. The voice sounded 100 per cent proof: gravelly, with a gallon of phlegm washing around in the throat. Five feet four, stocky as a bull, and with grizzled grey curls, Mailer was wearing the same clothes he'd worn six years ago at the UK launch of *Harlot's Ghost* – grey flannels, blue blazer with twinkling brass buttons – a sometime street-fighter now turned bizarrely preppy. There was just one thing new: a kipper tie in a dazzling aquamarine.

All that death and afterlife stuff was intended to turn our minds towards Mailer's new book, *The Gospel According to the Son*, a re-telling of the New Testament tale. Mailer recognised that this was a very un-Mailerish sort of subject. 'It's the sort of book I wouldn't have looked at 40 years ago.' He'd wanted to publish it anonymously, he said, but the American publishers had stamped on that idea.

Some critics have wondered whether he knew enough to re-write the gospels. Mailer's touching description of his own unpreparedness was as cunning as it was bizarre: 'Some books you come to, knowing little,' he said, 'with a sense of innocence.' Still, whether or not innocence actually means ignorance, Norman hadn't held back. He knew the original's limitations like the inside of his fist. 'It's a classic,' he said, 'but not always well written. It's a great story waiting to be told.'

So Norman told it, although it had taken him a little time to get the style right, toning it down, tuning it up …

But why in heaven's name, Bragg asked, hadn't he dug into Jesus like he dug into Marilyn Monroe or Muhammad Ali all those years ago?

All of a sudden, Norman turned Messianic. 'I wanted to tell the story, I wanted to reach people,' he said. 'I wanted to point out the compatibility between Christ and Marx, to re-emphasise the notion of caring. I believe in karma, an afterlife. I believe that we pay for our sins. I'm talking about Judaeo-Christian socialism here …'

As Norman walked up the side aisle to sign a few books, the music came surging again. This time it was the 'Hallelujah Chorus'.

Michael Glover

Reproduced opposite are the notes made by a Year 12 English class engaged in an exercise similar to that suggested on page 145 above. The class was asked to examine the review by answering the same questions as those listed there. Read Item 4 and then the students' notes on it. If you find these helpful, follow a similar strategy to plan and write your own analysis of Items 1 and/or 2 and/or 3.

WHAT DOES THE REVIEW SET OUT TO ACHIEVE?

- to judge how far the conversation was informative/entertaining/effective for the audience;
- to allow readers to decide whether to go and see it (and probably to suggest it wouldn't be worth their while!);
- to look at Mailer's motives for writing the book (also to question them: impression comes through that they may be dubious);
- to assess how worthwhile it was for Mailer to re-write the New T. (and to question his 'qualifications' for doing so);
- to criticise Mailer, his book and (to a lesser extent) the conversation with M. Bragg.

WHAT IS THE INTENDED AUDIENCE?

- 'Educated'/cultured types who might think of (a) reading the book (b) going to the conversation – it's printed in 'The Independent', a broadsheet newspaper. Wouldn't get reviewed in tabloids.
- People who already know something about Mailer's writing (calls him 'That Grand Old Pugilist of American Letters': 'old mate') and who may wonder what 'Stormin' Norman Mailer' is getting up to now.
- (Maybe) religious people who might find the whole thing offensive: 'set things going with a couple of readings at the lectern', etc.

HOW ARE THE PURPOSES ACHIEVED?

- Evaluation. On the surface it attempts to be balanced (typical of a review): 'Things started out promisingly enough' … 'The word, when it came, was endearingly human.' But it gets more critical as it goes on: 'It was bizarre … whether or not innocence means ignorance, Norman hadn't held back.' In the next-to-last para. Mailer comes over as a pompous egocentric, and there's sarcasm in the last para – contrast between 'sign a few books' and the Hallelujah Chorus.
- Mailer's motives. Writer casts a lot of doubt on these. E.g. Mailer gives a flip and stupid answer to MB's question 'But what exactly drove you to write it?'. Then he's described as 'bizarrely preppy': trying too hard to be 'controversial'. It's called, critically, 'a very un-Mailerish sort of subject' – and it's implied that he did it only for the money when Mailer lies about his reasons for writing the book: 'He'd wanted to publish it anonymously but the American publishers had stamped on that idea.' (Oh yeah, pull the other one!)

HOW DOES THE WRITER MAKE HIS CRITICISMS EFFECTIVE?

- Headline: a parody of 'And the word was with God'. Suggests Mailer is arrogant and setting himself up as God.
- Irony of 'Norman' as the new God: 'Norman' not a God-like name – same as 'The Life of Brian', but this is mockery of Mailer.
- Mailer says 'I've turned to blubber': emphasis on the physical, not the spiritual. He's a washed-out fatty, not the new messiah!
- Messiahs don't wear a 'kipper tie in dazzling aquamarine': Mailer is just a flash American Del-Boy, conning the public.
- 'A gallon of phlegm washing round in the throat' makes him seem repulsive and diseased – also effective use of over-statement.

THE STRUCTURE OF THE PASSAGE

- Backs up the irony of the whole thing (i.e. criticism). Starts by suggesting Mailer might turn out to be a 'saviour': serious tone.

- BUT: as passage goes on it emphasises (1) Mailer as a boxer (para 4) rather than a saviour – or even a novelist!; (2) Mailer happier 'digging' Marilyn Monroe and M. Ali than Jesus (para 7) – Bragg sending him up here; (3) passage ends with Mailer talking mumbo-jumbo (para 8) – this is the final, lasting impression of him: a senile high priest.

Picking up the attitudes: language and viewpoint

This section looks at examples of non-fictional prose where the main focus is on the writer's use of language to communicate feeling and point of view. The key questions to be addressed here are:

● Where does the writer 'stand'?

● How do the stylistic and other features of the piece indicate his or her attitude towards the chosen subject matter?

Relevant assessment objectives

All A level English courses are devised on the basis of a number of common assessment objectives which you can be asked to meet through various kinds of work on literary and non-literary texts. The material in this section should contribute to your fulfilling the following 'core' objectives:

● an ability to respond with understanding to texts of different types;

● an understanding of the ways in which writers' choices of form, structure and language express meaning;

● an ability to discuss [your] own and other readers' interpretations of texts;

● an ability to produce informed, independent opinions and judgements.

It is worth drawing attention to these objectives for A level English – they are not a complete list – since the items that follow may seem to you rather 'lightweight' compared with the kind of material covered in earlier chapters. Bear in mind, however, that it is not only the 'difficulty' of the text but also your techniques of responding to it that are being assessed. The objectives above can, and will, be met by detailed study of Shakespeare, Chaucer, T.S. Eliot or Jane Austen – to take four obvious examples. They will also be fulfilled by the nature of your engagement with the material exemplified by Items 5 and 6 on the following pages … which you should now read.

Contexts

Item 5 is made up of two pieces, both prompted by the end of Margaret Thatcher's career as prime minister. Item 5a is an edited extract from the *Diaries* of Alan Clark, minister of state at the Ministry of Defence during Mrs Thatcher's last government. He is describing how she consulted with senior Conservative colleagues before stepping down from the leadership contest which saw John Major elected as her successor. Item 5b is taken from *Thatcher for Beginners* (1997), which attempts to summarise the effects of her eleven years in power.

Item 6, 'Beloved and Bonk: Diary of a Divorce', is taken from an autobiographical account in a newspaper of a woman's marital break-up.

⟫⫯⟨⟩⫯○⫯⟨⟩⫯⟨

(5a) *from* **Diaries**
     by Alan Clark

Wednesday, 21 November

I went down the stairs and rejoined the group outside her door. After a bit Peter[1] said, 'I can just fit you in now – but only for a split second, mind.'

    She looked calm, almost beautiful. 'Ah, Alan ...'

    'You're in a jam.'

    'I know that.'   5

    'They're all telling you not to stand, aren't they?'

    'I'm going to stand. I have issued a statement.'

    'That's wonderful. That's heroic. But the Party will let you down.'

    'I am a fighter.'

    'Fight, then. Fight right to the end, a third ballot if you need to. But you'll lose.'   10
There was quite a little pause.

    'It'd be so terrible if Michael[2] won. He would undo everything I have fought for.'

    'But what a way to go! Unbeaten in three elections, never rejected by the people, brought down by nonentities!'

    'But Michael ... as *Prime Minister*.'   15

    'Who the fuck's Michael? No one. Nothing. He won't last six months. I doubt if he'd even win the Election. Your place in history is towering ...'

    Outside, people were doing that maddening trick of opening and shutting the door, at shorter and shorter intervals.

    'Alan, it's been so good of you to come in and see me ...'   20

    Afterwards I felt empty. And cross. I had failed, but I didn't really know what I wanted except for her still to be Prime Minister, and it wasn't going to work out.

Thursday, 22 November

Very early this morning the phone rang. It was Tristan[3].

    'She's going.'

    There will be an official announcement immediately after a short Cabinet, first   25
thing. Then the race will be on. Apparently Douglas[4] *and* John Major are going to stand. I said I thought it was crazy, Heseltine will go through between them. I could sense him shrugging. 'There you go.'

    Anyway, would I come over to his room at the Foreign Office and watch it from there?   30

    Afterwards, very *triste* and silent, I walked back to the MoD and sat in on a late (and unnecessary) Ministers' meeting. Tom[5] told us that it had been 'awful'. She started to read a prepared statement to them, then broke down, and the text had to be finished by the Lord Chancellor ...

    I didn't think I could bear it, but curiosity drew me into the Chamber for the   35
Lady's last performance ... She was brilliant. Humorous, self-deprecating, swift and deadly in her argument and in her riposte. Even Dennis Skinner, her oldest adversary, was feeding her lines; and at one point Michael Carttiss shouted, 'You could wipe the floor with the lot of 'em.'

    Too bloody true. What is to become of her? ... Can she just remain on the back   40
benches? It will be hard. What happens when she starts to be 'missed', and the rose-tinted spectacles are found in everyone's breast pocket?

⟫⫯⟨⟩⫯○⫯⟨⟩⫯⟨

[1] **Peter:** Peter Morrison, Mrs Thatcher's Personal Private Secretary

[2] **Michael:** Michael Heseltine, Mrs Thatcher's main rival in the leadership contest

[3] **Tristan:** Tristan Garel-Jones, Deputy Chief Whip

[4] **Douglas:** Douglas Hurd, Foreign Secretary

[5] **Tom:** Tom King, Defence Secretary and contender in the leadership contest

(5b)

from *Thatcher for Beginners*
by Peter Pugh and Carl Flint

The Lasting Effects of Thatcher

Thatcherism is British and for Britain. It is not an *ism* like "Marxism" or "Libertarianism" or even "Feminism", designed to embrace like-minded people across the world. It can be picked up by another nation state and applied to itself, but it is not an international idea as such.

As time puts perspective on the Thatcher years, it is already safe to say that there was . . .

A Thatcher Era

and that there has come into being something called . . .

Thatcherism

In looking at the *Thatcher Era*, we only have to think, was there a Callaghan era, a Heath era, a Wilson era? to see that it holds true.

Britain went into it . . .

a dispirited, second (or was it third?) division, overmanned, union-bullied, under-managed, poorly performing, bureaucratized, inefficient, subsidized, benefit-demanding, class-ridden society living with the comforting certainties of the Cold War

and came out of it . . .

a lively, definitely second division, relatively lean, union-cowed, well-managed, reasonably performing, not-quite-so-bureaucratized, less inefficient, still hopelessly subsidized and benefit-demanding, class-ridden society facing the uncertain realities of freed Communist states, most of whom quickly adopted Thatcherite practice.

"Thatcherism" has been dubbed as symbolizing greed, the triumph of the strong over the weak, materialism, little England and a world peopled only by philistines.

Others might see it as a creed which . . .

rewards effort

confronts bullies

faces up to difficult issues

realizes the strength of world competition

and stands up for what is right, not what is easy.

A major criticism of Thatcherism was its failure to establish an independent Bank of England which could, like the Federal Reserve Board in the USA and the Bundesbank in Germany, provide a strong bulwark against any future revival of inflation. Alex Brummer, City editor of *The Guardian*, writing immediately after Thatcher's resignation, supported an independent Bank of England: *Such a move . . . would provide reassurance on commitment to sound money while having the flexibility to use fiscal policy to do those things necessary to undo the wrongs of Thatcherism, which produced private prosperity but at a high cost of public squalor and financial hooliganism.*

(6)

BELOVED AND BONK
Diary of a divorce

My husband has just left me so the dog has begun to chase the chickens again. She has caught the sparks from the thunderbolt that has struck us all. This has meant that at moments of highest drama, such as – *ME*: 'Don't you remember making love in the shower when we had a flat full of guests?' *HIM*: 'I never liked that green paint in the bathroom,' we have to break off so I can scream myself hoarse at the bottom of the garden amid squawking fowls and a boxer with neon eyes.

It is the sort of thing we would have laughed ourselves silly over a few weeks ago but there seems to have been a bit of a sense-of-humour failure since Beloved came home and announced his imminent departure to be with Bonk in a Notting Hill love-nest.

It's all in a perfectly noble cause, mind you: Personal Growth – his – and as he so very generously says, mine too. Sweet, really. I spent my first night of personal growth lying face down on our lawn chewing grass and keening into the worm casts. I have been doing lots of similar enhanced development work every night since.

Sadly, Beloved finds my reactions a little embarrassing. Having been brave enough to break free from the constraining shackles of marriage, he is standing in a shiny new world washed clean of all the cloying shards of years of wasted past. So when I finally lost it yesterday, and smashed our entire dinner service (very neatly in a skip) and sliced up my arms for good measure, he was tight-lipped. He told me tersely to change my trousers because the children would be upset if they saw the blood. Later he asked if there was anything that 'sparked it off'.

At moments like this, headlines flash before my eyes – such as 'Aliens Stole My Husband'. Is this the same man who used to balance peanuts on his nose for my entertainment and do walrus impersonations?

Of course, those were the days when M & S boxers were acceptable and he was happy to cycle to work looking a total nerd in one of those back-to-front helmets. Nothing much short of Paul Smith and Calvin Klein on his botty these days, and precious little peanut balancing since he became a weekly boarder in London and could officially say he was a film director. Not a great deal of smiling, either. Do you ever see a film director smiling?

I blame it on the telly, driving nice staff out into the nasty corrupting world of freelancedom where they drink testosterone with egomania chasers. London media freelanceness did for Beloved, poor lamb. He rediscovered the joys of single life, this time not as a poor student but as a grown-up with serious dosh, glam job and a Clerkenwell flat. Coming home to a wife who knows her chickens by name and worries if the wind will snap her rudbeckias must have begun to seem a pretty unattractive option. I mean, compared with giving Bonk a once-over against the glittering backdrop of the City skyline …

So I'm coming to terms with it all by thinking of it as a style decision. A country wife and kids just didn't fit with Beloved's Criterion dinners and Armani trews. Like wearing wellies to the Baftas. With us still attached he could never have that ultimate media accessory: a divorce. It was simply a decision forced on him by circumstances.

So what man would fit my new style? What exactly does match a divorcee with two kids and a rudbeckia fixation? Well, let's put it this way – ain't no point ringing Alan Rickman and telling him I'm finally free. Something more countrified might be suitable and more accessible (since the rudbeckias and chickens don't allow travelling for sex). I've never really fancied anything in tweeds but after 20 years of regular delightful bonking and now two weeks without, I may have to lower my standards.

Or would it be simpler to have a sex clause in the divorce settlement agreement? You know, the cost of the mortgage, the Aga service and two sessions every month. I'll have to ask the lawyer. Watch this space.

Stevie Morgan

Suggested tasks

1 Compare the attitude towards Mrs Thatcher and 'Thatcherism' expressed by the writers of Items 5a and 5b respectively. Comment on the way in which their use of language, techniques of presentation and stylistic features reflect these attitudes.

2 Analyse the style in which Item 6 is written to show how it conveys Stevie Morgan's attitude towards (a) her husband, 'Beloved', and (b) her own situation. Pay particular attention to the writer's:

● choice of vocabulary and imagery;

● tone and register;

● organisation of the whole piece.

Suggested approach

It is sound advice to remember that writers always start with a blank sheet of paper. Everything they produce results from a series of choices, ranging from the overall construction of a piece to the selection of individual words. It may include presentational devices such as lay-out, headings and illustrations, as in Item 5b. It will certainly involve grammatical devices such as syntax (that is, the structure of a sentence or sentences), punctuation, tense-selection, first- or third-person address and so on. In an effective piece of writing, everything 'counts' and contributes to the successful communication of meaning.

This being so, it is vital that your own approach to analysing pieces of writing like Items 5 and 6 is both systematic and precise. A framework for helping it to be so is given below: discuss it with your teacher, making sure that you have a secure understanding of the terminology used.

Features of Writing	Examples
Lexical (relating to word-use)	vocabulary choice; imagery; idiom; slang; tone; register; word-play (e.g. puns, 'double entendres')
Grammatical (relating to sentence-use and 'parts of speech')	word-order; sentence structures; punctuation; choice of tense; first- or third-person address; Standard English/non-standard forms; use of dialogue; 'rhythm' of sentences
Organisational (relating to structural patterns)	text-related forms (e.g. linear narrative structure for story, logical discursive structure for argument); paragraph links, including contrasts; sequencing of subject matter; degrees of formality; length
Presentational (relating to conventions of print and publishing)	lay-out/format; illustrations; type-faces; headings and sub-heads; interaction between graphics and text

This framework, though far from complete, provides a basis for analysis. It is useful for discussion and note-making, but it will not serve as a model for your own considered written responses to a passage. That depends on the nature of the task set and your teacher's advice about how to shape and structure an answer.

To end this section, use the framework as a tool for exploring another text: Item 7 (pages 154–5). This is a journalistic piece written in 1711 by Joseph Addison and printed in *The Spectator*. It is one of a series of articles about 'Sir Roger', an acquaintance of Addison's, who was a country squire. Most of the tenants on his estate depended on him for their livelihood. In Item 7, Addison describes a typical Sunday service in his parish church.

Your task is to deduce Addison's attitude towards Sir Roger from the way in which the article is written. Do this in class or group discussion, referring to the framework above as you talk.

⋗┼◀▸⋯○⋯◀▸┼⋖

(7) *from* **Sir Roger at Church**

by Joseph Addison

My friend Sir Roger, being a good churchman, has beautified the inside of his church with several texts of his own choosing; he has likewise given a handsome pulpit cloth, and railed in the communion table at his own expense. He has often told me that, at his coming to his estate, he found his parishioners very irregular[1]; and that, in order to make them kneel and join in the responses, he gave every one of them a hassock and a   5
Common Prayer book, and at the same time employed an itinerant singing master, who goes about the country[2] for that purpose, to instruct them rightly in the tunes of the Psalms; upon which they now very much value themselves, and indeed outdo most of the country churches that I have ever met.

As Sir Roger is landlord to the whole congregation, he keeps them in very good order, and   10
will suffer[3] nobody to sleep in it besides himself; for if by chance he has been surprised into a short nap at sermon, upon recovering out of it he stands up and looks about him, and if he sees anybody else nodding, either wakes them himself, or sends his servant to them. Several other of the old knight's particularities[4] break out upon these occasions; sometimes he will be lengthening out a verse in the Singing-Psalms half a minute after the   15
rest of the congregation have done with it; sometimes, when he is pleased with the matter of his devotion, he pronounces 'Amen' three or four times to the same prayer; and sometimes stands up when everybody else is upon their knees, to count the congregation, or see if any of his tenants are missing.

I was yesterday very much surprised to hear my old friend, in the midst of the service,   20
calling out to one John Matthews to mind what he was about, and not disturb the congregation. This John Matthews, it seems, is remarkable for being an idle fellow, and at that time was kicking his heels for his diversion. This authority of the knight, though exerted in that odd manner which accompanies him in all circumstances of life, has a very good effect upon the parish, who are not polite[5] enough to see anything ridiculous in his   25
behaviour; besides the general good sense and worthiness of his character makes his friends observe these little singularities as foils that set off rather than blemish his good qualities.

As soon as the sermon is finished, nobody presumes to stir till Sir Roger is gone out of the church. The knight walks down from his seat in the chancel between a double row of his   30
tenants, that stand bowing to him on each side, and every now and then inquires how such a one's wife, or mother, or son, or father do, whom he does not see at church – which is understood as a secret reprimand to the person that is absent.

The chaplain has often told me that upon a catechizing day, when Sir Roger has been pleased with a boy that answers well, he has ordered a Bible to be given him next day for   35
his encouragement, and sometimes accompanies it with a flitch of bacon to his mother. Sir Roger has likewise added five pounds a year to the clerk's place; and, that he may

---

[1] **irregular**: i.e. in attending church
[2] **country**: the local parish
[3] **suffer**: permit
[4] **particularities**: eccentricities
[5] **polite**: refined

encourage the young fellows to make themselves perfect in the church service, has promised, upon the death of the present incumbent[1], who is very old, to bestow it according to merit.

The fair understanding between Sir Roger and his chaplain, and their mutual concurrence in doing good, is the more remarkable because the very next village is famous for the differences and contentions that rise between the parson and the squire, who live in a perpetual state of war. The parson is always preaching at the squire, and the squire, to be revenged on the parson, never comes to church …

Feuds of this nature, though too frequent in the country, are very fatal to the ordinary people, who are so used to be dazzled with riches that they pay as much deference to the understanding of a man of an estate as a man of learning; and are very hardly[2] brought to regard any truth, how important soever it may be, that is preached to them, when they know there are several men of five hundred a year who do not believe it.

40

45

50

---

[1] **incumbent**: i.e. the church clerk
[2] **very hardly**: with great difficulty

Transforming texts: summary and adaptation

All examining boards require you to re-write one kind of non-fiction text in a different non-fictional style. In part, this is a summarising task: without being able to see to the heart of the original, it is obviously impossible to adapt it meaningfully into another form. Text-transformation also tests your understanding of the formal, stylistic and linguistic features of whatever genre you are asked to turn material from the original into. You are cast in the role of author working with given information in order to write, for example, an instructional leaflet, a circular letter or an entry in an encyclopaedia. Hence you also need to show your awareness of the typical purpose of, and readership for, the text-type you are asked to produce. The readership is normally specified: 'A leaflet for adults with non-specialist knowledge of the subject', or 'A teenage magazine aimed principally at boys'.

In practice

Item 8 below, 'On Shaky Ground', is a review of two books about expeditions to Mount Everest. In it the author, herself a mountain writer, reflects on the fact that conquering Everest has become 'the ultimate package tour'.

Read the review. Then, using material from it, write an open letter to members of the British Amateur Climbing Association who may be planning to scale mountains like Everest as a form of holiday. The letter should make clear the risks of doing so and end with a recommendation. Assume an intelligent adult readership.

Your letter should be no longer than 200 words. You should concentrate on (a) selecting appropriate content based on the review, and on (b) the way in which you organise your writing.

---

⑧ # *On shaky ground*

Conquering Everest may be the ultimate package tour, but climbers' ethics are at an all-time low. AUDREY SALKELD reads two survivors' chilling accounts.

Late in the afternoon of May 10, 1996, in a mess tent at the foot of Mount Everest, I was typing up news of the first summit successes of the season when, feeling cold, I went outside to fetch a warmer jacket. Bubbling up the valley towards base camp was a pillar of purplish-black cloud. This was the fatal storm racing in that would catch out climbers from the three expeditions who had gone for the top from the Nepalese side. When darkness fell, more than 20 people were strung out along the dangerous southeast ridge of Everest, struggling to regain their camp on the South Col. Others were trapped on the opposite side of the mountain. Eight people failed to make it back. Two others, critically frostbitten, were later plucked from above the Khumbu Icefall in one of the most daring helicopter rescues ever.

Jon Krakauer, the author of **Into Thin Air: A Personal Account of the Everest Disaster** (Macmillan £16.99) was one of those climbing the mountain that day. An experienced mountaineer, he had been sent by an American magazine to report on the growing and controversial phenomenon of commercial ascents of the world's highest mountains. Climbing Everest was becoming the ultimate package holiday. Krakauer's companions on an expedition led by Rob Hall, a New Zealand mountaineer, who was the leading

---

practitioner in this new form of tourism, included people whose climbing skills could best be described as modest. They had paid up to £42,000 each in the hope of standing on top of the world, and were drawn, so Krakauer supposed, by dreams of minor celebrity or career advancement. This was no climbing team of shared ambition: each client was here essentially for himself. 'Scribbling constantly, quietly recording their words and deeds in order to share their foibles with a potentially unsympathetic public' was an undercover role in which Krakauer felt awkward. Months later, with the mountain and its monumental tragedy behind him, he was no longer so sure of the motivations of his fellow-members, any more than he felt he still knew his own.

The danger of climbing with guides, he discovered, was that it blurred your personal responsibility. It was too easy to relinquish to them your mountaineering judgment and, to an extent, your conscience as well. Krakauer is now tormented that, on regaining the South Col camp during the night of the storm, he huddled exhausted in his tent, unaware that, a short distance outside, two of his party lay exposed and dying on the hard, wind-whipped ice. Even worse, his mistaken identification of a hooded figure in the dark may well have contributed to the death of one of the guides in his team. Survivor guilt haunts him.

Into Thin Air is an honest, compelling story of what many believed was a tragedy waiting to happen. Slanting through the relentless build-up of events are moments of heroism and astonishing fortitude. The pathos of Rob Hall's last radio messages to his pregnant wife in New Zealand, when, helpless and isolated at the South Summit, he might as well have been Major Tom in outer space; the miracle of Beck Weathers, twice given up as beyond help, willing himself to stand up and blunder, blind and maimed, back to a life he refused to leave – these are powerful moments which Krakauer handles masterfully.

He does not shrink from pointing out where he believes commercial concerns, petty rivalries or oxygen deficiency led to misguided decisions. Krakauer confesses that his frankness has angered some, and upset friends and relatives of a few of the victims, but he has raised issues that need to be discussed.

Joe Simpson, too, is all for widening the high-altitude debate. In **Dark Shadows Falling** (Cape £15.99), his concern is that the strong ethics and selfless instincts that have characterised mountaineering in the past are being eroded by modern-day ambition, selfishness and greed. He is shocked that, on the north side of Everest in 1996, as on other occasions, climbers blinkered by summit fever callously walked past others stricken to the point of death, without helping, comforting, or even, as he tells it, experiencing any qualms.

Lonely deaths on lofty mountains have a strong place in Simpson's heart. He was himself once alone and given up for dead, on an Andean peak. And his superhuman effort then in extricating himself from a crevasse, and crawling with a shattered leg down a mountain, stemmed more out of the desire not to die alone than any survival urge. When he reads that a Japanese climber has said: 'Above 8,000 metres is not a place where people can afford morality', he is chilled and angered.

Should high-altitude mountaineering be more strictly controlled; should bottled oxygen be restricted for use in medical emergency and not as an aid to climbing? Would that control the numbers on Everest and unlock the traffic jams? And even if so, how do you shore up sagging ethics? Simpson and Krakauer pose the questions; the answers prove more elusive. 'If shutting the door on man's last imploring gesture, or avoiding eye contact while climbing sternly past three dying men, are the requisite skills for modern high altitude climbing, then I want none of it,' Simpson concludes.

Audrey Salkeld is a mountain writer and historian

Sample answers

Below are two responses by Year 12 English students to the task set on page 156. Read and compare them. Pay particular attention to how well they satisfy the requirements outlined there.

Answer 1

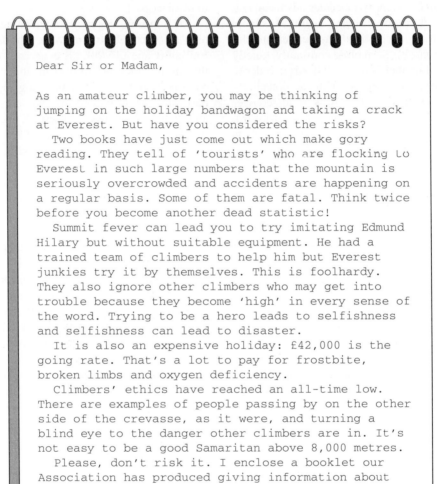

Dear Sir or Madam,

As an amateur climber, you may be thinking of jumping on the holiday bandwagon and taking a crack at Everest. But have you considered the risks?

Two books have just come out which make gory reading. They tell of 'tourists' who are flocking to Everest in such large numbers that the mountain is seriously overcrowded and accidents are happening on a regular basis. Some of them are fatal. Think twice before you become another dead statistic!

Summit fever can lead you to try imitating Edmund Hilary but without suitable equipment. He had a trained team of climbers to help him but Everest junkies try it by themselves. This is foolhardy. They also ignore other climbers who may get into trouble because they become 'high' in every sense of the word. Trying to be a hero leads to selfishness and selfishness can lead to disaster.

It is also an expensive holiday: £42,000 is the going rate. That's a lot to pay for frostbite, broken limbs and oxygen deficiency.

Climbers' ethics have reached an all-time low. There are examples of people passing by on the other side of the crevasse, as it were, and turning a blind eye to the danger other climbers are in. It's not easy to be a good Samaritan above 8,000 metres.

Please, don't risk it. I enclose a booklet our Association has produced giving information about smaller mountains you can conquer with ease and safety. Happy climbing!

Yours sincerely,
Chris Bonnington.
(president BACA)

Evaluate this answer by considering:

- How effective is the use made of the original material?
- How apt are the letter's contents to its purpose?
- How appropriate to the specified readership is the language and tone?
- How well-planned and organised is the letter?
- How clearly does it communicate?

In the light of these criteria, discuss with your teacher a suitable grade for this answer on a scale of A–E.

Now compare it with the second example.

Answer 2

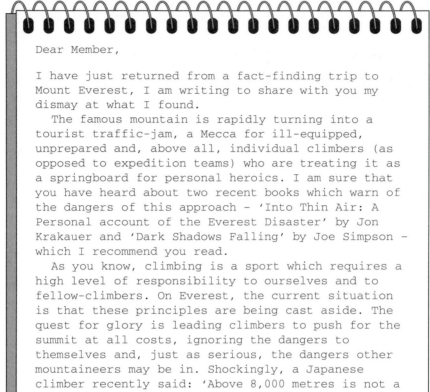

Dear Member,

I have just returned from a fact-finding trip to
Mount Everest, I am writing to share with you my
dismay at what I found.

The famous mountain is rapidly turning into a
tourist traffic-jam, a Mecca for ill-equipped,
unprepared and, above all, individual climbers (as
opposed to expedition teams) who are treating it as
a springboard for personal heroics. I am sure that
you have heard about two recent books which warn of
the dangers of this approach – 'Into Thin Air: A
Personal account of the Everest Disaster' by Jon
Krakauer and 'Dark Shadows Falling' by Joe Simpson –
which I recommend you read.

As you know, climbing is a sport which requires a
high level of responsibility to ourselves and to
fellow-climbers. On Everest, the current situation
is that these principles are being cast aside. The
quest for glory is leading climbers to push for the
summit at all costs, ignoring the dangers to
themselves and, just as serious, the dangers other
mountaineers may be in. Shockingly, a Japanese
climber recently said: 'Above 8,000 metres is not a
place where people can afford morality.' The spirit
of comradeship and camaraderie is being betrayed by
such callous and insensitive attitudes.

I therefore appeal to you to uphold the best
traditions of our sport and our Association by
refusing to take part in the 'Everest circus'. I am
sure you will agree that the ethics of
mountaineering are more important than self-
glorification.

Yours faithfully,
D.J. Brown
(for the British Amateur Climbing Association)

Assess this answer by applying the same criteria as those you used for Answer 1. Again, discuss with your teacher a suitable grade.

Now make a check-list of Do's and Don't's to consult whenever you attempt a text-adaptation task. If you asked examiners for their advice, they would suggest the following points to guide you:

- It is less important to use all, or most, of the original material than to select those parts of it that best suit the purpose of the task.

- Your change from one language mode to another should be determined more by the nature of the readership in question than by any other single consideration.

- Tone, idiom and register are as important as vocabulary when adapting material for a different purpose and readership – as is your decision about the degree of formality/informality it will be appropriate to use.

- Whatever form you are required to adapt the original into, its cohesiveness (i.e. the way in which the whole thing hangs together) is a critical factor.
- Marks are deducted in the exam for overstepping the word-limit and for inaccuracy in your own expression.

Further practice material

Item 9 below is a newspaper article about an army recruitment drive targeting homeless young men. It appeared in *The Guardian* in October 1997. Read it carefully, then attempt one (or more) of the tasks printed on page 161.

⑨
Now the Army steps down into the gutter

Decca Aitkenhead

There has always been something vaguely troubling about the army recruitment ads which come on the telly just at that dank, disappointing hour of Sunday when you are starting to wish you had done something with your weekend. Like late night 'Party!' chat-lines, the timing is cruel, picking off the casualties of bedsit gloom with the vulture touch of Moonies outside a cold railway station.

Billy hasn't seen any of the army ads, though. This is because Billy doesn't have a television – on account of not actually having anywhere to live. He hangs around Piccadilly Gardens in Manchester, sleeps over grates in China Town, and has been homeless for the past four of his 19 years. In that time, he has had a number of offers of a bed in return for various services. Now, through the Big Issue, he has heard about a new army recruitment drive being launched amongst the homeless, and thinks he might be interested. Yeah, he shrugs. Why not?

A sergeant has been touring hostels in Leeds, inviting homeless men to 'Look at Life' – the title of a recruitment open day. About 30 came along on Wednesday, for a bit of a chat and, of course, something to eat.

The army is having some trouble persuading 'ordinary' people to join up, and if the 'Look at Life' day is considered a success, it may extend its hostel tours nationwide in a drive to fill its 5,000 squaddies shortfall with the homeless.

'There are a lot of well-qualified people out there who have dropped out of life,' enthused Colour Sergeant John Dent. 'We can offer work.' It's getting cold in Piccadilly Gardens now and Billy and his friends are hoping he comes to Manchester soon.

Well it's a bold enough initiative, certainly. Most homeless charities have sounded slightly thrown by the plan, suggesting as it might a sort of broad-mindedness not typically associated with the armed forces. Nobody wants to seem ungenerous about such a scheme – and so official misgivings have been confined to the practical.

Crisis feel obliged to point out that something like one in four of all homeless men have actually been in the army already, and that it was in fact the difficulty of fitting into civilian life which put them on the streets in the first place. The 'skills for life' with which recruits are apparently equipped appear, in the light of this research, a little doubtful.

Go down to the Strand in London and, sure enough, you can find an ex-serviceman in a doorway within minutes. 'I did seven years,' says one. 'Done three in a mental hospital since I come out. All they taught me was how to murder. Who wants to know how to murder?' The man next to him thinks he'd quite like to, but then reflects that he'd rather just get drunk.

So then there's also the problem that many youngsters living on the streets are struggling with drink and drug problems; not areas the army is famous for tackling with sensitivity. Others have severe mental health and behavioural difficulties. Outreach workers who help the homeless find jobs describe an ongoing process of emotional and practical support which is fairly tricky to envisage in a military environment. As one charity director puts it simply, 'A lot of them are very damaged young people. They will jump at any opportunity to get off the streets. Then it will backfire – and their lives will have failed again. They are just setting them up to fail yet again.'

All of these are excellent reasons to doubt the wisdom of the scheme. What hasn't been pointed out, however, amid all the polite comments, is an alternative objection: that Billy, say, might indeed make a splendid and happy soldier, but that to go trawling the streets and hostels in the hunt for fresh squaddies is not just ambitious, but actually immoral.

It is not exactly controversial to state that homeless people are vulnerable. That's why drug dealers are so attached to them, and why pimps looking for new girls, and businessmen looking for a bit of rough trade, and cults looking for new blood, make their way to Piccadilly Gardens with such unfailing regularity. If you want someone to do something most people with a modicum of choice in the matter would rather not do, you head straight for the homeless. And now Her Majesty's Forces are joining the long and shabby queue.

It would be plainly naive not to acknowledge the forces of supply and demand; most Big Issue sellers, for example, would probably prefer to sell BMWs, and beggars, quite literally, cannot be choosers. The army has always drawn many of its lower ranks from disadvantaged lads with nothing else to do. But the difference between broadcasting ads between Heartbeat and London's Burning to bored teenagers who want to get away from their mum, and recruiting a cold, homeless man who wonders how else he'll make it through the winter, is a moral chasm.

When you join the army, it is not like joining a factory. You sign up and they own you, unless you can buy yourself out, which is an unlikely option for someone who only joined because he was penniless. And the thing about being in the army which they tend not to mention, when they're showing you your warm bunk and giving you your hot meal, is that you're signing up to the possibility that you might get killed.

Lots of men and women agree to this arrangement all the time, and that is fine – if a little baffling. It is not fine, but grotesque, to go exploiting the very people who are in no position to make a 'choice' in any meaningful sense at all.

Ironically, the only moral indignation expressed this week over the relationship between the armed forces and the homeless was provoked by a different story. The Admiralty Arch in Trafalgar Square has been proposed as a homeless shelter this winter, an enterprising plan which indicates a much healthier order of priorities – and brings to mind another solution. The problem of homelessness is huge and unarguable; the point of the army, on the other hand, is increasingly unclear. Rather than use the homeless to save the army, then, perhaps we could get rid of the army, and use the defence budget to save the homeless instead.

Use material from the article to undertake one or more of the following tasks:

1 Imagine you are a member of the army recruitment team responsible for planning the 'Look at Life' open day described in paragraph 3 of the article.

A pamphlet encouraging the homeless to enlist and emphasising to them the benefits of army life is to be distributed during the open day. Write this pamphlet, using no more than 300 words.

Assume a fairly diverse readership in terms of social background: homelessness is not exclusive to the educationally or socially 'deprived'.

2 The writer of this article is strongly opposed to the army's initiative. Consider her reasons carefully. Then write a letter to the editor of *The Guardian* from someone who is basically sympathetic to the recruitment drive, though not necessarily in favour of it.

Address what you take to be the main issues raised by Decca Aitkenhead. The letter, intended for publication in a broadsheet newspaper, should be no longer than 300 words.

3 *Decca Aitkenhead claims that army recruiting among the homeless is 'actually immoral'.*

Script two statements to be made on the radio programme *The Moral Maze*: one from the director of a homeless charity who agrees with this view, and one from an army recruitment officer who does not.

Each statement should be confined to 300 words. Bear in mind that the statements are intended to be spoken. Assume an intelligent adult audience.

Making the most of drafting

The difficulty as well as the compressed nature of text-adaptation work makes drafting and redrafting essential, if you are to achieve it successfully. Drafting does not mean 'write it quickly in rough first'. Work as hard on your draft as you do on your final version – and spend more time writing it. Ideally, show your draft to your teacher and include explanatory notes on:

- the vocabulary, tone and register you have used, bearing in mind purpose and specified readership;

- the structural principles on which you have based your writing;

- how you have switched language modes between the original material and the text-type you are producing.

The feedback you get from your teacher will help more than anything else to improve your 'best' version. Use it.

You can practise your drafting skills by working with a partner and interviewing each other in turn. The subject should be 'My views on: the monarchy/legalising soft drugs/abortion/blood sports' … etc. Choose something about which you feel strongly.

As your partner speaks, jot down the main points she or he makes. Then write up a careful 100 word account of what was said, trying to reflect your partner's views and her or his personality as it emerged during the interview.

Show your writing to your partner. Re-work it together until you are both satisfied that it accurately reflects the content and the 'flavour' of the interview.

Comprehension, comment, analysis: exemplar material and tasks

Different examining boards have different approaches to 'comment and analysis' work on non-fiction texts. In this section, therefore, a range of material is provided for practising the particular skills required by various A level syllabuses. The approaches suggested in Sections 6.1 to 6.3 remain relevant. However, the purpose here is to illustrate the specific demands made in external exams on your understanding and appreciation of non-fiction. For this reason, the material that follows is presented in the formal way in which you will find it in A level English papers.

Example 1

Item 10, 'Escape from School', is an extract from the journalist René Cutforth's autobiography *Order to View*. He is recounting an incident that occurred during his private schooling in the Midlands. The school's headmaster, nicknamed Old Kip, based his approach to discipline on the principle of 'moral responsibility'.

Read the extract carefully, then answer the following questions.

(a) Present clearly and concisely the reasons why René Cutforth related better to the policeman and his wife than he did to Mr Seaton and Old Kip.

(b) What does the passage reveal about the writer's temperament when he was a boy? Suggest, with reasons, how old you think he was when he escaped from school.

(c) Make a comparative analysis of the speech styles of the policeman and Old Kip, noting features such as vocabulary, idiom and register.

(d) Comment on the significance of the phrase 'moral responsibility' within the extract as a whole.

(e) Evaluate the effectiveness of this piece as an example of autobiographical writing. You should comment on René Cutforth's style, taking account, among other things, of diction, syntax and overall structure in relation to his purposes as you understand them.

>━◆━○━◆━<

⑩ Escape from School

by René Cutforth

Mr Seaton was a new master who'd become devoted to Old Kip's ideas, and had even invented a new variety of moral responsibility. He was the mathematics master, and his new invention was that you marked your own maths papers according to a complicated system which I never understood. At the end of the week he asked you what your marks were, and you told him on your 'Scout's honour'. I never had the remotest idea 5 what my marks were and I used to award myself a figure I hoped would be low enough not to attract attention, and high enough to keep me out of trouble. But one morning I had the misfortune to be asked first, and I said 85, glibly enough, and then realized in the silence that that was very high indeed. So I said, 'Oh – no sir, I mean 35,' and I peered at my exercise to make it appear that I'd mistaken a three for a an eight. Mr 10 Seaton came striding up and, of course, was unable to find evidence of either figure, among the muddled miseries of my calculations. So he began to shout. 'Stand up, boy. Admit, boy, you have no idea. Does your Scout's honour mean nothing to you? Are you prepared to cheat and lie your way through life?' He went on and on and finally barked out: 'I shall inform the headmaster that I've a cheat in my form.' 15

It was the last lesson in the afternoon of a perfect July day. Mr Seaton, I knew, would inform the headmaster at dinner that night. The school would be summoned after lunch the next day. Meanwhile there was an hour's free time before tea. The heavy sweet smell of the country drifted through the elm avenue where the rooks were cawing away like mad, the classroom was dusty, ink-stained, and suddenly very narrow and confining 20 like a jail. Outside you could hear the country breathing sleepily and calmly in the sunshine. I made up my mind. I'd go – now. And with that decision, all in a second, I was as happy as Larry. I went out onto the lawn, and stood on top of the north bank among the trees for a minute or two looking around. And then I slipped through the elm avenue, under the cawing rooks, over the wall, over the road, and onto the field path 25 which led winding up and down a thick green slope, to the field of white stones which was the limit of my explorations on Sunday walks.

For the rest of that summer evening I loafed through the sweet grass, and the long ditches full of ragged-robin, where the cow parsley was up to my waist, entirely at one with the universe: I sucked grasses, climbed trees, avoided villages, paddled in streams, 30 and finally, when it began to grow dark, I found a cow shed, in a paddled patch of sun-baked mud in a thread-bare field on a western slope, and lay down in some old-smelling hay inside, and went to sleep. That mood was still with me in the morning. A wonderful morning with the sun sparkling all new on everything, and a soft wind and a glittering green downward slope to start my journey with, and in this delightful world, 35 there was no washing.

But now I was getting near Leicester, and the villages grew more and more frequent and soon they were continuous. I was very tired, and going very slowly. A cold wind blew up and though I tried hard to skirt Leicester and get out into the country again, I only half succeeded, and spent most of the day bitterly among the tramlines. Clouds covered the 40 sky. At about seven o'clock that evening, clogged with fatigue, I was plodding along a black road, through rows of ugly miners' cottages in a cold rain. I'd nothing left but obstinacy. And about a mile out of Desford on the north road towards Ashby, a bicycle came suddenly up from behind me and stopped, barring my way. It was an enormous fat scarlet policeman, with a heavy old-Bill moustache. 'Where y' going lad,' he said, 45 beaming at me through the rain. 'I'm just walkin',' I said. 'Ah, walkin' are you?' He looked me up and down. 'Well, what about a bite to eat?' 'Yes,' I said, 'I could do with that.' 'Then us'll just tek a little walk back and fix it up,' he said. We walked back to a miner's cottage of blackened red brick, and there was his wife, if possible redder and larger than he was. A huge fire, what they call a collier's fire in those parts, filled the 50 grate and half the chimney. It was as hot as the tropics, and what small space was left in the room when these enormous figures sat down was filled with china dogs, bowls of plants, shepherdesses and pictures of virgins locked out in the snow.

There was a fat cat, and a proper black kettle singing on the hob. They stuffed me with bacon and eggs, and bread and butter and jam, enough tea to float a battleship. They 55 laughed all the time. 'Eat up, lad. That's right. Never let 'em get you down,' said the policeman. 'And how are you, eh? Fit as a fiddle, eh? Now I suppose your name – it couldn't be Cutforth, could it?' 'Yes, it is,' I said. 'Well you've done a fair walk,' he said. 'How did you like it?' I said that up till today I've never liked anything better. 'That's the stuff, lad. Well, I'll just go and do a bit of telephoning, and I'll be back.' 60

When he came back he said, 'Now, how did you come to start this bit of a walk, like?' I thought he was a very sensible man. He appeared to have no moral responsibility of any kind. So I told him the whole story, with an imitation of Old Kip holding forth about the 'disapproval of his fellows'. The policeman and his wife rocked to and fro beating their sides in an ecstasy of laughter. 'Nay,' the policeman said. 'Nay, it sounds a proper rum auction, that school. And that Kip is a proper comic cut.' Now this was to me an entirely new idea. It had never occurred to me that it was possible to criticize the set-up. Actually to think of the school in that lordly way as a 'rum auction' and old Kip as a 'proper comic cut' – it was a new and welcome outlook. 65

'I can see,' the policeman went on, 'as you'd no other course, but to get out and keep cheerful. I never could abide a whinger. A whinging kid I cannot stomach. Your dad – I've just rung him on the phone, and he'll be here directly. Your dad, I suppose, being a gentleman, won't have the guts – er – to give that young master a bloody nose same as I would. But take my advice, lad – you go back to that school, and face 'em out, and never let 'em get you down.' My father arrived in the car shortly afterwards, and my new friend immediately changed into a comic turn himself, touching his forelock and saying 'Here's my best respects,' and being tipped very heavily. 70 75

It was decided that I should go back, and two or three days later my father left me in Old Kip's study. He said, 'So you have decided to return. I think that is a wise decision. The boys have been prepared for your reappearance among them. I think an attitude of bravado will not go down at all well. You will receive no punishment. But I wish you to realize some part of the great anxiety of which you have been the cause. There is just one thing: your behaviour has caused grave sorrow to Mr Seaton, and he's waiting in the next room to receive your apology should you wish to give it. But I leave it to you. It is your own moral responsibility. Shall I tell him to come in?' I took a deep breath and shouldered my moral responsibility. 'No, Sir,' I said. And went in to tea to face the school. 80 85

Example 2

Item 11 is from the Diary of Samuel Pepys. The extract was written during the Great Fire of London in 1666.

Read the extract carefully, then undertake the following tasks.

(a) Write a full commentary on the stylistic features of this passage that are typical of diary writing. If you wish, make comparisons with the writing of other diarists to illustrate your answer.

(b) (i) Use material from the extract to write a report on the Fire of London in the style of *either* a contemporary broadsheet *or* a contemporary tabloid newspaper.
　　(ii) Explain how and why your choice of language differs from that of the original.

⑪ *from the* Diary of Samuel Pepys

September 5, 1666

I lay down in the office upon W. Hewer's quilt, being mighty weary and sore in my feet with going till I was hardly able to stand. About 2 in the morning my wife calls me up and tells of new cries of 'Fire!' – it being come to Barking Church, which is the bottom of our lane. I up; and finding it so, resolved presently to take her away; and did, and took my gold (which was about £2350), W. Hewer, and Jane down by Poundy's boat to 5

Woolwich. But Lord, what a sad sight it was by moonlight to see the whole City almost
on fire – that you might see it plain at Woolwich, as if you were by it. There when I came,
I find the gates[1] shut, but no guard kept at all; which troubled me, because of discourses
now begun that there is plot in it and that the French[2] had done it. I got the gates open,
and to Mr Shelden's, where I locked my gold and charged my wife and W. Hewer never   10
to leave the room without one of them in it night nor day. So back again, by the way
seeing my goods well in the lighters at Deptford and watched well by people. Home, and
whereas I expected to have seen our house on fire, it being now about 7 o'clock, it was
not. But to the fire, and there find greater hopes than I expected; for my confidence of
finding our office on fire was such, that I durst not ask anybody how it was with us, till I   15
came and saw it not burned. But going to the fire, I find, by the blowing up of houses and
the great help given by the workmen out of the King's yard, sent up by Sir W. Penn, there
is a good stop given to it, as well at Mark Lane end as ours – it having only burned the dial
of Barking Church, and part of the porch, and was there quenched. I up to the top of
Barking steeple, and there saw the saddest sight of desolation that I ever saw. Everywhere   20
great fires. Oil cellars and brimstone and other things burning. I became afeared to stay
there long; and therefore down again as fast as I could, the fire being spread as far as I
could see it, and to Sir W. Penn's and there eat a piece of cold meat, having eaten
nothing since Sunday but the remains of Sunday's dinner …

Thence homeward, having passed through Cheapside and Newgate Market, all burned   25
– and seen Anthony Joyce's house in fire. And took up (which I keep by me) a piece of
glass of Mercer's Chapel in the street, where much more was, so melted and buckled
with the heat of the fire, like parchment. I also did see a poor cat taken out of a hole in
the chimney joining to the wall of the Exchange, with the hair all burned off the body
and yet alive. So home at night, and find there good hopes of saving our office – but   30
great endeavours of watching all night and having men ready; and so we lodged them
in the office and had drink and bread and cheese for them. And I lay down and slept a
good night about midnight – though when I rose, I hear that there has been a great
alarm of French and Dutch being risen – which proved nothing. But it is a strange thing
to see how long this time did look since Sunday, having always been full of variety of   35
actions, and little sleep, that it looked like a week or more. And I had forgot almost the
day of the week.

><+>•<+>•O•<+>•<+><

[1] **gates**: the City gates
[2] **the French**: there was a popular theory that the fire had been started by the French as a prelude to their planned
invasion of London

Example 3

Item 12 is a review by the novelist and literary historian Peter Ackroyd of three biographies of Jane
Austen. Read the review several times, then answer the following questions.

(a) According to this article, why is the conventional image of Jane Austen as a 'literary maiden
aunt' a distorted one? Present your answer in the form of a summary of no more than 300 of
your own words.

(b) Write a commentary on the techniques Peter Ackroyd uses to persuade his readers that 'she was
sick and wicked'.

(c) Write a letter of between 200 and 300 words to Peter Ackroyd from a reader who, having read
his article, thinks it to be unfairly biased. Focus on the way the article is written and presented,
rather than on its factual content or your own view of Jane Austen.

(12) *Real girl power: Peter Ackroyd on three biographies that trace Jane Austen's journey from spinster to literary celebrity*

She was sick and wicked

When a woman of Jane Austen's acquaintance was delivered of a dead child, the novelist brightly remarked that the still-birth was probably the result of shock when the wife happened 'by chance to look at her husband'. It is a joke in the worst possible taste, and hardly reflects the 'gentle Jane' of literary stereotype, but it has the merit of being entirely characteristic. There is her famous remark, on hearing of an English defeat in Portugal: 'How horrible it is to have so many people killed! And what a blessing that one cares for none of them.'

Of course the varnish has been scraped off the portrait of this particular 'literary maiden aunt' on previous occasions, but these three new biographies help to complete the restoration. Of course it is always irritating when a biographer finds that his or her subject has been adopted by another writer, but the volumes under review have the virtue of being quite distinct.

The impressions of Austen's character, for example, are analogous without being identical. Myer depicts Austen as a kind of outsider, 'tougher, more irritable and more sardonic' than is usually considered; Nokes has discovered within her writing 'a restless, reckless undercurrent of frustration', while Tomalin, in turn, diagnoses the problems attendant upon 'the dryness and coldness about her heart'. The last seems most convincing. As Austen remarked of one of her own characters, she had 'no more heart than a stone to people in general'.

People in particular were of course quite another matter, and the domestic interiors contained

---

JANE AUSTEN
A Life
By Claire Tomalin
Viking, £20
ISBN 0 670 86528 1

JANE AUSTEN
By David Nokes
Fourth Estate, £20
ISBN 1 85702 419 2

JANE AUSTEN
A Biography
By Valerie Grosvenor Myer
Michael O'Mara Books, £18.99
ISBN 1 85479 213 X

---

within these biographies are always interesting. The facts are familiar enough. After some brief forays into female education, she never strayed beyond the enclosure of her family circle. All her life she remained a spinster, dependent upon the kindness of her siblings; but if her life of general poverty remained a constant source of vexation, her social insignificance helped to fuel her perceptions as well as her resentment. To some she seemed 'dowdy', even 'prim', but she was spirited enough when it suited her. One contemporary described her as a 'butterfly'. But she was not a butterfly at all. She was a hawk. 'Pictures of perfection,' she once wrote, 'make me sick and wicked.'

Her brother wrote that hers was 'not by any means a life of event', but nothing sensational necessarily needs to occur to any writer. She only had to look into herself to find all the horrors and ambitions of the greater world. There is often the hunt for some 'problem' which might explain her, when in fact the beauty of her writing suggests that there was no real problem at all. The fault lay in others, and it seems likely that she suffered all her life from being

underestimated; she rarely had the confidence to challenge those who took her for granted, and instead indulged her sick or wicked thoughts within her letters to her sister.

The publication of *Sense and Sensibility*, when she had reached what seemed to her to be the dim and dreary age of 36, changed all that. This novel was followed by *Pride and Prejudice*, which had in fact been composed some 15 years before, and all at once the spinster became a literary celebrity. She was perhaps gratified by her success in more than one respect: she described each novel as her 'darling child'. But, in characteristic 18th-century fashion, she also decided to put her offspring to work. 'I shall try to make all the money … I can of it,' she wrote.

With the subsequent publication of *Emma* and *Mansfield Park* her originality and wit were widely remarked, although the periodicals were happy to emphasise that her writing was 'inoffensive' and 'harmless'. Many of her admirers urged her to attempt something heroical or historical, but she knew that her apparent limitations were not limitations at all. Hence her famous remark about working upon two inches of ivory.

Ivory, however, is very tough. That is why Tomalin's fine phrase, 'economic romance', is an appropriate description for all of Austen's fiction. Her novels are as concerned with money, and the power of money, as those of Balzac; both writers were conveying the vagaries of an unsettled society in which value lay only in capital and credit. Hers was by no means the soft or comfortable world to be found in film and television adaptations. It was an anxious civilisation moved by 'debt and scandal' (among other subjects Austen touches upon sodomy and incest) while at the same time fuelled by avarice and hypocrisy. It was a society in which the unsuccessful simply disappeared from sight.

Her own family were not immune from such pressures, and these biographies all suggest that they could be as greedy as any of their contemporaries. It may be that Austen, as her parents'

seventh child, had the advantage of being able to observe her elders behaving in less than an impeccable manner. Certainly she saw through all the conventions by which the Austens and others were supposed to live. She had a clear eye which she turned upon herself as deliberately as she trained it upon others. She once described herself as a 'wild Beast' but, in fact, she was only a human being stripped bare of all pretences.

Of the three works under review, that of Valerie Grosvenor Myer is the least satisfying. Nokes

is good on Jane Austen's relationship with others, Tomalin on Austen's relationship with herself. Nokes is copious, Tomalin is more controlled. Nokes has written his life from the perspective of the family, standing by and watching their reactions; Tomalin is more dispassionate and combative. This reviewer would award the palm to Tomalin, although Nokes is never very far behind. But why speak of competition, when Austen herself found all the ways of the world highly comical?

Example 4

The nineteenth-century author William Cobbett wrote a series of letters to his son instructing him in 'proper behaviour' for a young man entering adulthood. Item 13 below is an extract from the letter in which Cobbett gives advice about the duties of a husband.

Read the extract closely, then undertake the following tasks:

(a) Summarise Cobbett's views on marriage in no more than 300 of your own words.

(b) Analyse the lexical and stylistic techniques that Cobbett uses to develop his argument. Say briefly how effective you judge them to be.

(c) Addressing some of the points Cobbett makes, write about husband–wife relations from a *contemporary* viewpoint. (It may or may not be your own.) Limit yourself to a maximum of 500 words and use whatever form seems most appropriate to the task.

⤜┤◄►┄O┄◄►┤⤛

⑬ Advice to a Husband

by William Cobbett

A husband thus under command [of his wife] is the most contemptible of God's creatures. Nobody can place reliance on him for anything; whether in the capacity of employer or employed, you are never sure of him. No bargain is firm, no engagement sacred, with such a man. Feeble as a reed before the boisterous she-commander, he is bold in injustice towards those whom it pleases her caprice to mark out for vengeance. 5
In the eyes of neighbours, for friends such a man cannot have, in the eyes of servants, in the eyes even of beggars at the door, such a man is a mean and despicable creature, though he may roll in wealth and possess great talents into the bargain. Such a man has, in fact, no property; he has nothing that he can rightly call his own; he is a beggarly dependent under his own roof; and if he have anything of the man left in him, and if 10
there be a rope or river near, the sooner he betakes himself to the one or the other the better. How many men, how many families, have I known brought to utter ruin by the husband suffering himself be to subdued, to be cowed down, to be held in fear, of even a virtuous wife! What, then, must be the lot of him who submits to a commander who, at the same time, sets all virtue at defiance! 15

Women are a sisterhood. They make common cause on behalf of the sex; and, indeed, that is natural enough, when we consider the vast power the law gives us over them. The law is for us, and they combine, wherever they can, to mitigate its effects. This is perfectly natural, and, to a certain extent, laudable, evincing fellow-feeling and public spirit; but when carried to the length of 'he shan't', it is despotism on the one side, and 20 slavery on the other. Watch, therefore, for the incipient steps of encroachment; they come on so slowly, so softly, that you must be sharp-sighted. If you perceive them, put at once an effectual stop to their progress. Never mind the pain that it may give you: a day of pain at this time will spare you years of pain in time to come. Many a man has been made miserable, and made his wife miserable too, for a score or two of years, only 25 for want of resolution to bear one day of pain: and it is a great deal to bear; it is a great deal to thwart the desire of one whom you so dearly love, and whose virtues daily render her more and more dear to you. But (and this is one of the most admirable of the mother's traits) as she herself will, while the tears stream from her eyes, force the nauseous medicine down the throat of her child, whose every cry is a dagger to her 30 heart; as she herself has the courage to do this for the sake of her child, why should you flinch from the performance of a still more important and sacred duty towards herself, as well as towards you and your children?

Am I recommending tyranny? Am I recommending disregard of the wife's opinions and wishes? Am I recommending a reserve towards her that would seem to say that she was 35 not trustworthy, or not a party interested in her husband's affairs? By no means: on the contrary, though I would keep anything disagreeable from her, I should not enjoy the prospect of good without making her a participator. But reason says, and God has said, that it is the duty of wives to be obedient to their husbands; and the very nature of things prescribes that there must be a head of every house, and an undivided authority. And 40 then it is so clearly just that the authority should rest with him on whose head rests the whole responsibility, that a woman, when patiently reasoned with on the subject, must be a virago in her very nature not to submit with docility to the terms of her marriage vow.

>–!–◄►–•–◯–•–◄►–!–◄

Chapter 7 Past historic – or is it?

 7.1 **Forming a dialogue with the text**

Main text: *Bleak House*, Charles Dickens

 7.2 **Metaphysically modern?**

Main texts: 'Twicknam Garden', John Donne
'To My Inconstant Mistris', Thomas Carew

 7.3 **Looking through contemporary eyes**

Main texts: Preface to the second edition of *Wuthering Heights*,
Charlotte Brontë
Wuthering Heights, Emily Brontë

Forming a dialogue with the text

Over and above Shakespeare, a fair chunk of your A level syllabus may be made up of literature from the past, written between 1370 and 1900. All students feel apprehensive about this. The language of 'classics' like Dickens, Milton, Marlowe or Chaucer can look dauntingly difficult at first sight. The subject matter may seem remote from your own interests. Flick through the Introduction and Notes to any edition of (say) Ben Johnson's play *The Alchemist* (1605) – an old A level favourite – and you'll find an alarming amount of 'background' material on Elizabethan science and society, the classical unities of Aristotelian drama and the theory of humours propounded by the Greek philosopher Galen. You can be forgiven for thinking: 'Do I have to take all this on board before I'm ready even to start reading the text?'

The purpose of this chapter is to encourage you to answer 'No'. Of course, writers in the past brought to their work certain assumptions about human life which are different from ours. Of course, the forms and structures they used for their writing belong more to their own day and age than to the present. Of course, language-use changes over time. Life evolves through the centuries; it is hardly surprising that language and literature, arguably the richest records of human life and nature, evolve with it. You need no stack of commercially produced 'study guides' to do your understanding of this evolution for you. Keep faith with your own ability – and with your teachers'.

De-mystifying a 'classic'

The prime necessity when you first encounter a 'big' work from the past is to get yourself onto its wavelength. This section proposes one way of doing so by carrying on your own dialogue with the text.

Dickens's *Bleak House* was published in 1853. Chapter 1 describes a London law court – the Court of Chancery – in which the Lord Chancellor is hearing an endless case about a will on an exceptionally foggy afternoon. The extract below is from the beginning of Chapter 2. Read it to yourself, carefully and with an open mind.

From **Bleak House**

by Charles Dickens

It is but a glimpse of the world of fashion that we want on this same miry afternoon. It is not so unlike the Court of Chancery but that we may pass from one scene to the other, as the crow flies. Both the world of fashion and the Court of Chancery are things of precedent and usage: oversleeping Rip Van Winkles who have played at strange games through a deal of thundery weather; sleeping beauties whom the knight will wake one day, when all the stopped spits in the kitchen shall begin to turn prodigiously!

It is not a large world. Relatively even to this world of ours, which has its limits too (as your Highness shall find out when you have made the tour of it and are come to the brink of the void beyond), it is very little speck. There is much good in it; there are many good and true people in it; it has its appointed place. But the evil of it is that it is a world wrapped up in too much jeweller's cotton and fine wool, and cannot hear the rushing of the larger worlds, and cannot see them as they circle round the sun. It is a deadened world, and its growth is sometimes unhealthy for want of air.

My Lady Dedlock has returned to her house in town for a few days previous to her departure for Paris, where her ladyship intends to stay some weeks, after which her movements are uncertain. The fashionable intelligence says so for the comfort of the Parisians, and it knows all fashionable things. To know things otherwise were to be unfashionable. My Lady Dedlock has been down at what she calls, in familiar conversation, her 'place' in Lincolnshire. The waters are out in Lincolnshire. An arch of the bridge in the park has been sapped and sopped away. The adjacent low-lying ground for half a mile in breadth is a stagnant river with melancholy trees for islands in it and a surface punctured all over, all day long, with falling rain. My Lady Dedlock's place has been extremely dreary. The weather for many a day and night has been so wet that the trees seem wet through, and the soft loppings and prunings of the woodman's axe can make no crash or crackle as they fall. The deer, looking soaked, leave quagmires where they pass. The shot of a rifle loses its sharpness in the moist air, and its smoke moves in a tardy little cloud towards the green rise, coppice-topped, that makes a background for the falling rain. The view from my Lady Dedlock's own windows is alternatively a lead-coloured view and a view in Indian ink. The vases on the stone terrace in the foreground catch the rain all day; and the heavy drops fall – drip, drip, drip – upon the broad flagged pavement, called from old time the Ghost's Walk, all night. On Sundays the little church in the park is mouldy; the oaken pulpit breaks out into a cold sweat; and there is a general smell and taste as of the ancient Dedlocks in their graves. My Lady Dedlock (who is childless), looking

out in the early twilight from her boudoir at a keeper's lodge and seeing the light of a fire upon the latticed panes, and smoke rising from the chimney, and a child, chased by a woman, running out into the rain to meet the shining figure of a wrapped-up man coming through the gate, has been put quite out of temper. My Lady Dedlock says she has been 'bored to death'.

Therefore my Lady Dedlock has come away from the place in Lincolnshire and has left it to the rain, and the crows, and the rabbits, and the deer, and the partridges and pheasants. The pictures of the Dedlocks past and gone have seemed to vanish into the damp walls in mere lowness of spirits, as the housekeeper has passed along the old rooms shutting up the shutters. And when they will next come forth again, the fashionable intelligence – which, like the fiend, is omniscient of the past and present, but not the future – cannot yet undertake to say.

Sir Leicester Dedlock is only a baronet, but there is no mightier baronet than he. His family is as old as the hills, and infinitely more respectable. He has a general opinion that the world might get on without hills but would be done up without Dedlocks. He would on the whole admit nature to be a good idea (a little low, perhaps, when not enclosed with a park-fence), but an idea dependent for its execution on your great county families. He is a gentleman of strict conscience, disdainful of all littleness and meanness and ready on the shortest notice to die any death you may please to mention rather than give occasion for the least impeachment of his integrity. He is an honourable, obstinate, truthful, high-spirited, intensely prejudiced, perfectly unreasonable man.

Sir Leicester is twenty years, full measure, older than my Lady. He will never see sixty-five again, nor perhaps sixty-six, nor yet sixty-seven. He has a twist of the gout now and then and walks a little stiffly. He is of a worthy presence, with his light-grey hair and whiskers, his fine shirt-frill, his pure-white waistcoat, and his blue coat with bright buttons always buttoned. He is ceremonious, stately, most polite on every occasion to my Lady, and holds her personal attractions in the highest estimation. His gallantry to my Lady, which has never changed since he courted her, is the one little touch of romantic fancy in him.

Indeed, he married her for love. A whisper still goes about that she had not even family; howbeit, Sir Leicester had so much family that perhaps he had enough and could dispense with any more. But she had beauty, pride, ambition, insolent resolve, and sense enough to portion out a legion of fine ladies. Wealth and station, added to these, soon floated her upward, and for years now my Lady Dedlock has been at the centre of the fashionable intelligence and at the top of the fashionable tree.

Now re-read the extract, pen in hand, and personally annotate a photocopy of the text as shown below. The idea is not to make profound statements but to conduct your own private conversation with the text and its author as you read.

It is useful, though not obligatory, to divide your statements – which will normally be no more than a single word or a short phrase – into two broad categories:

Comment	Response
• events (what's happening)	• personal thoughts and feelings
• impressions of character	• anticipations of the story
• style / language / tone	• judgements
• links and cross-references	• questions about meaning and effect

Below, the first and fifth paragraphs are given as examples of this method in practice. Add to the statements; change them; delete them if they seem to you misguided. Personally annotate the remaining paragraphs yourself.

In Fashion

Contrasts with law court in ch. 1

It is but a glimpse of the world of (fashion) that we want on this same miry afternoon. It is not so unlike the Court of Chancery but that we may pass from the one scene to the other, as the crow flies. Both the world of fashion and the Court of Chancery are things of (precedent) and usage: oversleeping Rip Van Winkles who have played at strange (games) through a deal of thundery weather; sleeping beauties whom the knight will wake one day, when all the stopped spits in the kitchen shall begin to turn prodigiously!

Link

Stuck in the past?

Key word: makes the law seem a 'game'

Really? How?

Who ?!

HELP! What's all this about?

***

Sir Leicester (Dedlock) is only a baronet, but there is no mightier baronet than he. His family is as old as the hills, and infinitely more respectable. He has a general opinion that the world might get on without hills but would be done up without Dedlocks. He would on the whole admit nature to be a good idea (a little low, perhaps, when not enclosed with a park-fence), but an idea dependent for its execution on your great county families. He is a gentleman of strict conscience, disdainful of all littleness and meanness and ready on the shortest notice to die any death you may please to mention rather than give occasion for the least impeachment of his integrity. He is an honourable, obstinate, truthful, high-spirited, intensely (prejudiced,) perfectly (unreasonable) man.

Sounds sterile, inhuman

Sarcastic

Social snob

Sounds ironic

Words in this list are contradictory

Is this his own opinion?

His value system?

Vain, self-important

Like his wife, isn't he?

Ah! Now we know for sure — a bigot

Key word: Dickens's judgement of him

Benefits – and a note of caution

A level *students* have found this method helpful for the following reasons.

- It encourages concentrated, rather than 'lazy', reading: you 'see more' if you are doing something active instead of letting the text wash over you.

- It 'catches' ideas as they occur, which may otherwise evaporate.

- It provides a 'running script' from which more considered notes can be compiled later.

- It allows you to react in your own language, not necessarily the 'approved' vocabulary of formal A level essays.

- It enables you to make personal responses to a challenging text without the need to 'go public' in class discussion.

A level *teachers* have found this method valuable for the following reasons.

- If students make these personal annotations in advance of a lesson – as opposed to 'Read Chapter 2 before next Tuesday' – class discussion flows better, is more focused, and tends to go deeper.

- More time can be spent in class on what students really need to be helped with – such as style and effect – rather than what they are quite capable of seeing for themselves.

- Personal annotations guarantee that all students have actively tackled the text on their own and are therefore more likely to have developed an individual perspective on it.

- For the teacher who opts to read and monitor this kind of work, it can be looked through quickly and is easy to comment on; it is also useful for carrying on a written dialogue with students.

- It is logistically impossible, and educationally undesirable, to 'cover' in class the whole of a bulky text exhaustively: personal annotations encourage students to take responsibility for their own study.

However, both students and teachers have found this method self-defeating unless it is used selectively. You will have no difficulty understanding why. It works best when key points in the text have been reached and/or when everyone is in danger of being overwhelmed by the length and complexity of an A level text, particularly a novel. It is also a useful prelude to other methods of study described later in this chapter.

The real value of this approach to a 'classic' is that it takes away the sense of the text as a literary monument which can only be accessed by 'teacher-telling' or by recourse to second-hand material disguised as A level 'pass notes'.

Metaphysically modern?

The large body of poems written between 1580 and 1680 rarely escapes the attention of A level examiners. It is often assumed that this is because of their highly individual form and style – which is undoubtedly true, up to a point. However, chief examiners are just as concerned to set for A level 'early' poets whose subject matter and themes are likely to strike a chord with contemporary students' feelings and experiences. Paradoxical as it may sound, poets like John Donne, writing 400 years ago, appear so frequently on English syllabuses partly because of their modernity.

The purpose of this section is twofold: (a) to help you make a genuinely personal response to seventeenth-century metaphysical poetry, and (b) to raise your awareness of those aspects of structure, style and language that characterise it. In the end, these purposes are inseparable: the second is implicit in the first.

Metaphysical poetry – not 'metaphysics'

Of all the terms ever coined to describe different forms of poetry, 'metaphysical' is perhaps the most unfortunate. It makes the poems it purports to define sound like a branch of either science or philosophy, or both. For the moment, then, put it to one side and concentrate on reading the poem below simply as a poem: first to yourself, referring carefully to the footnotes, than aloud with a partner. On each reading, let yourself by guided by the punctuation: don't read 'line by line' but from pause to pause – comma to comma, comma to semi-colon, comma to full stop.

Born in 1572, John Donne was educated in Oxford and went on to study law at Lincoln's Inn. However, his career was effectively ruined when his secret marriage to Ann More was discovered by her father, an establishment politician, who promptly disinherited her and had Donne imprisoned. Not surprisingly, Donne's early poems deal with the pleasures and pains of secular love. In 1615 he was ordained a priest, later becoming Dean of St Paul's. Donne's last poems dramatise his often anguished struggle to submit himself to the austere disciplines of Christian faith.

This poem is dated 1610. Because Donne's mistress has been unfaithful to him, their love affair has come to an end. He tries to relieve his distress by visiting a garden where the spring flowers are in full bloom.

Twicknam Garden

Blasted with sighs, and surrounded with teares,
    Hither I come to seeke the spring,
    And at mine eyes, and at mine eares,
Receive such balmes[1] as else cure every thing;
    But O, self traytor, I do bring   5
The spider love, which transubstantiates[2] all,
    And can convert Manna to gall[3],
And that this place may thoroughly be thought
    True Paradise, I have the serpent[4] brought.

[1] **balmes**: soothing remedies for pain
[2] **transubstantiates**: (1) changes one substance into another; (2) transforms bread and wine into the body and blood of Christ at Communion
[3] **Manna to gall**: manna is a wafer used in the Communion service; gall is blood or bitter-tasting bile
[4] **serpent**: traditionally, the sin of envy is represented by a serpent; in Paradise, the devil took a serpent's form

'Twere wholesomer for mee, that winter did   10
    Benight the glory of this place,
    And that a grave frost did forbid
These trees to laugh, and mocke mee to my face;
    But that I may not this disgrace
Indure, nor yet leave loving, Love let mee[1]   15
    Some senseless peece of this place bee;
Make me a mandrake[2], so I may groane here,
    Or a stone fountain weeping out my yeare.

Hither with christall vyals[3], lovers come,
    And take my teares, which are loves wine,   20
    And try[4] your mistresse Teares at home,
For all are false that tast not just like mine;
    Alas, hearts do not in eyes shine,
Nor can you more judge womans thoughts by teares,
    Than by her shadow, what she wears.   25
O perverse sex, where none is true but shee,
    Who's therefore true, because her truth kills mee.

John Donne

>─◄>─○─◄>─◄

[1] **let mee**: Donne is addressing Love directly – 'allow me to'
[2] **mandrake**: a poisonous plant shaped like the human body, which was supposed to shriek when uprooted
[3] **vyals**: glass containers for chemicals; also drinking vessels
[4] **try**: test out, experiment on

Feeling out the meaning

No poem, whether written in 1610 or earlier this year, gives up the whole of its meaning immediately. More than any other literary form, poetry is typified by its compression. You are likely to find a degree of feeling 'packed' into the brief span of a poem more dense than that incorporated into (say) a three-act play or a short story. Whoever said, 'Prose is extensive, poetry is intensive' was guilty of over-simplification but not of inaccuracy.

As will be clear from your reading of 'Twicknam Garden', poetry like Donne's is remarkably dense with feeling: it's a kind of force-field of personal emotion, though far from an 'uncontrolled outpouring'. One useful way of clarifying to yourself both the depth of emotion it contains and the way in which the expression of this emotion is 'shaped' is to identify several focal-points of feeling in the course of the poem. Then work outwards from each, amplifying them by personal responses to further details in the text. This works particularly well if you can, without distorting the poem's meaning, locate one major 'focal-point' in each stanza, as shown in the diagram on page 178.

Either by yourself, or preferably with a partner, use this method to highlight the points of feeling in the whole poem. (Draw a diagram using the same headings of 'Focal-point of feeling', 'Related feelings' and 'Lines'.) Especially when you are working out the emotional content of a poem written in stanzas, this approach is often more effective than general class discussion. It also gives you a confident basis for further work, since you are discovering meaning for yourself: you will frequently be surprised or reassured by the extent of what you discover about poems written in the past.

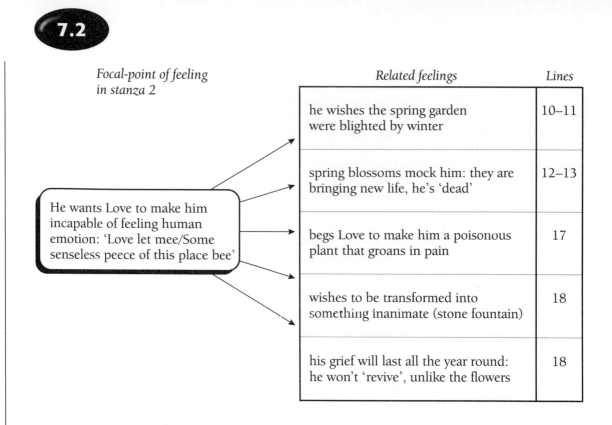

Focal-point of feeling in stanza 2

Related feelings	Lines
he wishes the spring garden were blighted by winter	10–11
spring blossoms mock him: they are bringing new life, he's 'dead'	12–13
begs Love to make him a poisonous plant that groans in pain	17
wishes to be transformed into something inanimate (stone fountain)	18
his grief will last all the year round: he won't 'revive', unlike the flowers	18

He wants Love to make him incapable of feeling human emotion: 'Love let mee/Some senseless peece of this place bee'

Giving a shape to feeling

If poets merely allowed their most intense feelings to overflow on to the page like molten lava, they may well feel satisfied that they had 'unburdened' themselves. However, lava being a shapeless mass, it is unlikely that they would convey their feelings very clearly to us. In common with other modes of literature, poetry communicates because it is crafted language – and the chief elements of the poet's craft are form, style and diction (that is, particular word-choices). These are the means by which poets, like other writers, give shape to their feelings: a shape that is in itself an integral part of the poem's 'meaning'.

Seventeenth-century 'metaphysical' poetry is distinguished by formal and stylistic elements that – though far from unique to it – are most commonly associated with Donne. Before going further with your work on 'Twicknam Garden', consider for the purpose of demonstration part of another Donne poem, 'The Sunne Rising'.

Here his mood is completely different from that of 'Twicknam Garden'. He is joyously in love with his mistress, and she with him. As they lie together in bed, he feels playfully resentful that the sun is rising, thus calling them from their pleasure to face the commonplace occupations of a new day:

> Busie old foole, unruly Sunne,
> Why dost thou thus
> Through windows and through curtaines call on us?
> Must to thy motions lovers seasons run?

Donne goes on to claim that the union between himself and his mistress is so total that they are nothing less than the whole world to each other. He compares the 'landscape' of her body to all the countries on earth combined together; he himself is the 'prince' of this kingdom, to whose rule she ecstatically surrenders.

The poem concludes:

> She'is all States, and all Princes, I;
> Nothing else is.
> Princes doe but play[1] us; compar'd to this,
> All honor's mimique[2]; all wealth alchimie[3].
> Thou sunne art halfe as happy as wee,
> In that the world's contracted[4] thus;
> Thine age askes ease[5], and since thy duties bee
> To warme the world, that's done in warming us.
> Shine here to us, and thou art every where;
> This bed thy centre is, these wall, thy spheare[6].

Throughout this whole stanza, as throughout the whole poem, Donne's expression of feeling is developed along the line or axis of one extended and consistent idea: since he and his mistress make up a world complete in itself, the sun's job is done by shining only on them. They are elevated by their love to universal sovereignty. Therefore it follows that:

- she is all countries in one; he is the ruler of these countries;

- political rulers have less power than Donne and his mistress because they aren't empowered by love;

- love's riches are greater than money; therefore all financial currencies are inferior to the lovers' emotional 'wealth';

- their bedroom walls define the limit of the universe; the bed, the 'throne' of their kingdom, is therefore at its very centre.

Feeling fused with intellect: wit, conceit and paradox

It will be obvious by now that Donne's passionately happy feelings about being in love are conveyed not by an outpouring of molten lava but through a carefully constructed line of reasoning to which the reader is held. (Note the number of 'therefores' in the summary above.) Make a proposition or a hypothesis – 'My mistress and I are rulers of the world' – and see what leads on from it … a, b, c, etc. In Donne's day, this technique of deductive reasoning, or *syllogism*, was termed *wit*, which does not mean 'humour' but 'intellectual inventiveness'. As in 'The Sunne Rising', it is always exercised in a highly concentrated way: the a's, b's and c's succeed one another thick and fast.

Seventeenth-century wit is characterised further by its fondness for images – metaphor, simile, personification – to follow through a line of reasoning. Donne and his contemporaries called images *conceits* (a variant form of mental 'conceptions'). They tend to be comparisons that 'juxtapose two things which are patently unlike, or which we should never think of together, in such a way that we feel their incongruity', as Helen Gardner defines it in her edition of the metaphysical poets (Penguin). Thus their ingenuity or novelty – even outrageousness – is what tends to be most striking. Donne's comparison of his bedroom to the universe is a typical metaphysical conceit, as is the likening of his mistress to 'all States'. Work out for yourself why there is an illogical logic in the line, 'Thou sunne art halfe as happy as wee'.

[1] **play**: act the parts that are really ours
[2] **mimique**: a pale imitation of the power we possess
[3] **alchimie**: a debased and fraudulent currency
[4] **contracted**: confined to where we are
[5] **askes ease**: makes you tired and in need of rest
[6] **spheare**: world, globe

Finally, metaphysical poets make frequent use of *paradox* – the discovery of a likeness between two things which we normally think not only to be incongruous but also contradictory, for example, 'Shine here to us, and thou art every where'. This technique often reflects the depth and complexity of feeling in poetry like Donne's and is deliberately used to do so. Sometimes the paradoxes will strike us as merely 'clever', a form of intellectual showing-off. More commonly, their impact is genuine because they throw new light on areas of experience which we have 'never thought of like that before'.

The structure and style of 'Twicknam Garden'

Now turn back to your work on 'Twicknam Garden'. Bearing in mind the points above, examine how the poem's structure is based on a set of oppositions of ideas which include:

Positives	Negatives
spring	winter
life	death
pleasure	pain
paradise	wilderness
animate	inanimate
wine	tears
truth	falsehood
substance	shadow
spiritual	carnal

Discuss as a class how these oppositions allow Donne to clarify and convey his feelings through syllogism, paradox and the use of conceits.

Do you think that the complex formal organisation of the poem works against Donne's expression of powerful feeling or enhances it?

Finally, consider the tone and rhythm of the poem. It has become commonplace to say that Donne's style often appeals to modern readers because it is colloquial: in other words, it has the rhythms and verbal texture of the 'speaking voice' rather than of the 'written word'. What examples of this can you find in 'Twicknam Garden'? Discuss them and say how far you find them to be effective.

Ancient or modern – or neither?

If you have worked through this section in detail, you will by now have 'got inside' a metaphysical poem that is one of the most difficult you could have been asked to tackle. (Few poems on your A level syllabus will pose more of a challenge to your understanding and response.) Do you now see it as a literary dinosaur, or as a poem that has something to offer a modern reader? On the basis of the work you have done, how important is the distinction between 'ancient' and 'modern'?

For comparison

On page 181 is a second metaphysical poem comparable in theme to 'Twicknam Garden'. It was written about twenty years later, probably in the 1630s. Read the poem first to yourself, then aloud with a partner.

Thomas Carew (1594–1640) was educated at Oxford and, like Donne, trained for a career in law. He was, however, less interested in study than in the pursuit of pleasure: evidently he applied himself to his law-books very little and established a reputation as a great libertine in his life and talk. He embarked on a political career with the help of his relative, Sir Dudley Carleton, who found him a post with the Ambassador of Venice, from which he was dismissed in disgrace for an indiscretion. He fought in the Civil War on the Royalist side but died in 1640 before they were defeated.

In this poem Carew's mistress, like Donne's, has been unfaithful ('inconstant'). He addresses his poem to her.

To My Inconstant Mistris

When thou, poore excommunicate[1]
    From all the joyes of love, shalt see
The full reward, and glorious fate,
    Which my strong faith shall purchase me,
    Then curse thine own inconstancie.   5

A fayrer hand than thine shall cure
    That heart, which thy false oathes did wound;
And to my soule, a soule more pure
    Than thine, shall by Loves hand be bound,
    And both with equall glory crown'd.   10

Then shalt thou weepe, entreat, complaine
    To Love, as I did once to thee;
When all thy teares shall be as vaine
    As mine were then, for thou shalt bee
    Damn'd for thy false Apostasie[2].   15

Thomas Carew

Follow the same procedure as you used on 'Twicknam Garden' for 'feeling out the meaning' (pages 177–8 above) and examining the poem's style and structure.

Then, in discussion or writing (or both), make a detailed comparison between the two poems, paying particular attention to:

- the subject matter and each poet's attitude towards it;

- the use of language and imagery;

- the way the poems are constructed.

End by saying which of the two poems you find more effective.

[1] **excommunicate**: a person banished from the Church
[2] **Apostasie**: abandoning of religious faith

Looking through contemporary eyes

Personal response?

The purpose of this final section is to help you answer a question that every A level student asks at some stage during the course: namely, how valid is it to respond to literature written in the past from a 'modern' viewpoint that is highly personal to yourself? To put it in another, rather simplistic way: for the exam – or for coursework – do you have to try to write about (say) an eighteenth-century text as if you were an eighteenth-century reader?

All A level English examiners would offer the following view. To wilfully distort any work of literature in order to drag it screaming 'Relevant!' into the present day, regardless of its author's evident intentions, is an act of cultural vandalism. But exactly what an author 'intends' is often genuinely open to interpretation. As long as the text in question will support a variety of views (including 'modern' ones) when it is read with informed intelligence and without personal bias, an individual interpretation of it is not merely justified: it is absolutely essential.

This kind of personal response is what examiners look for and reward very highly when they find it – as long as you can convince them that your own interpretation is solidly rooted in the text, supported by evidence from the text and informed by a coherent overview of the text (rather than a selective and partial view). Personal response does *not* mean: 'I'll see in this book whatever I choose to see, as long as it caters to my own view of the world rather than to what the author wrote.' Personal response *does* mean: 'I've been as open as possible to what the book is communicating to me, trying to deduce as much as I can from the text about its author's purposes. Now, what do I think?'

Contrasting viewpoints

The only practical way to settle the question with which this section opened is by demonstration. On pages 183–6 is a coursework assignment on Heathcliff in Emily Brontë's *Wuthering Heights*, written in 1997, exactly 150 years after the novel was first published (Item B). The essay is strongly personal and deals with the topic 'Do you feel any sympathy for Heathcliff?' from a contemporary viewpoint. The starting-point for this essay was class discussion of another 'essay' dealing with the same topic, written in 1850 by Emily Brontë's sister, Charlotte (Item A). (Note that Charlotte Brontë refers to Emily as 'Ellis Bell', the pseudonym under which *Wuthering Heights* was published.)

Your first task is to compare the view of Heathcliff presented in the two pieces of writing. Then discuss with your teacher your response to the way the coursework essay is written in relation to whatever texts from the past you are studying, particularly novels. Consider whether its conclusions should be deemed less valid than those of Charlotte Brontë, given that she was writing in the same day and age as Emily and that she knew her sister's character intimately.

(A) *Preface to the second edition of* **Wuthering Heights**

by Charlotte Brontë

> Had Ellis Bell been a lady or a gentleman accustomed to what is called 'the world', her view of a remote and unreclaimed region, as well as of the dwellers therein, would have differed greatly from that actually taken by the homebred country girl. Doubtless it would have been wider – more comprehensive: whether it would have been more original or more truthful is not so certain ...
>   5

I am bound to avow that she had scarcely more practical knowledge of the peasantry[1] amongst whom she lived, than a nun has of the country people who sometimes pass her convent gates. My sister's disposition was not naturally gregarious[2]; circumstances favoured and fostered her tendency to seclusion; except to go to church or take a walk on the hills, she rarely crossed the threshold of home. Though her feeling for the people around was benevolent, intercourse[3] with them she never sought; nor, with very few exceptions, ever experienced ... Hence it ensued that what her mind gathered of the real concerning them, was too exclusively confined to those tragic and terrible traits of which, in listening to the secret annals of every rude vicinage[4], the memory is sometimes compelled to receive the impress[5]. Her imagination, which was a spirit more sombre than sunny, more powerful than sportive, found in such traits material whence it wrought creations like Heathcliff, like Earnshaw, like Catherine. Having formed these beings, she did not know what she had done ...

Heathcliff stands unredeemed; never once swerving in his arrow-straight course to perdition[6], from the time when 'the little black-haired, swarthy thing, as dark as if it came from the Devil', was first unrolled out of the bundle and set on its feet in the farmhouse kitchen, to the hour when Nelly Dean found the grim, stalwart corpse laid on its back in the panel-enclosed bed, with wide-gazing eyes that seemed 'to sneer at her attempt to close them, and parted lips and sharp white teeth that sneered too'.

Heathcliff betrays one solitary human feeling, and that is *not* his love for Catherine, which is a sentiment fierce and inhuman: a passion such as might boil and glow in the bad essence of some evil genius; a fire that might form the tormented centre – the ever-suffering soul of a magnate from the infernal world; and by its quenchless and ceaseless ravage effect the execution of the decree which dooms him to carry Hell with him wherever he wanders. No; the single link that connects Heathcliff with humanity is his rudely confessed regard for Hareton Earnshaw – the young man whom he has ruined; and then his half-implied esteem for Nelly Dean. These solitary traits omitted, we should say he was child neither of Lascar[7] nor gipsy, but a man's shape animated by demon life – a Ghoul ...

Whether it is right or advisable to create things like Heathcliff, I do not know: I scarcely think it is.

[1] **peasantry**: country people
[2] **gregarious**: outgoing, extrovert
[3] **intercourse**: contact, conversation
[4] **rude vicinage**: rural environment
[5] **impress**: stamp, form
[6] **perdition**: damnation
[7] **Lascar**: native Indian

(B) Do you feel any sympathy for Heathcliff?

It is not hard to understand why many readers of *Wuthering Heights* agree with Charlotte Brontë that Heathcliff is less of a human being than some kind of 'demon driven purely by malice and evil'. The novel is full of characters who view him in exactly this way. Isabella calls him 'fierce, pitiless, wolfish ... a lying fiend, a monster' after he marries her not out of love but 'so that I should be Edgar's proxy in suffering, till he could get a hold of him'. Heathcliff spreads 'suffering' to almost everyone – in particular, Hindley, Hareton, even his own son Linton – and does so without compassion for his victims. We have Heathcliff's own word for this:

> 'I have no pity! I have no pity! The more the worms writhe, the more I yearn to crush out their entrails!'

Even Cathy, whom he calls 'my love, my life, my soul', accuses him of being her murderer: 'You have killed me – and thriven on it.' How is it possible to feel any sympathy for a 'thing' (Charlotte Brontë) like this, or not to echo Isabella in asking: 'Is Mr Heathcliff a man? If so, is he mad? And if not, is he a devil?'

I shall argue that the traditional view of Heathcliff as 'a deformed monster' (E.P. Whipple) is both over-simplistic and seriously outdated. In my view, Emily Brontë portrays him as a vulnerable human being whose actions, if they cannot all be excused, can be understood in terms of why he is treated by others and by what he learns from the circumstances in which he find himself. Literally 'finds himself', since perhaps the most important fact about Heathcliff is that his destiny is in effect decided for him when he is brought as a 'vagabond' to Wuthering Heights and is immediately cast in the role of disempowered outsider. The view that Heathcliff is an inhuman force who acts on others entirely according to his own 'fiendish' will is, in my opinion, contradicted by the text. He is acted upon, not only during his childhood but also after Cathy's death, by forces over which he has little control, including his own psyche. What he calls his 'moral teething' is dictated by the selfishness, the cruelty and the malice with which he meets. From this he learns that the only way to survive is to emulate it. Like the rest of us, his behaviour is, to a large extent, conditioned. In this sense, he becomes a villain because he is first made into a victim and, despite the 'revenge' he takes into his own hands, he remains so to (and beyond) his death. It is for this reason that I find it possible to sympathise with him, as I believe Emily Brontë intended her readers to do.

Modern psychology tells us that adult character is largely formed by our childhood experiences. Heathcliff learns early in life that he is unwanted (except by Mr Earnshaw and, later, Cathy) in the tightly self-protective world of Wuthering Heights. 'We don't take kindly to foreigners here, Mr Lockwood,' says Nelly Dean, whose first action towards Heathcliff – already christened 'that gipsy brat' by Mrs Earnshaw – is to 'put it on the landing of the stairs, hoping it would be gone by morning'. It is already clear that the orphaned Heathcliff is not going to find a surrogate mother in either of these women, neither of whom even acknowledge him as a human being (Nelly first refers to him as 'it'). He is only given a name to indulge Mr Earnshaw's selfish fancy for a substitute son: 'Heathcliff' is 'the name of a son who died in childhood'. The young Hindley needs to practise exercising an authority based on economic power – he is the future master of Wuthering Heights – over a subservient, and Heathcliff is the ideal candidate: 'You beggarly interloper' is a message Hindley reinforces by physical violence, and later, when he has assumed ownership of the Heights, 'he drove [Heathcliff] from their company to the servants, and indicated that he should labour out of doors instead'. As Cathy writes in her diary, 'Hindley swears he will reduce him to his right place.'

Not only, then, is Heathcliff displaced; he is dispossessed, told he is an 'imp of Satan', denied 'the instructions of the curate', and taught repeatedly that he has neither identity nor status. He learns to define himself by what he is excluded from. Crucially, this includes wealth. When he and Cathy 'scamper' rebelliously across the moors to Thrushcross Grange and gaze in at its 'pure white ceiling bordered by gold, a shower of glass drops hanging in silver chains from the centre, and shimmering little soft tapers', Heathcliff is actually looking at what, in a class-bound society based on money and privilege, he cannot have – except by taking it forcibly or by learning the lesson of how it uses violence to protect itself against a 'gypsy' intruder like himself ('Run, Heathcliff, run! They have let the bull-dog loose, and he holds me').

On this journey of discovery, Heathcliff learns an even more painful lesson: the Linton world of wealth which debars him does not debar Cathy, his 'soul-mate'. In fact, the novel's symbolism makes clear that, because she has a social status which Heathcliff lacks, Thrushcross Grange almost 'seizes' Cathy and claims her as its own: '"Skulker has caught a little girl, sir," he replied, "and there's a lad here who looks an out-and-outer."'

From this point on, Heathcliff is separated from the one person who has shown him love and affection in a world hostile above all to his lack of economic identity. It is not necessary to make a Marxist analysis in order to see that Cathy and Heathcliff are forced apart by the class difference between them, nor to understand the significance of Heathcliff's comment, 'If Cathy had wished to return, I intended shattering their great glass panes to a million fragments unless they let her out.'

To me, the strongest reason for feeling sympathy with Heathcliff is that 'they' do not let Cathy out – nor, in my opinion, does she ever completely 'wish to return' to the man she later describes as being 'more myself than I am ... he's my soul'. I would argue that, from the point at which she allows Edgar Linton to enter her life (if not her soul), Cathy makes Heathcliff more of a victim than anyone else has done. Nelly Dean describes Cathy as a 'spoiled child' and my argument is based on the same view. Like all children who never fully grow up, Cathy lives much of her life through fantasy, which is the ultimate expression of ego. Right to the end of her life, a 'virtual suicide', Cathy fails to de-centre (to borrow a term from Freud). The consequences for Heathcliff are devastating. Seeing their effect on him surely leaves us no option but to feel pity as we empathise with his pain.

Cathy's fantasy is this:

> 'Every Linton on the face of the earth might melt into nothing before I could come to forsake Heathcliff ... I shouldn't be Mrs Linton were such a price demanded! He'll be as much to me as he has been all his lifetime.'

The pragmatic Nelly knows what the price is that is 'demanded'. She responds to Cathy's plan to sustain her twin loves for Edgar and Heathcliff by pointing out that the latter will feel rejected by her marriage to the former, just as he was when he overheard Cathy say that it would 'demean' her to marry him. Cathy dismissed this as 'nonsense'. Manifestly, it is *not* nonsense. With stunning naivety, the child-woman goes on to claim: 'This is for the sake of one [i.e. Heathcliff] who comprehends in his person my feelings to Edgar and myself.'

It is so obvious that Heathcliff, of all people, does *not* comprehend that the only conclusion I can draw from Cathy's declaration of her love for him – 'If all else perished and he remained, I should still continue to be' – is that she is unconsciously exploiting Heathcliff to fulfil her own impossible ideal: the simultaneous love and devotion of two men, which will then free her from the adult necessity to commit herself to a choice between them. In order to do this, Cathy would have to accept that maturity imposes limitations on what, as children, we believe we can have because we imagine ourselves to be loved by all and loveable to all. This is, in fact, precisely how Cathy still thinks of herself:

> 'How strange! I thought, though everybody hated and despised each other, they could not avoid loving me.'

I believe, therefore, that it is possible to see Heathcliff as a casualty of Cathy's infantile fantasy, even before she is forced by Edgar into making an adult decision:

> 'Will you give up Heathcliff hereafter, or will you give me up? It is impossible for you to be my friend and his at the same time; and I absolutely require to know which you choose.'

Cathy's reaction to this is to will her own death in order to escape the dilemma she has placed herself in. Heathcliff is surely right to say to her: 'You have killed yourself ... I have not broken your heart – you have broken it – and, in breaking it, you have broken mine.' His suffering here draws out our deepest pity. It will be, as he tells her, a terrible 'anguish' to him for Cathy to 'escape into that glorious world and to be always there'. To me, her 'solution' is a profoundly selfish one, and the selfishness of it increases my sympathy for Heathcliff; he is left to face the real world without her:

'I cannot live without my life! I cannot live without my soul!'

This outburst may sound sentimental, but it is actually nothing less than the truth. From the point when Cathy dies, Heathcliff does not 'live': he merely endures. As Pauline Nestor comments: 'Throughout the rest of his life, Heathcliff is consumed with frustration, finding himself both literally and figuratively haunted by the endless deferral of satisfaction.' His only chance of happiness in a world inimical to him (as we have seen) has been thwarted by Cathy's egotism. It is no consolation to him, more like agony, to hear her say, 'That's not my Heathcliff. I shall love mine yet, and take him with me.'

She does not, of course, take him with her – only her vision of him. Instead, she torments him – at least this is the effect – with glimpses of the love she has betrayed:

> 'I could almost see her, and yet I find I could not! I ought to have sweat blood then, from the anguish of my yearning ... To be always disappointed! It racked me!'

Some readers would argue that to be 'racked' is what Heathcliff deserves. After Cathy's death, he embarks on a campaign of vengeance against both families so brutal that it makes every reader recoil in horror; it is here that one understands why Charlotte Brontë took the view of him that she did ('Heathcliff never swerves in his arrow-straight course to perdition'). Perhaps his attempt, unsuccessful in the end, to reduce Hareton to a state of total degeneracy is the most shocking example of all.

Yet what else is he doing than paying back the inhumanity which the 'older generation' have taught him? He has learned, not least from Edgar, that power is derived from money and ownership, so he determines to become master of both the Heights and the Grange. He has learned that to survive is to be ruthless, and he does not by any means have a monopoly of the violence in the novel, as Hindley and Isabella show.

However, I do not believe that Heathcliff's barbaric behaviour is motivated solely by hatred of those who have hated or mistreated him. As he says, his revenge is in the end futile:

> 'But where is the use? I don't care for striking, and I can't take trouble to raise my hand – I have lost the faculty for enjoying their destruction.'

Psychologically, his greatest wish is to exhaust his capacity for living in order to die – to be, as he believes, with Cathy in her 'glorious world' beyond the anguish with which her loss has 'racked' him for twenty years. Mixed with revulsion at his vindictive sadism, it is difficult not to feel a measure of sympathy with such passionate 'yearning'.

It is conventional to see the ending of *Wuthering Heights* in a romantic way. Much as I would like to share the view that the love of Cathy and Heathcliff transcends the boundaries of death, I do not think Emily Brontë 'forces' this conclusion on her readers. The text can support a different reading. This is my final reason for sympathising with Heathcliff: he dies in the belief that 'there is one who won't shrink from my company', but it may be he dies deluded in thinking so.

It must be significant that Emily Brontë leaves it to Lockwood, the novel's ultimate (and consistently mistaken) romantic, to hint at a transcendently happy union for Cathy and Heathcliff beyond the grave: 'I wondered how any one could ever imagine unquiet slumbers for the sleepers in that quiet earth.' Is this ending in harmony with the rest of a novel which has been chiefly about exclusion, loss and unfulfilment? According to my interpretation, *Wuthering Heights* was not written as 'the greatest love story ever told'. It is primarily a psychological exploration of a man who suffers and who causes suffering to others. That is why Heathcliff is both pitiable and terrifying. Pity and terror are the elements of tragedy, and to me the book is Heathcliff's tragedy. It would be more consistent with the novel as a whole to see the ending as a confirmation of this tragedy rather than as (to me) a piece of trite Victorian sentimentality.

Chapter 8 Arguing your case

Questioning A level questions

'Always answer the question.' This is obviously good advice – but, of course, you already know it. No one fails on purpose to 'answer the question' unless they are attempting A level Suicide. This is why you feel like screaming (or transferring to Sociology) when you get back an essay that suggests your whole time was spent not addressing the question asked.

A better starting-point is to 'question the question'. There are at least two good reasons for doing this. Firstly, it is exactly what A level examiners do when they mark your essays, as the 'key words' section a little further on shows. Secondly, apart from the unseen and/or context questions, your A level English grade depends entirely on how well you write essays in answer to set questions – and how well you answer an essay question depends on how adept you become at seeing its implications. This is a skill that can be learned by everyone: it is not a 'gift' that some have and some haven't. This section demonstrates how to acquire that skill.

Typical questions – and how to understand them

Listed below is a selection of questions of the kind generally asked at A level. Study the way in which they are worded. For the purpose of this activity, it does not matter whether or not you know the texts to which they refer.

Shakespeare

1. Do you think that Hamlet is mad at any point in the play? [AEB, 1996]

2. The role of Shylock has been interpreted by actors in a variety of ways. From your reading of *The Merchant of Venice*, do you regard Shylock as more a tragic hero than a comic villain? [NEAB, 1996]

3. 'Cordelia's death is dramatically unnecessary and totally undeserved.' What is your response to this comment on King Lear? [O&C, 1996]

4. 'In dying, as in living, Roman values prove to be more powerful than Egyptian values.' Discuss this view of *Antony and Cleopatra*. [O&C, 1995]

5. In what ways do Caliban and Ariel contribute to the dramatic interest of *The Tempest*? [NEAB, 1995]

Other drama

6. 'Marlowe failed to find a single unifying theme in *Edward II*.' Discuss this view. [O&C, 1995]

7. Jonson claimed that he was writing with a clear moral purpose. Does *The Alchemist* support this view? [AEB, 1996]

8. In what sense do you think either *Comus* or *Samson Agonistes* qualifies for inclusion in the 'Drama' section of this paper? [AEB, 1996]

9. 'Williams is much more interested in dramatising the psychological conflicts between his characters than in creating for them a convincing social world.' How far would you agree with this view of *A Streetcar Named Desire*? [UCLES, 1996]

10. What means does Bennett use to engage you with the characters he has created in *Talking Heads*? Write about one or more of the monologues. [NEAB, 1996]

Poetry

11. In the 'General Prologue', how far do you agree that Chaucer does not judge wickedness but is simply amused by it? [AEB, 1995]

12. What part does Donne's 'wit' (that is, intelligence and inventiveness) play in his poetry? [AEB, 1996]

13. 'In *Songs of Innocence and Experience* Blake is concerned with loss, not of childhood but of the mature individual's child-like vision of existence'. Discuss. [UCLES, 1996]

14. 'Browning admires those who embrace the promises and opportunities of life as opposed to avoiding life's challenges.' Discuss the *Selected Poems* in the light of this comment. [NEAB, 1995]

15. 'Larkin is anti-modern, anti-religion, anti-women. Is there anything he stands for?' Write your answer by examining the poetry of *The Whitsun Weddings*. [O&C, 1995]

Prose

16. '*Gulliver's Travels* provokes laughter and indignation – and both are learning experiences for the reader.' With reference to two books of *Gulliver's Travels*, consider this view of Swift's satirical methods and their effectiveness. [UCLES, 1996]

17. Is *Wuthering Heights* anything more than a violent melodrama? [AEB, 1996]

18. 'In *The Mill on the Floss* George Eliot's portrayal of Maggie's relationships with Philip Wakem and Stephen Guest is a powerful exploration of sexual energy and sexual desire.' Discuss. [UCLES, 1996]

19. In *Tess of the d'Urbervilles*, how much sympathy do you have for Angel Clare? [AEB, 1994]

20. 'Bold' is a word that has often been used in praise or criticism of *Beloved*. What do you think is most excitingly and successfully bold about the book? [O&C, 1995]

Key words: a platform for constructing argument

Whatever else you have concluded about the demands of A level questions, you will be aware by now that you are invariably required to argue a case. Take the example above (17) on *Wuthering Heights*. To write a relevant answer, you would have to 'argue through' the following points:

● How far, and in what ways, is the novel 'violent'?

● Is the novel actually a 'melodrama'?

● Does the term 'violent melodrama' accurately or adequately describe the novel?

● … and, if not, what else is there in the novel over and above violent melodrama?

Pause to think about these 'questions within the question'. Apart from the novel's title, the examiners have used seven words. Yet all of the points above are either an explicit or an implicit part of what the question asks you to do.

When A level examiners meet to agree how they will mark candidates' answers, they identify key words in each question. They use these for assessing how well any question has been answered, and they give marks accordingly. First and foremost, they do not judge what you write but whether you have based your answer on the key words (that is, on the demands of the question set).

With this in mind, look back to questions 1, 10, 11 and 20. The examiners' key words for each of these would be:

1. you, mad, any point

10. means, use, engage you, one or more

11. how far, you, judge, simply amused

20. praise, criticism, you, most excitingly, (most) successfully, bold

Discuss with your teacher what you can learn from the examiners' basic approach to marking. For future reference, make careful notes on the conclusions you draw.

Now look at the following questions and identify the key words in them. It does not matter whether you know the texts to which they refer.

21. 'The Wife of Bath is blind to the possibilities of truly satisfying relationships between men and women.' Do you agree with this comment on the Prologue and Tale? [O&C, 1995]

22. Consider the dramatic function of the comic characters in *Henry V*. How effective do you find them? [AEB, 1993]

23. '*Dr Faustus* is a ramshackle, badly-constructed play containing a few passages of wonderful poetry.' Discuss. [NEAB, 1996]

24. 'To achieve lasting happiness the characters in *Pride and Prejudice* must learn to temper their inclinations with prudent judgement.' With this comment in mind discuss Austen's portrayal in the novel of any two of the following relationships: Elizabeth and Darcy; Jane and Bingley; Charlotte and Mr Collins; Lydia and Wickham. [UCLES, 1996]

25. Choose three poems by Sylvia Plath in which the feeling of terror is dominant. What do you think is distinctive about the way Plath presents this feeling? [AEB, 1996]

Towards arguing your own case

This section has listed twenty-five questions on different A level texts. Choose one on a text that you are studying. Use what you have learned about how to respond to a question to plan an answer that is as relevant as you can make it. Remember that (a) A level questions require you to construct or conduct an argument, and (b) the commonest key word used by examiners is 'you'.

If you feel sufficiently confident, work on your own. Otherwise make your plan in class discussion with your teacher.

What is a well-argued A level essay?

Reproduced on pages 192–5 are two answers, written in exam conditions, to the question: 'Do you agree that *Macbeth* fails as a tragedy because we are unable to feel either admiration or sympathy for its hero?' Your task is to decide (a) how adequately each of them deals with the question, and (b) how effectively each candidate argues his or her case. Read them both twice, with real care and concentration.

(If you are not familiar with *Macbeth*, your teacher should give you a brief summary of its plot and of the character of Macbeth himself.)

Candidate A

Do you agree that Macbeth fails as a tragedy because we are unable to feel either admiration or sympathy for its hero?

Macbeth is the tragedy of a basically good man who is destroyed by his fatal flaw of ambition. It is not only his own ambition but Lady Macbeth's as well, so I can feel sympathy for Macbeth in this respect, without her influence he would probably not have murdered Duncan: 'We will proceed no further in this business.' The play is a tragedy because it glimpses what Macbeth could have been like without his 'vaulting ambition'. It is important to remember that the play is also about Scotland and the damaging effects on it of Macbeth becoming king: 'Alas poor country, almost afraid to know itself.' This is a major part of the tragedy.

Before he is gripped by ambition, Macbeth is admired by everyone. Shakespeare builds up this picture of a hero in battle so we can see his potential:

> 'For brave Macbeth – well he deserves that name –
> Disdaining fortune, with his brandished steel,
> Which smoked with bloody execution,
> Like valour's minion.'

He fights for Scotland, not for his own glory, and is rightly rewarded by Duncan:

> 'What he hath lost, noble Macbeth has won.'

He is favourably compared with the Thane of Cawdor who betrayed his country. A picture is painted of Macbeth as a brave and loyal warrior, 'It is a peerless kinsman'.

It would be wrong to say that all sympathy for Macbeth is lost before and after Duncan's murder. Macbeth is not a cold-blooded murderer, he agonises with himself about the evilness of what he is doing:

> 'He's here in double trust;
> First as I am his kinsman and his subject,
> Strong both against the deed; then as his host,
> Who should against his murderer shut the door,
> Not bear the knife myself.'

This is where the contrast with Lady Macbeth brings out his human side, he has a sense of morals but she has given herself over to evil ('Come you spirits that tend on mortal thoughts, Unsex me here'). She simply says 'A little water clears us of this deed', but Macbeth knows that he will never be free from his guilt:

> 'Methought I heard a voice cry "Sleep no more!"'

It is obviously wrong for him to murder, but it is tragic to see the way he suffers for it.

I feel the most sympathy for Macbeth in the banquet scene where he completely breaks up:

> 'It will have blood, they say; blood will have blood.'

This is the man who was a heroic warrior, 'Bellona's bridegroom', now being reduced to a gibbering wreck. He has to suffer alone, Lady Macbeth cannot get through to him and his only companions now are the witches. It is tragic to see how he believes it when they deceive him:

> ' … for none of woman born
> Shall harm Macbeth.'

He is now totally in the grip of evil, but I feel pity for his isolation and the difference in what he has been reduced to.

Things have got totally out of control and Macbeth's tragedy also becomes Scotland's tragedy. Because he is being led by evil forces he cannot do anything about, Lady Macduff's children are killed on Macbeth's instructions and the whole country is filled with blood:

> 'I think our country sinks beneath the yoke;
> It weeps, it bleeds, and each new day a gash
> Is added to her wounds.'

Scotland's ruin reflects the ruin in Macbeth, adding to the effect of tragedy. It happens on a large scale and gives a greater sense of waste.

Finally, I feel sympathy for Macbeth when he can see no point in life at the end of the play:

> 'Life's but a walking shadow, a poor player
> That struts and frets his hour upon the stage
> And then is heard no more.'

The witches and his fatal flaw have brought him to this pitiful state. But he does not die a coward's death by killing himself, like Lady Macbeth, he returns to being what he was at the start of the play:

> 'Come wind, come wrack,
> At least we'll die with harness on our back.'

Although he has done evil, Macbeth dies bravely as a warrior should and admiration can be felt for this.

In conclusion, I do not think *Macbeth* fails as a tragedy. Shakespeare takes us inside Macbeth's mind and shows us all his suffering because of one fault in his character. A man to be pitied as well as condemned.

Candidate B

Do you agree that Macbeth fails as a tragedy because we are unable to feel either admiration or sympathy for its hero?

According to Aristotle, tragedy should give rise to feelings of pity and terror. To some extent, *Macbeth* does both. The sense of pity is evoked by the spectacle of a once-virtuous man being horrifically destroyed by evil. The consequences of this process spread far beyond Macbeth and affect almost every other character in the play. From this arises the feeling of terror – that evil, once set in motion, can annihilate virtually everything in its path.

The witches represent the force of evil in the play. Their aim is to seize on whatever is morally good and turn it into the opposite of itself:

> 'Fair is foul, and foul is fair'.

In this topsy-turvy moral world, the world of *Macbeth*, virtue becomes vice and vice becomes virtue. Hence Macbeth's 'good' qualities – patriotism, loyalty, courage and conscience – are nullified by the influence of Lady Macbeth, the witches' human representative. In the scene where she persuades Macbeth to commit himself to the 'sacrilege' of murdering his king, she overturns these qualities one by one and makes them seem to him like weaknesses rather than the strengths that they are:

> 'Art thou afeard
> To be the same in thine own act and valour
> As thou art in desire?'

Like the witches, Lady Macbeth 'equivocates' with the truth. Under her spell, Macbeth performs the murder with his moral sense completely disordered:

> 'Away, and mock the time with fairest show:
> False face must hide what the false heart does know.'

He has allied himself with the unnaturalness which in *Macbeth* is always a signifier of evil. As a result, to use the Porter's words, he will in the future 'equivocate [himself] to hell'.

Hell is a state of mind, and it is the state in which Macbeth lives for most of the play. Because he has 'murdered' his own morality, he has also murdered his capacity to live a normal, constructive life. The consequences are truly terrible:

> 'I am in blood
> Stepped in so far, that should I wade no more
> Returning were as tedious as go o'er.'

This is the logic of damnation. Macbeth has no purpose in living except to act unconsciously (at least until near the end of the play) as an agent of the witches' will and as a channel for the evil they embody. After the Banquet Scene he is barely recognisable as a human being at all:

> 'From this moment
> The very firstlings of my heart shall be
> The firstlings of my hand.'

He becomes like some impersonal, irresistible destructive force, beyond the reach of moral and humane feeling.

The manner of his death merely confirms this impression. It is without nobility or anything remotely approaching heroism:

> 'It is a tale
> Told by an idiot, full of sound and fury,
> Signifying nothing.'

Macbeth has ceased to be human. He has been diminished to 'nothing', a man without identity whose only surviving instinct is to blindly destroy the identity of others:

> 'Lay on, Macduff,
> And damned be him that first cries "Hold, enough".'

But Macbeth has been 'damned' from the moment he committed himself to the wholesale destruction of everything that gives meaning to life by surrendering his own identity to evil.

Macbeth is a play that resists categories. It comes nearest to being a morality play; its overall effect is to provoke horror and revulsion rather than the sense of catharsis which Aristotle maintained was the function of tragedy. To conclude with Malcolm's words, it 'pours the sweet milk of concord into hell'.

For this activity, you will find it helpful to have to hand a photocopy of both essays.

Work with a partner. Put yourself in the place of an A level examiner. Assess the answers above as argued essays by following, in order, these instructions:

- Number the paragraphs in each essay. (Candidate A has written seven, Candidate B six). Strictly in the light of the question set, decide how far each paragraph is relevant to it by using a scale of 1–4, where 1 = 'a completely relevant paragraph' and 4 = 'an almost irrelevant paragraph'.

- Still assessing paragraph by paragraph, use the same scale to assess how well the candidates make clear the topic of each paragraph and how well they stick to it without digressing. (1 = 'a very clear and consistent paragraph', 4 = 'an unclear and incoherent paragraph'.)

- Use the same scale to give a single 'score' to the whole of each essay for the variety of material drawn on to develop the argument. You should look for the use each candidate makes of reference to different parts of the play while still remaining relevant to the question. (1 = 'excellent variety: all relevant', 4 = 'little variety: mostly not relevant'.)

- Use the same scale to give a single 'score' to the whole of each essay for the use of quotation from the text to back up points that develop the argument. (1 = 'points consistently supported by suitable quotation', 4 = 'little or no suitable quotation'.)

- Look again at the first paragraph of each essay. How well does it lay the basis for the argument to be followed in the whole essay? (1 = 'very well', 4 = 'not at all'.)

If you have followed the above procedure systematically and with care, you have done exactly what A level examiners do with each answer they mark. They will, of course, do the same with yours.

Now add up the 'scores' you have given to each essay. Award Candidate A one overall score between 4 and 20 to show how effective you judge his or her essay to be as a relevant answer based on argument. Do the same for Candidate B.

As a class, discuss your findings and how you arrived at them. Then with your teacher study the marking grid on page 199. It is used by one A level board to assess essays written on set texts under exam conditions. Consider the criteria used to allocate grades from U ('fail') to A. How many of these, particularly in the last two columns, relate to the ability to *argue* effectively?

For future reference, make your own notes on what you have learned from this activity about the characteristics of a good/average/bad argued essay on an A level text.

The essay reproduced below, written in exam conditions, earned an 'A' grade for the qualities you have been considering in this section: well-constructed argument which is relevant to the question asked. Study it carefully. Then make a list of the strengths of the essay as a piece of argued writing, preferably without referring back to the work you did earlier.

(If you are not familiar with *Hamlet*, your teacher should give you a brief summary of its plot, its main characters, and its 'revenge' theme. Better still, watch the 1996 Kenneth Branagh film video.)

>–¦–‹◆›–◦–‹›–¦–‹

'Hamlet is more concerned with reforming his mother's morals than with avenging his father's murder.' What is your response to this comment?

There is evidence in the play for agreeing with this comment. After telling Hamlet to revenge his 'foul and most unnatural murder' at the end of Act I, the Ghost has to return at the end of Act III to remind him to put everything from his mind except Claudius:

> 'Do not forget, this visitation
> Is but to whet thy almost blunted purpose.'

5

This comes at the very point when Hamlet is condemning his mother for her disgusting morals:

> 'Nay but to live
> In the rank sweat of an enseamed bed
> Stewed in corruption, honeying, and making love
> Over the nasty sty.'

10

It does seem here that Hamlet has been sidetracked from his revenge by his horror at his mother. However, I believe this idea is based on only a narrow view of the whole play, as I shall try to show.

The first question is, between the Ghost's two appearances has Hamlet's famous 'delay' been caused only, or mainly, by his disgust with Gertrude? I would argue it hasn't, that there are many other reasons. The main one is that he has had to make himself certain whether 'the spirit that I have seen' is really his father's ghost, because it:

15

> 'May be a devil, and the devil …
> Abuses me to damn me.'

20

Unless he gets this evidence, his revenge against Claudius cannot go ahead without the risk that it is his morbid imagination creating something that is unreal. Therefore he needs to stage the Mousetrap play before he can proceed. When Claudius's reaction confirms his guilt, Hamlet shows signs that he will 'sweep to my revenge':

> 'Now could I drink hot blood,
> And do such bitter business as the day
> Would quake to look on.'

25

He only goes to his mother's closet because he has been commanded to, on Claudius's instructions (via Polonius), to distract him from revenge.

It is true that the news of Gertrude's 'frailty' plunges Hamlet into deep melancholy. But it is not so much her morals alone as what he has to confront about the whole of life that numbs his will to take revenge. Her immorality and deceit are, to him, only symptoms of the general condition of the world:

30

> '… this goodly frame the earth seems to me a sterile promontory … why,
> it appears no other thing to me but a foul and pestilent congregation of
> vapours.'

35

To Hamlet, human life as a whole is like 'an unweeded garden that grows to seed'. Faced with this he wants only to have no part in it ('To die, to sleep; to sleep, perchance to dream'). While he is in this mood, any thoughts of his revenge for his father and reforming his mother are equally laid aside.

40

I believe he only manages to focus himself back on his revenge by working himself up into a rage against Claudius through his attack on his mother's morals. The height of his fury in the Closet scene comes not when he is taking his mother to task but when he imagines Claudius taking over his father's place as her husband and as Denmark's king:

> 'A murderer and a villain,
> A slave that is not twentieth part the tithe
> Of your precedent lord, a vice of kings,
> A cutpurse of the empire and the rule …'

45

This is the point where the Ghost intervenes. After this, we see a calmer, more balanced Hamlet, after he has partly restored his relationship with his mother:

50

> 'Once more good night,
> And when you are desirous to be blessed,
> I'll blessing beg of you.'

According to this argument, Hamlet is only able to get things back in perspective and return to his revenge because he has 'burned out' from his system the poison of his mother's wickedness and heard her repentance for it: 55

> 'Thou turn'st mine eyes into my very soul,
> And there I see such black and grained spots
> As will not leave their tinct.'

He talks about being a 'scourge and minister' in this scene. Being a 'minister' to Gertrude seems to allow him to go on without diversion to concentrate on being a 'scourge' to Claudius. Therefore we could say that he is not *distracted* from his revenge by concerning himself with his mother but that he becomes more single-minded about it as a result of his interview with her, as he shows in the scene shortly after when he decides: 60 65

> 'O from this time forth,
> My thoughts be bloody, or be nothing worth.'

The difference between the Hamlet who promised to 'sweep' to revenge in Act I and the Hamlet who actually does it in Act V becomes clear if we compare him with Laertes. Laertes wants only revenge for his father, a purely private and personal revenge: 70

> 'O thou vile king,
> Give me my father.'

On the other hand, Hamlet in Act V is not acting any longer for himself alone, either towards his mother or his father. He sees himself now as an instrument of Providence who must purge the whole world of Claudius's villainy: 75

> '… is't not perfect conscience
> To quit him with this arm? And is't not to be damned,
> To let this canker of our nature come
> In further evil?'

He says 'our' nature, not 'my' nature. Hamlet has come to see that there are more important things involved in ridding human life of its Claudiuses than a mother's sins or even a father's murder. All that matters is to put himself at the service of the 'divinity that shapes our ends', to act on behalf of humanity as a whole against the sort of evil that Claudius represents: 'The readiness is all.' 80

I would agree, therefore, that Hamlet's shock and disillusionment at finding out about his mother is a step on the way to him finding out about life in general, how evil it can be, and discovering a role for himself to remove this evil. In order to reach this point, he has both to come to terms with Gertrude's 'rank corruption' and to kill the 'incestuous, murderous, damned Dane', as he swore to his father's Ghost that he would. But beyond this, he has to be 'constant to my purposes' and be 'ready' to act on the part of mankind in general, not just for himself. 85 90

MARKING GRID 1996

Reproduced by permission of the Associated Examining Board

GRADE	LEVEL	MARKS	TEXTUAL GRASP AND APPRECIATION	CONVEYING THE TEXT (AND ANSWERING RELEVANTLY)	QUALITY OF EXPRESSION
U	1	1–3	Narrative approach with frequent misreadings.	Mere assertion of points of view. Often irrelevant answer.	Frequent weaknesses of expression. Excessive, aimless quotation. Misunderstood technical terms.
N	1	4–6	Merely accurate storytelling. A skimpy reading.	Difficulty in engaging with question. Assertive comments largely underdeveloped and unsupported.	Simple expression. Flawed, but conveying basic ideas. Paraphrase plus lengthy quotation. Unassimilated notes.
E	2	7–8	Response to surface features of text. Basic and generalised but usually accurate response.	Some awareness of effect of text on selves. An attempt to use specific details to support points made.	Expression generally able to convey ideas. Greater variety of vocabulary and sentence structure. Paraphrase with some embedded ideas. Quotation often overlong. Technical terms or unassimilated notes may be intrusive.
D	2	9–10	Some awareness of implicit meaning. Straightforward approach. Response to obvious contrasts and comparisons.	Can explain moods and feelings in text. Becoming aware of effect on reader of scene or events. At least implicit relevance to question.	Adequate expression matching understanding. More sophisticated vocabulary; structure of response can be identified. Quotation probably overlong but sometimes analysed. Fair grasp of technical terms and some ability to use notes.
C	3	11–13	Beginnings of appreciation of language and style. Secure knowledge and understanding of text. Awareness of subtlety. Closer reading becomes obvious.	Can see alternative interpretations and/or pursue strong personal response. Analysing. Exploring. Clearly aware of effect on reader of scene or event. Coherent, shaped and relevant response.	Expression clear and controlled. Paraphrase rare. Well structured with links between sentences and paragraphs. Wide vocabulary. Neat and purposeful use of short quotation as part of structured argument. Technical terms and assimilated notes become integral part of informed personal response.
B	3	14–15	*Answers in this category will have some of the following characteristics in addition to all those in Level 3*		
A	4	16–20	Insight. Conceptualised response. Confident exploration of ideas, language, style. Autonomy as reader.	Overview. Mastery of detail of text. Originality.	Mastery of structure. Confidence in expression. Rarely at a loss for the right word. Skilful use of quotation and close analysis of it. Technical terms and secondary sources enhance response to text.

8.3

Practising the basics of written argument

This section asks you to put into practice what you have learned from sections 8.1 and 8.2 about how to plan and write an argued essay at A level.

The texts you will use are two very short stories comparable in subject matter and style. (They also provide useful practice material for the 'unseen'). Depending on your present degree of confidence in arguing a case, you can choose to work on one or both of them.

Now read the stories through, twice, before following the instructions on page 203.

Now read the stories through, twice, before following the instructions on page 203.

>—⊹—◇—⊹—≺

(A) The Breadwinner

by Leslie Halward

The parents of a boy of fourteen were waiting for him to come home with his first week's wages.

The mother had laid the table and was cutting some slices of bread and butter for tea. She was a little woman with a pinched face and a spare body, dressed in a blue blouse and skirt, the front of the skirt covered with a starched white apron. She looked tired   5 and frequently sighed heavily.

The father, sprawling inelegantly in an old armchair by the fireside, legs outstretched, was little too. He had watery blue eyes and a heavy brown moustache, which he sucked occasionally.

These people were plainly poor, for the room, though clean, was meanly furnished,   10 and the thick pieces of bread and butter were the only food on the table.

As she prepared the meal, the woman from time to time looked contemptuously at her husband. He ignored her, raising his eyebrows, humming, or tapping his teeth now and then with his finger-nails, making a pretence of being profoundly bored.

'You'll keep your hands off the money,' said the woman, obviously repeating   15 something that she had already said several times before. 'I know what'll happen to it if you get hold of it. He'll give it to me. It'll pay the rent and but us a bit of food, and not go into the till at the nearest public-house.'

'You shut your mouth!' said the man, quietly.

'I'll not shut my mouth!' cried the woman, in a quick burst of anger. 'Why should I   20 shut my mouth? You've been boss here for long enough. I put up with it when you were bringing money into the house, but I'll not put up with it now. You're nobody here. Understand? *Nobody*. I'm boss and he'll hand the money to me!'

'We'll see about that,' said the man, leisurely poking the fire. Nothing more was said for about five minutes.   25

Then the boy came in. He did not look older than ten or eleven years. He looked absurd in long trousers. The whites of his eyes against his black face gave him a startled expression.

The father got to his feet.

'Where's the money?' he demanded.   30

The boy looked from one to the other. He was afraid of his father. He licked his pale lips.

'Come on now,' said the man. 'Where's the money?'

'Don't give it to him,' said the woman. 'Don't give it to him, Billy. Give it to me.'

The father advanced on the boy, his teeth showing in a snarl under his big moustache. 35

'Where's the money?' he almost whispered.

The boy looked him straight in the eyes.

'I lost it,' he said.

'You – *what*?' cried his father. 40

'I lost it,' the boy repeated.

The man began to shout and wave his hands about.

'Lost it! *Lost it!* What are you talking about? How could you lose it?'

'It was in a packet,' said the boy, 'a little envelope. I lost it.'

'Where did you lose it?' 45

'I don't know. I must have dropped it in the street.'

'Did you go back and look for it?'

The boy nodded. 'I couldn't find it,' he said.

The man made a noise in his throat, half grunt, half moan – the sort of noise that an animal would make. 50

'So you lost it, did you?' he said. He stepped back a couple of paces and took off his belt – a wide, thick belt with a heavy brass buckle. 'Come here', he said.

The boy, biting his lower lip so as to keep back the tears, advanced, and the man raised his arm. The woman, motionless until that moment, leapt forward and seized it. Her husband, finding strength in his blind rage, pushed her aside easily. He brought the 55 belt down on the boy's back. He beat him unmercifully about the body and legs. The boy sank to the floor, but did not cry out.

When the man had spent himself, he put on the belt and pulled the boy to his feet.

'Now you'll get off to bed,' he said.

'The lad wants some food,' said the woman. 60

'He'll go to bed. Go and wash yourself.'

Without a word the boy went into the scullery and washed his hands and face. When he had done this he went straight upstairs.

The man sat down at the table, ate some bread and butter and drank two cups of tea. The woman ate nothing. She sat opposite him, never taking her eyes from his face, 65 looking with hatred at him. Just as before, he took no notice of her, ignored her, behaved as if she were not there at all.

When he had finished the meal he went out.

Immediately he had shut the door the woman jumped to her feet and ran upstairs to the boy's room. 70

He was sobbing bitterly, his face buried in the pillow. She sat on the edge of the bed and put her arms about him, pressed him close to her breast, ran her fingers through his disordered hair, whispered endearments, consoling him. He let her do this, finding comfort in her caresses, relief in his own tears.

After a while his weeping ceased. He raised his head and smiled at her, his wet eyes 75 bright. Then he put his hand under the pillow and withdrew a small dirty envelope.

'Here's the money,' he whispered.

She took the envelope and opened it and pulled out a long strip of paper with some figures on it – a ten shilling note and sixpence.

(B) ## The Examination Result

by Alun Williams

Happened about thirty years ago. I was eleven. We were just the five brothers at home: Cornelius, Emlyn, Emrys, Edwin and myself. My mother had died when I was two and I remembered nothing of her. There was no photograph of her in the house. My father, during the three years he survived, had destroyed them all to blunt the stab of recollection.

This fact had a curious effect on Cornelius. He saw it as the chief defeat of his life and made sure that Emrys, Emlyn and Edwin won their scholarships and made their way to the Grammar School. But it was on me that he centred his greatest hopes. He said that we four would blaze a trail of glory through the Grammar School with me providing the brightest flames at the rear, the last and best.

Cornelius had started a small business and by means of working from dawn to midnight was doing quite well. Cornelius was a very bright lad. He had won a scholarship to the Grammar School, but had been unable to take it up because mother's illness ate up the money in the house and made my father ignore everything except her.

Each evening after work or at slack periods during the hours when I helped him in the shop he checked on the state of my English and arithmetic. He brought me a little library of good books and saw that I read them. 'I'm willing to work in that shop,' he would say. 'For you I would work right through the night, clean the floor of the potato shed with my own body, but don't you let me down, any of you. That's all I ask.' His eyes would settle, green and intense, on me. 'You especially.'

And so we came to the spring of the year in which I was to sit the scholarship examination for Grammar School. The golden weather came soon that year and Cornelius kept me back from the lovely beckoning slopes on which I wanted to play with my friends.

'Time for that later', he said. 'I do without things I want, a lot of things. So can you with a prize like that at stake.' I can still see the strain and sadness on his face as he said that. I heard later that he told the girl he was friendly with that he would not marry until I, the youngest of the brothers, had completed a course at the University, ten or eleven years to go. She said could not wait so long and left him.

I got wound up with anxiety a week before the examination. I had violent stomach cramp. At school I would sit without a word in the corner of the concrete-covered yard, not even lifting my head when my friends crowded round me and told me to stop being moody. I said nothing about this to Cornelius in case he might think I was making excuses in advance.

On the day of the examination, every inch of my being was in a turmoil. The pain got right into the nib and made it blunder foolishly. I made every mistake in arithmetic and spelling within reach. The exam was held in the art room of the Grammar School. The walls were hung with plaster casts of tigers' mouths and human lips, utterly silent and utterly threatening. As I left the room at the end of the afternoon, even the air through which I walked seemed to crumble in ruin.

It was on a Friday that our headmaster, old Mr Robias, ordered the whole school to be brought into the main hall. He said that school had had a triumph. We had twice as many pupils on the list as any other school in the area.

He read out the names. My senses picked up every speck of sensation as the loud, proud baritone voice boomed out its message. My name was not called.

I was the first out of the hall. I ran alone on to the hillside that rose steeply behind the street in which I lived. I sat down, my back tight against a small wild apple tree that had a hole in it into which my back fitted. It had been mine since early childhood. It was where I went whenever I felt too angry, lost or cheated. My eyes were fixed on the back of our house, on the kitchen door through which Cornelius would pass at a quarter to six when he came home for tea.

I grew hungry. When Cornelius came into sight and put his hand on the latch of the kitchen door it had the effect on me of a summons. I got up and made my way down to the house, my mind and heart empty of everything except my fear.

When I went in, my brothers were seated at the table, eating in silence. Not one of them looked up as I came in. I sat on my chair. There were pockets of thunder in all four corners of the kitchen. I was excited by the sight of food but my fingers could not bring themselves to approach it.

'Well?' said Cornelius.

'I didn't pass,' I said. I wanted to run, but my legs had worked themselves round the legs of the chair and would not budge.

Cornelius stood up and threw his knife and fork on the plate with a terrifying clatter. He leaned over and hit my face with his full strength. The blow toppled me off the chair. I heard a few vague little sounds of protest from Emrys, Emlyn and Edwin. I shouted something angry, a formless childish oath that caught up a thousandth of the rage and bewilderment I felt.

Cornelius raised his arm again, but I slithered along the floor and shot my hand up to the latch of the door. The iron latch had been worn thin and sharp by age and use. I felt it cut my skin. But the door opened and I rushed out. No one followed.

60

65

Choose to write on one of the following. Take as much time as you feel you need. Plan and draft your work before producing a final version, which should be between three and four pages long.

- On 'The Breadwinner'

  1. Compare the behaviour of the three characters in the story. Which of them does the author present the most sympathetically and which the least? Justify your opinion by close reference to the way the story is written.

  2. 'The conflict at the heart of the story is not between Billy and his father but between his parents.' Do you share this view? Justify your opinion by close reference to the way the story is written.

- On 'The Examination Result'

  1. Is Cornelius presented in a completely unfavourable light or are we asked to sympathise with him to some extent? Justify your opinion by close reference to the way the story is written.

  2. 'The conflict at the heart of the story is not between Cornelius and Alun (the author): it is within Alun himself.' Do you share this view? Justify your opinion by close reference to the way the story is written.

- On both stories together

  'Each family is working out its own problems and frustrations through the son. The boys themselves are blameless.' Do you agree? Make close reference to the way the stories are written to support your opinion.

Assessing yourself and getting feedback

On a separate sheet of paper, describe in confidence to your teacher any difficulties you find in constructing or conducting written argument. These might arise from the task you have just completed or be of a more general kind, or both. It is sometimes easier to express them in the form of questions.

Hand in this sheet along with your essay. Your teacher will respond in writing to the specific points you raise.

Producing the evidence: how to use reference and quotation

No essay question can be successfully 'argued' in general terms alone: evidence from the text is always required. However, if reference and quotation are not used appropriately they can actually obscure an argument – or at least be irrelevant to your 'case' – instead of assisting it. This section demonstrates how to use 'quotes' as an integral part of building up an argued essay. It is one of the most important A level skills you need to acquire – and, like every other aspect of your ability to argue on paper, it can be learned.

Use versus usefulness

Good argued essays use close reference to the text in order to support, or back up, key points in the development of an argument. Poor argued essays use close reference to the text as a substitute for any real argument at all. Below are examples of each, drawn from A level exam work.

Example A

> 'The Lake Isle of Innisfree' gives a romantic view of Ireland: 'There midnight's all a-glimmer and noon a purple glow'. Yeats's idea of paradise is 'a small cabin of clay and wattles made'.

Consider why the quotations here add *nothing* to the candidate's statements about Yeats's 'romantic view of Ireland' or his 'idea of paradise'.

Example B

> In 'Byzantium', Yeats visualises the afterlife and encourages us to consider the unity of the natural and spiritual worlds. The 'fury and the mire of human veins' is contrasted with a spiritual image, 'Shade more than man, more image than a shade'. Here Yeats is suggesting that our physical body is actually a way of imprisoning the soul and that, with death, the soul can finally become free.

Consider why the quotations here are used both to illustrate and develop the candidate's commentary.

Going round in circles

Some uses of quotation gain credit for illustrating a statement but fail to carry forward the point being made to the next stage in the argument. Consider why, in the example below, quotation is used in a merely 'circular' way rather than in a 'progressive' one.

> Throughout the play, Tennessee Williams presents Blanche Dubois as unstable, vulnerable and scared: '(stage direction) She is seated in a tense, hunched position.' This presents the audience with the scared and vulnerable side of Blanche. Williams's choice of words allows the audience to see that she is scared.

Making quotations work for you

Examiners will reward you highly for providing quotations if you use them for the reasons listed in the table on page 205 under 'Plus'. They will not reward you at all if you use them for the reasons listed under 'Minus'.

Plus	Minus
To illustrate a *specific* point – not a general one – in your argument	To show that you have read and remembered the text
To take your analysis of the subject matter and/or style of the text a step further	To paraphrase or summarise what the text is about
To show that you can integrate details from . the text into your argument about some aspects of the novel/play/poem as a whole	To let the author's words do your arguing for you instead of doing it yourself
To show that you are able to make a personal response to the author's style and use of language	To show that you have remembered your teacher's advice to 'use quotes' in the exam

For future reference, make notes on what you have learned from this section so far about the importance of building quotation into your writing.

Doing it well: two demonstrations

Below are extracts from two A level essays. Consider why an examiner would give both of them high marks for the way they employ quotations.

>─┤◄►─○─◄►├◄

Example A

In his poem 'The Flea', Donne is trying to persuade a woman who is reluctant to have sex with him to actually do so. At the beginning, his tone is a mixture of mock-serious and playful:

> 'Mark but this flea, and mark in this
> How little that which thou deny'st me is.'   5

His comment to the woman, 'Mark but …' and 'mark in this' suggests someone putting forward a rational argument. He is using persuasive tactics based on logic rather than flattery or force, as we might expect. The emphasis in the second line falls on 'How little', in order to underplay the importance of the woman's virginity.

Donne then develops his argument that sex is not such a big issue by turning his   10
attention to what the flea has done, which is bitten them both:

> 'It sucked me first, and now sucks thee,
> And in this flea our two bloods mingled be.'

On the level of argument, Donne is still trying to seduce the woman by logic: just as, if they do go to bed together, their bodily fluids will 'mingle', so they 'mingle' in the flea.   15
In fact, he says, they have already done so: 'sucked me' … 'now sucks thee'. Mischievously, he is suggesting that having sex will therefore be merely a sort of action replay of the way their 'two bloods' have already mixed together. The logic of this is pretty weak, but Donne is now trying another seduction tactic as well by using language with sexual overtones ('sucked … sucks') to tempt the woman into bed.   20

Example B

Cathy tells Nelly Dean about her love for Heathcliff by comparing it with her love for Edgar which is 'like the foliage in the woods'. She means that it won't last, it will change just as winter 'changes the trees' by killing off their leaves, etc. Like Edgar with his money and posh house, the 'foliage' may be attractive on the outside, however it has nothing deep down to keep it going. This is different with her love for Heathcliff. He is   5
not attractive, 'a source of little visible delight', because he has nothing to give her except love. But Cathy thinks his and her love 'resembles the eternal rocks beneath', meaning it will last and be forever ('eternal'). Rocks 'beneath' ground can't be seen but they lie very deep and they are 'necessary' as a foundation for the landscape. This is how Cathy sees her love for Heathcliff, being 'necessary'. She is like the landscape, she   10
would fall apart if her eternal rocks, i.e. Heathcliff, were as she says 'annihilated'.

One of the reasons why these students use quotations well is that they build them into the structure of their own sentences. As a final thought about 'quoting', consider why this is an effective strategy when arguing a case.

Opening up: what to include in your first paragraph, and why

Why first paragraphs matter more than you think

It is an over-statement to say that examiners know by the time they have read your first paragraph what mark they will give to the whole essay – an over-statement, but not by much. This is because first paragraphs usually indicate:

- whether you are going to answer the question asked or the question you would like to be asked;
- whether you are going to argue or merely 'tell the story';
- whether you are going to write your own essay or a 'prepared' one based on someone else's material;
- whether or not you have anything interesting, intelligent or relevant to say.

With these points in mind, consider what the opening paragraphs below from A level essays suggest about the kind of argument that is going to follow. Whether or not you know the texts concerned is immaterial. Give each of them a mark between 1 and 5.

1. What connections do you see between the three groups of characters – the lovers; the Athenian workmen; the fairies – in *A Midsummer Night's Dream*?

    At first sight, there is little connection between these three sets of characters. They come from completely different worlds. However, they all contribute to the theme of love, particularly its folly and its fickleness. At the end of the play it is important that characters from all walks of life are brought together in the Duke's palace, showing unity and helping the play to have a happy ending in the traditions of comedy.

2. Pope's poetry has been described as 'superficial'. What qualities in 'The Rape of the Lock' and 'Epistle to a Lady' in your opinion give them depth?

    Pope says at the start of 'The Rape of the Lock': 'What mighty causes rise from trivial things'. However, he has his tongue in his cheek, the poem is not really trivial because it has a lot more depth to it than meets the eye. It is showing how young women think themselves to be more important than they really are. Pope's way of showing this is known as mock Epic, and this is what gives depth to his poetry.

3. 'Wordsworth is better at description than narrative.' Examine this view.

    I will show in this essay that Wordsworth is better at description than narrative. This is mainly because 'The Prelude' Books 1 and 2 doesn't really tell a story, it is autobiographical, but it is full of brilliant descriptions like the famous skating passage where you can almost hear the sound of skates on the ice: 'All shod with steel we hissed across the polished ice'. There are a lot of 's' sounds in this description which makes you really hear what is happening, typical of Wordsworth's skill of description.

4. How important is Mr Emerson in *A Room with a View*?

    Mr Emerson is in many ways the novel's main character as far as its themes are concerned. He represents a liberal, enlightened attitude to life, in stark contrast to the narrow-minded conventionality of characters like Charlotte Bartlett and (particularly)

Cecil. It is between these two 'views' of how to live a fulfilled life that Lucy is caught in the first half of the book, and it is Mr Emerson who opens her eyes so that she has 'room' to choose between them in the second. The fact that, as George's father, he actively encourages his son's courtship of Lucy, and that she ultimately commits herself to George, underlines Mr Emerson's importance. He is the truth-teller in a novel about the importance of being true to one's own instinctive feelings:

'Yes, for we fight for more than Love or Pleasure: there is Truth. Truth counts, Truth does count.'

5. Explore the purpose and effects of Miller's interweaving of past and present in *Death of a Salesman*.

Arthur Miller's use of flashback sequences is very effective. It has several reasons. First it shows how Willy's mind is growing confused by mixing together things from the past and present. Secondly, it helps us to see the importance to Willy of Ben, a figure of the past. Finally it proves that the play is happening more in Willy's mind than in the outside world, which is why the house is described as 'transparent'.

Introducing through summary

'Summary' suggests a conclusion. In A level essays, it is more useful when it comes at the beginning rather than at the end. In other words, your first paragraph should summarise the main points of the argument you will then go on to write. 'One point per sentence' throughout the first paragraph is a safe rule-of-thumb. This is why the example above on *A Room with a View* is excellent; why the example on *A Midsummer Night's Dream* is just adequate; and why the example on Wordsworth is very weak.

Improving your own practice in writing 'first paragraphs'

- When you draft an A level essay, get into the habit of writing (not planning) your first paragraph last. Work out why for yourself.

- As you revise any text, brainstorm first paragraphs on imagined essay questions round the class. Support, question and constructively criticise each other's contributions. Sharing the task gives everyone confidence.

- Especially as the exam approaches, set yourself (if your teacher doesn't!) ten or twelve possible questions on each of your set texts. First practise writing a full first paragraph (between six and ten lines); then practise *thinking* it. At the point when you can do the latter consistently well, you are ready to face the most difficult challenge of an A level examination: writing 'to time' a sequence of essays, each of which is based on arguments relevant to the question asked.

Chapter 9 'I know what I want to say, but ...': how to write what you mean

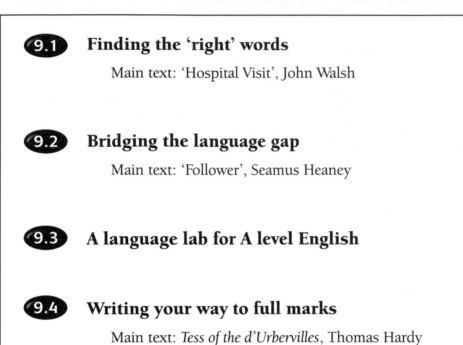

9.1 Finding the 'right' words

Main text: 'Hospital Visit', John Walsh

9.2 Bridging the language gap

Main text: 'Follower', Seamus Heaney

9.3 A language lab for A level English

9.4 Writing your way to full marks

Main text: *Tess of the d'Urbervilles*, Thomas Hardy

Finding the 'right' words

Read the poem below. Then write a critical analysis of it, paying particular attention to the poet's observations and feelings while he is in the hospital. You should comment on his choice of language and on such matters as imagery, verse form, sound and rhythm.

Do this task under examination conditions. You are allowed fifteen minutes reading time and one hour to write your analysis.

Hospital Visit

The hospital smell
combs my nostrils
as they go bobbing along
green and yellow corridors.

What seems like a corpse   5
is trundled into a lift and vanishes
heavenwards.

I will not feel, I will not
feel, until
I have to.   10

Nurses walk lightly, swiftly,
here and up and down and there,
their slender waists miraculously
carrying their burden
of so much pain, so   15
many deaths, their eyes
still clear after
so many farewells.

Ward 7. She lies
in a white cave of forgetfulness.   20
A withered hand
trembles on its stalk. Eyes move
behind eyelids too heavy
to raise. Into an arm wasted
of colour, a glass fang is fixed,   25
not guzzling but giving.
And between her and me
distance shrinks until there is none left
but the distance of pain that neither she nor I
can cross.   30

She smiles a little at this
black figure in her white cave
who clumsily rises
in the round swimming waves of a bell
and dizzily goes off, leaving behind only   35
books that will not be read
and fruitless fruits.

John Walsh

Evaluating your own work

Before handing in what you have written, add to your script:

- an indication of what you found most difficult, particularly in terms of writing down your responses to the poem. Show this in whatever way seems clearest: underlining, notes in the margin, comments at the end, and so on;

- a request for your analysis either to be given an A level mark/grade or not.

You may find it helpful to take this a step further and write on a separate sheet of paper an honest statement – which your teacher will read in confidence – of how you felt while doing this task. Similar self-reviews by A level students who have preceded you include:

> I CAN'T do this! It sends me completely brain dead. I just stared at the poem for ages, then at the instructions, then at the poem again … I don't know what to say about 'his choice of language' (isn't that his business anyway!) – are you supposed to say something really profound like 'his use of words is very good'? I don't suppose they'd put it on A level if it wasn't good, would they?

> If I knew how to plan what to write, I think I'd be OK (more or less!) – but I DON'T know (how to plan, I mean), so everything I put down gets mixed up with everything else … HELP!!

Post mortem

As a class, discuss frankly with your teacher the written work you have done on 'Hospital Visit'. This should take place not less than a week after it was handed in.

Follow your own agenda. Your conversation might cover:

- the difference between being able to talk well and write well about literature, especially poetry, at A level – and how to close the 'gap';

- whether there is a 'special' language that examiners expect you to use when they ask you to attempt this kind of exercise;

- what sort of things you should be looking for when you have to comment on 'such matters as imagery, verse form, sound and rhythm'.

A personal action plan

Following this discussion, draw up your own action plan for improving your level of performance in writing a critical analysis. Expend real thought and time on this; it is by far the most important self-help strategy you can employ in order to make progress.

When you have finished, show the plan to your teacher. She or he will almost certainly be able to add important points to it, or modify the ones you have made.

Bridging the language gap

This section contains an A level coursework essay on the poem 'Follower' by Seamus Heaney. It was written by a student in Year 12 during the autumn half-term.

Read the poem to yourself, twice. Then immediately afterwards read the student's essay on it.

>—|—◆>—·O·—<◆—|—<

Follower

My father worked with a horse-plough,
His shoulders globed like a full sail strung
Between the shafts and the furrow.
The horses strained at this clicking tongue.

An expert. He would set the wing　　　　　　　　5
And fit the bright steel-pointed sock.
The sod rolled over without breaking.
At the headrig, with a single pluck

Of reins, the sweating team turned round
And back into the land. His eye　　　　　　　　10
Narrowed and angled at the ground,
Mapping the furrow exactly.

I stumbled in his hob-nailed wake,
Fell sometimes on the polished sod;
Sometimes he rode me on his back,　　　　　　　15
Dipping and rising to his plod.

I wanted to grow up and plough,
To close one eye, stiffen my arm.
All I ever did was follow
In his broad shadow round the farm.　　　　　　20

I was a nuisance, tripping, falling,
Yapping always. But today
It is my father who keeps stumbling
Behind me, and will not go away.

Seamus Heaney

>—|—◆>—·O·—<◆—|—<

A Critical Appreciation of 'Follower'

This poem is about the relationship of Seamus Heaney and his father. When he was young, Heaney looked up to his father, he seemed to him a good farmer and a strong man. He wanted to 'grow up and plough' like him. But at the end of the poem, Heaney's father seems to have grown old and useless, Heaney doesn't admire him any more and just wants him to 'go away'.　　　　5

　　In the poem, their relationship changes. At first, Heaney sees his father as 'an expert', because he can do all the jobs on the farm in such a perfect way:

　　'The sod rolled over without breaking.'

This shows he was good at ploughing. He could work out how to plough a field without measuring it, just by looking at it and taking it from there:　　　　10

'His eye
Narrowed and angled at the ground
Mapping the furrow exactly.'

As a boy, Heaney obviously loved his father, they were very close. He used to go out
working with him in the fields: 15

'He rode me on his back'

showing the closeness there was between them. Like a lot of boys, he wanted to be
like his father when he grew up:

'I wanted to grow up and plough'.

Although he was a 'nuisance', his father put up with him, probably because he was   20
his son and also too young to do much to help.

   At the end of the poem, things have changed, though. Probably because his
father is now too old to work, Heaney thinks he gets in the way:

'But today
It is my father who keeps stumbling   25
Behind me'.

He has no patience with his father because he interferes with the work on the farm.
He seems to wish he was dead, 'and will not go away'.

   In my opinion, Heaney doesn't come out of the poem very well. His father was
very kind to him as a boy, very patient, and let him follow in his 'broad shadow' as   30
if he was protecting him. But at the end he doesn't give back to his father what he
got from him as a child. I think in the poem Heaney is trying to say that this is typical
of the younger generation who are often ungrateful to their parents. This is probably
the main theme of the poem. It could also be about the difference between being
a farmer like his father and being a poet which Heaney is. Maybe he thinks that   35
farming is a bit beneath him because it is manual work, whereas writing poetry
needs academic qualifications. To me, Heaney seems a snob.

⊱┼◄⟩┄○┄⟨►┼⊰

Evaluating someone else's work

Make your own assessment of the essay on 'Follower'. Use the following yardsticks:

- How clearly has the poem been understood?

- Are key points adequately supported by quotation from the text?

- Does the analysis show a strong element of personal response to the poem?

- Does the style in which the essay is written indicate fluency and a wide range of vocabulary?

- Is response to the poem's meaning combined with a detailed response to the poet's style and
  technique?

Combining these five yardsticks together, award the essay an A level grade on the scale A to F
(F = Fail).

Now compare your assessment with (a) that of at least one other person in your class, and (b) that
of your teacher. If there are differences, discuss the reasons for them.

A language lab for A level English

At some point during the course, virtually every student concludes that the two most difficult challenges of A level English are (a) commenting on an author's style and technique, and (b) finding a suitable language in which to do so.

Some time ago, a Year 13 English class began their A level year by building up (with assistance from their teachers) a 'language lab' to help them meet these challenges. The result of their work is reproduced below.

If you find this helpful in extending the range of your own written expression, try, as a class, to develop your own version of it. Build it up gradually, using a class file from which individual photocopies can be made. The examples you include in it will carry more weight if they are taken directly from your own essays and other forms of written response to literature.

Common expressions: single words

Use these words as alternatives to:

puts over / gets across / brings out

(a) **evokes**, as in 'Yeats evokes an impression of peacefulness by the way in which he …'

Or 'Donne's use of a dramatic opening to this poem evokes the feeling that …'

(b) **conveys**, as in 'Emily Brontë conveys the impression that Heathcliff is an outsider by …'

Or 'This whole scene from *Antony and Cleopatra* conveys a strong sense of pathos.'

(c) **suggests**, as in 'Lawrence suggests that humans do not value natural life by the way in which he …'

Or 'The slow passage of time is suggested by the halting, laboured rhythm of the closing lines of the poem.'

(d) **depicts**, as in 'The opening paragraph depicts a scene of bleak desolation.'

Or 'Chaucer depicts the Wife of Bath as an aggressively independent woman.'

(e) **portrays**, as in 'Shakespeare portrays King Lear as a man more sinned against than sinning.'

Or 'In the sleep-walking scene, Lady Macbeth is portrayed as a woman whose mind is tortured by guilt and fear.'

makes clear / gets clear / shows clearly

(a) **evident**, as in 'Dickens's sympathy for Joe is evident from the way he describes …'

Or 'It is evident that Tess is presented by Hardy as a "pure woman" because …'

(b) **focuses**, as in 'Tennessee Williams focuses on Blanche's restless insecurity by …'

Or 'Our attention is focused on the way in which Macbeth becomes increasingly isolated.'

(c) **clarifies**, as in 'Jane Austen clarifies the reader's attitude towards Fanny Price when she …'

Or 'Dryden's scornful feelings towards Thomas Shadwell are further clarified by his use of the sarcastic phrase …'

(d) **apparent**, as in 'The impression that life is futile is made apparent by the metaphor comparing existence with …'

Or 'Iago's real feelings towards Othello become apparent at the point when …'

carries on further / keeps going / adds to

(a) **develops**, as in 'The poem's theme is developed further by the way that …'

(b) **sustains**, as in 'Ted Hughes sustains the mood of violence and aggression in the second stanza by …'

(c) **elaborates**, as in 'Forster elaborates on Lucy's naive and inexperienced response to life when he …'

(d) **extends**, as in 'The imagery of battle is extended by the simile comparing Belinda to …'

made stronger / made to stand out / made more obvious

(a) **reinforces**, as in 'Romeo's death reinforces the impression of two lovers being at the mercy of fate.'

(b) **enhances**, as in 'In *Waiting for Godot*, Beckett enhances the sense of hopelessness by …'

(c) **intensifies**, as in 'The way in which the Athenian workmen perform their play intensifies the mood of comic release.'

(d) **highlights**, as in 'Jonson highlights Sir Epicure Mammon's obsession with fabulous riches by …'

(e) **underlines**, as in 'Milton underlines his determination to "justify the ways of God to men" by describing …'

coming before / coming after / coming one after the other / next to last / next to

(a) **preceding**, as in 'In the preceding stanza, Sylvia Plath has described how terrified of her father she feels.'

(b) **subsequent**, as in 'During subsequent scenes, the convicts show a growing enthusiasm for staging the play.'

(c) **consecutive**, as in 'The three consecutive comic chapters lighten the mood of an otherwise sombre novel.'

(d) **penultimate**, as in 'The poem's ending highlights the theme Owen has explored in the penultimate stanza.'

(e) **juxtaposes**, as in 'In order to bring out the contrast between them, Marvell juxtaposes these two key ideas.'

Common expressions: contexts

Use these words accurately by looking at the context.

repetition / reiteration

(a) 'The poet's frequent repetition of the soft '1' sounds evokes a feeling of …'

(b) 'The reiteration of the phrase "Lord have mercy on us" conveys the writer's fear of imminent death'.

(c) 'The reiterated adjective "mellow" enhances the impression of …'

emphasis / emphasises

(a) 'At the opening of the play, the emphasis is on Willy Loman's sense of confusion.'

(b) 'Later on in the poem, the emphasis changes; it now falls on the way in which …'

(c) 'As the novel develops, Lawrence emphasises the fact that each generation faces a different set of challenges.'

compare / contrast

(a) 'The tree is compared with a skeleton to indicate that the whole world of nature seems to be dying.'

(b) 'Hamlet's feelings about his father's death are strongly contrasted with those of Claudius and Gertrude.'

(c) 'There is a sustained contrast in the novel between those characters who are capable of compassion and those who are not.'

explicit / implicit

(a) 'By showing that Macbeth is a warrior, Shakespeare makes his lack of physical fear quite explicit.'

(b) 'Implicit in Lady Macbeth's comment "What beast wasn't then / That made you break this enterprise to me?" is the accusation that her husband does not possess manly courage.'

Commenting on imagery: simile, metaphor, personification, symbolism

Golden rules

(a) NEVER make vague generalisations, as in 'There is a lot of imagery in this poem.'

(b) ALWAYS be specific – explain the meaning of an image and describe its effects, as in 'The image comparing two lovers with the feet of a pair of compasses shows how, though separated by distance, they remain emotionally and spiritually linked together.'

(c) Best verbs to describe a writer's use of imagery: 'The poet **employs** a simile comparing x with y …'

Or 'The military metaphor **used** in the first line of the speech is part of a pattern of imagery which extends through the whole scene.'

Simile – acceptable usages include:

(a) 'The poet uses a simile comparing his lover's eyes with the sun to suggest the way in which she illuminates his life.'

(b) 'The simile comparing imagination with a flash of lightning makes clear the sudden, unpredictable way in which a mental connection between two ideas can be made.'

Metaphor – acceptable usages include:

(a) 'Hughes uses a metaphor to compare the effect of turbulent winds on the landscape with a wild stampede of cattle.'

(b) 'The sun is described metaphorically as "the eye of heaven".'

(c) 'Metaphorically speaking, the solid-seeming house is, under the assault of the storm, like a fine glass goblet which is fragile and easily shattered.'

(d) 'The metaphorical phrase "There's daggers in men's smiles" suggests that, beneath a façade of friendliness, no one can be trusted: anyone might be a dangerous traitor.'

Personification – acceptable usages include:

(a) 'The personified description of the house as "mean" and "slit-eyed" suggests that, like its owner, it conveys a feeling of miserliness and a lack of warmth.'

(b) 'The twigs are personified as "aged hands", evoking the impression that, like an old person's fingers, they are gnarled, thin and bony.'

Symbolism – acceptable usages include:

(a) 'The caged bird is a symbol of the captive imagination.'

(b) 'The sick rose symbolises the death of young love.'

(c) 'Symbolically, the grinning skeleton represents the triumph of death.'

(d) 'The fast-withering grass is symbolic of the transience of human life.'

Commenting on the sound of words

Golden rules

(a) NEVER generalise. The effects produced by sound will be local and specific; they will never apply to a whole poem or to the whole of a speech in a play.

(b) ALWAYS link comments on sound to your understanding of the meaning, following Alexander Pope's observation that 'The sound must seem an echo of the sense.'

(c) Distinguish between consonant and vowel sounds. Consonant sounds apply to all the letters of the alphabet except 'a', 'e', 'i', 'o' and 'u'.

Acceptable ways of commenting on the effect of word-sounds include:

(a) 'The hard "t" sound which is reiterated in the opening two lines reinforces the impression of the rough wind cutting through the "bladed atmosphere".'

(b) 'The succession of full, rounded vowel-sounds evokes a sense of rich spring growth. Together with the mellow "m" and "sh" sounds, they convey a feeling of ripe fulfilment in the world of nature.'

Useful adjectives

These adjectives are useful for describing the effects produced by certain vowel and certain consonant sounds. ALWAYS check their exact meaning.

Vowel sounds	Consonant sounds
broad / open	soft / mellow
clipped / terse	hard / harsh
drawn out / expansive	liquid / lilting
heavy / weighty / laboured	hushed / sibilant
rounded / flat	sonorous
thin / spare / taut	aggressive / vigorous
brisk / staccato	explosive / dynamic

Alliteration – acceptable usages include:

(a) 'The "f" sound is alliterated throughout these two lines, enhancing the impression of a boat moving swiftly through the water and creating flying foam as it slices the waves.'

(b) 'The alliterated "w", together with the weighty, dragging vowel sounds, has the effect of creating a mournful mood.'

(c) 'In the first stanza, the heavy alliteration of the "p" and "d" sounds adds to the impression of footsteps plodding relentlessly onwards.'

Onomatopoeia – acceptable usages include:

(a) 'The onomatopoeic word "thump" which ends this line suggests an aggressive knocking on the solid oak door.'

(b) 'The word "batter" in "Batter my heart" is onomatopoeic, giving the impression that Donne wants God to break forcefully through his own resistance to salvation from sin.'

Commenting on rhythm

Golden rules

(a) NEVER generalise. The effects produced by rhythm will be local and specific; they will never apply to a whole poem or to the whole of a speech in a play.

(b) ALWAYS link comments on rhythm to your understanding of the meaning. Writers, especially poets, use rhythm to reinforce the thoughts and feelings they wish to convey: any comment on rhythm that does not acknowledge this will be irrelevant.

(c) ALWAYS look for two aspects of rhythm as a starting-point for commenting on it – *speed* (or pace) and *variations* (or 'departures from regularity').

Acceptable usages include:

(a) 'The rhythm of the line is slowed down by the succession of long, drawn-out vowel sounds. This laboured pace reinforces the impression of exhaustion as the weary soldiers drag themselves back to the trenches.'

(b) 'The pace of these lines is accelerated by the brisk monosyllables ("skip", "flit", "jig") which help to evoke a mood of carefree enjoyment as the children play happily in the park.'

(c) 'In these heavily punctuated lines the rhythm is halting and tentative, reflecting the way in which Hamlet finds extreme difficulty in rousing himself to act.'

Adjectives for describing rhythm

Useful adjectives for describing the rhythm of a line, or a sequence of lines, include:

> disjointed, fragmented, laboured, pedestrian, halting, faltering, staccato, turbulent, lively, brisk, animated, swelling, smooth, even-paced, regular, fluid.

Adjectives best avoided include:

> flowing, jerky, choppy, fast.

Commenting on verse form or 'versification'

Golden rules

(a) NEVER make generalisations about the form of a whole poem. It is not a matter of analysis, merely of observation, to write: 'This poem is a sonnet ...' or 'The poem has seven stanzas ...' or 'Othello's speech is in blank verse ...' or 'This stanza rhymes ABAB ...' or 'There is a mixture of long and short lines in the poem ...' – and leave it at that.

(b) ALWAYS focus on the part rather than the whole – single, specific instances such as the effects of versification within a couplet, a line, or a half-line. As ever, relate the resulting comments clearly to meaning.

(c) The most common aspects of verse form on which comment is expected are: word order (or 'syntax'); line length; rhyme; and the poet's/playwright's use of punctuation and syllables. In practice, these will often overlap with each other; they will also frequently be linked with the effects of sound and rhythm (see above).

Example of comment on word order

> Pears from the boughs hung
> Golden, the street lay still and cool.

The poet places 'Golden' at the start of line two in order to emphasise the rich, burnished colour of the fruit, an effect heightened by the contrast with the 'still' and 'cool' street. In addition, the fact that 'Golden', with its two heavy syllables, follows an unpunctuated open-ended line indicates how the ripe fruit bends the bough from which it is hanging.

Example of comment on line length

> He sipped with his straight mouth,
> Softly drank through his straight gums, into his long slack body,
> Silently.

The first line is monosyllabic; its even, measured rhythm suggests the way in which the snake drinks in a relaxed and unhurried manner. The second line, with its broader and drawn-out vowel sounds, is far longer, giving an impression of the slow lengthy passage of water through the snake's seemingly endless body. The placing of the single word 'Silently' on a separate line draws attention to the aura of calm stillness surrounding the snake – and also suggests, perhaps, something sinister about the snake, as if, though now relaxed, its body is latent with potential power and violence.

Example of comment on rhyme

> Twenty-one years have passed away;
> Tomorrow is another day.

The rhyme here has the effect of drawing a contrast. In the first line, the poet reflects on the fleeting passage of time; his tone is melancholy and wistful, as though he is reproaching himself for wasting opportunities which have slipped by. In the second line, however, the tone changes to one of optimism and the poet makes a resolution to face the future with more determination. His sense that many years have 'passed away' is offset by his consoling awareness that there will be 'another day' in which to live more purposefully.

Example of comment on punctuation

> No, I'll not, carrion comfort, Despair, not feast on thee.

The tortured syntax of this line, with its heavy punctuation and reiteration of negatives ('No ... not ... not'), evokes the poet's anguished struggle to resist falling into despair. He holds back the word 'Despair' until half way through the line, as if by postponing naming it he will be more able to avoid it. The frequent punctuation gives to the line a disjointed rhythm, evoking the impression of a man wrestling in some spiritual vortex against an enemy which threatens to overwhelm him. The short, panting phrases reinforce this sense of bitter struggle, as if the effort of resistance all but exhausts him.

Example of comment on closed-ended (or 'end-stopped') lines

> The hands of the clock are still.
> Its eyes are blind.
> This house has died.

The heavy end-stop concluding each line creates an inert, lifeless rhythm. Together with the emphatic monosyllables, this helps to suggest the way in which time has conquered the house. The image of the stopped clock serves to reinforce the impression of a house at the mercy of time's tyranny.

Example of comment on open-ended (or 'run-on') lines

> No more it opened with all one end
> For teams that came by the stony road
> To drum on the floor with scurrying hooves
> And brush the mow with the summer load.

All the lines in this stanza are open-ended, the effect being to suggest the way in which the barn used to be a scene of busy, ceaseless activity. This impression is heightened by the brisk rhythm of 'scurrying hooves' and the way in which the tempo of each of the last three lines increases towards the line-ending.

Example of comment on caesura (or 'middle-stop')

> The girl was beautiful; now she has died.

The poet wishes to dwell on the girl's beauty, as he makes clear by the lingering stress given to 'beautiful' by its placing immediately before the caesura. The antithetical balance of clauses which the caesura creates in this line draws an effective contrast between the beauty of the girl in her prime and its absence now that she is dead.

Examples of comment on syllables

(a)   The fair breeze blew, the white foam flew …

The poet is describing a boat being forced through the water at high speed. The succession of monosyllabic words, with their expansive vowel sounds, gives the impression of swift, surging forward movement – an effect heightened by the internal rhyme on 'blew' and 'flew' and by the regular rhythm of the two clauses separated by a caesura. The effect is of strong, rhythmic gusts of wind propelling the boat onwards.

(b)   But now they drift on the still water,
          Mysterious, beautiful.

The poet, by his use of two consecutive polysyllabic adjectives, emphasises the co-existence of mystery and beauty he perceives in the wild swans: each word has the same syllabic structure as the other and the balancing caesura brings them into closer relationship. In addition, the polysyllables, with their light vowel sounds, evoke an impression of the way the swans move across the 'still water' in a smooth, apparently effortless way.

A spelling check-list

Words most commonly misspelt include:

alliterated	develops	ironic	reiterates
alliteration	echoes	ironically	repetition
alliterative	effective	lyrical	repetitive
archaic	emphasis	metaphor	rhyme
beginning	emphasises	metaphorical	rhyming
caesura	evocative	monosyllabic	rhythm
climactic	evokes	onomatopoeia	rhythmic
commentary	focused	pathos	simile
communicates	focuses	perceives	stanza
comparative	generalisation	personified	successive
convey	generalised	playwright	symbolises
corresponding	heightened	portrays	tragedy
description	imagery	reinforces	tragic

Use the space below to write down the words that *you* have trouble spelling, including the names of characters in your set texts.

Writing your way to full marks

The essay printed in this section was written by a Year 13 student in one hour under exam conditions. It earned the maximum possible mark – a more common occurrence than you (and some of your teachers!) might think.

The student is writing on Thomas Hardy's *Tess of the d'Urbervilles*. The question focuses on Chapter 11 of Phase the First: The Maiden. It will obviously be beneficial for you to read, or re-read, the chapter.

At this stage in the book, Tess has left her secluded rural village to work on Alec d'Urberville's estate. Alec, a wealthy libertine who lives purely for pleasure, has for some time been attempting to seduce her; Tess's rebuttals merely increase his determination to do so. In the previous chapter, Alec has 'rescued' Tess from a quarrel with one of his former lovers. In Chapter 11, he takes her on horseback to an ancient forest, The Chase, where Tess loses her virginity to him.

Comment on the way in which Hardy presents the episode in The Chase in Chapter 11. What importance do you think it has to the novel as a whole?

This chapter marks the point at which Tess becomes a 'Maiden no More'. From now on 'this beautiful feminine tissue, practically blank as snow as yet' is 'doomed to receive' the consequences of being a woman who has, in the eyes of 'the social law', sinned against Victorian morality. The child she gives birth to after Alec makes her pregnant is appropriately named Sorrow. What happens in The Chase starts off a chain of events   5
during which Tess, however hard she tries, is shadowed by 'sorrow' and can never escape from it for long. It is the turning-point in her life, the real beginning of her tragedy:

> 'An immeasurable social chasm was to divide our heroine's personality
> thereafter from that previous self of hers who stepped from her mother's   10
> door to try her fortune …'

In this chapter, Hardy presents Tess as the innocent victim and Alec as the villain. Tess calls him 'treacherous' and Hardy portrays him entirely in this light. The fact that 'I don't quite know where I am myself' represents how Alec deliberately leads Tess astray so that he can force himself on her. This is underlined by the way 'he made a sort of couch or   15
nest for her in the deep mass of leaves'. She is trapped like one of the birds she is employed by Alec's mother to look after, at his mercy.

Tess's innocence and vulnerability are highlighted throughout the chapter. She is shown to be almost childlike, 'a white muslin figure he had left upon dead leaves … sleeping soundly'. Circumstances, as well as Alec himself, have worked against her. Because she   20
has 'risen at five o'clock every morning of the week', she is 'inexpressibly weary' – her 'sleepiness' and 'actual drowsiness' are referred to by Hardy several times. Alec takes advantage of this. Her 'simple faith' is no match for his cunning. She is presented as passive (as is shown by 'as the pale light lessened, Tess became invisible') whereas Alec is an alert and active sexual opportunist seizing his chance.   25

It is symbolic that 'a faint luminous fog … enveloped them'. Tess is confused and emotionally disorientated by Alec's wiles. He makes her feel indebted to him by telling her: 'By the bye, Tess, your father has a new cob today. Somebody gave it to him.' On top of this, he uses flattery – 'You know I love you, and think you the prettiest girl in the world' – and acts the part of the injured lover: 'Good God! What am I, to be repulsed   30 by a mere chit like you?' It is no wonder that, mentally, Tess is in a 'growing fog', like the atmosphere in the forest. Her uncertainty about what to feel is shown by the way she finds difficulty in finishing her sentences throughout the chapter:

'"I'm grateful," she repeatedly admitted. "But I fear I do not –"'

The whole setting for this chapter is highly symbolic. 'The Chase' describes Alec's prolonged sexual pursuit of Tess as well as the place where it finally succeeds. Hardy emphasises that it is 'the oldest place in England' with 'primeval yews and oaks', bringing out how Tess's violation is an age-old practice – she is not the first, and will not be the last woman to suffer it. For her, as for others, it will bring tragedy to her life, as the fact that 'The Chase was wrapped in thick darkness' symbolises. 'Darkness' also suggests Alec's villainy.

At the end of the chapter, Hardy asks: 'Where was Tess's guardian angel? Where was the providence of her simple faith?' Throughout the novel, Tess is shown to be a victim of Fate, as she is here. Circumstance and chance decide her destiny, rather than her own wishes (she is asleep when Alec violates her) or Christian Providence. *Tess* is a novel which challenges the Christian view of the world, as 'Tess's own people' do too. They 'never tired of saying in their fatalistic way: "It was to be."'

Therefore this scene in The Chase, which has deliberately pagan overtones ('some of Tess d'Urberville's mailed ancestors rollicking home from a fray'), sets the pattern for the book as a whole. Tess is always seen as a victim of arbitrary forces working to bring her down. 'Why it was', as Hardy says, ' ... many thousands of years of analytical philosophy have failed to explain to our sense of order.' From this point on, Tess is 'doomed' to be divided from the 'Pure Woman' she really is by 'an immeasurable social chasm' which brands her an adulteress, a bigamist and finally a murderess. Judged by Christian morality, she is guilty ('THY, DAMNATION, SLUMBERETH, NOT') – and 'The Woman Pays'. Judged by 'the natural law', she is innocent. 'There lay the pity of it.'

All things considered ...

Look back to the way in which you assessed the coursework essay in section 9.2. How well do the 'yardsticks' you used to do so apply to this essay?

Discuss with your teacher the possible reasons why the candidate's answer above reached full marks. What can you learn from it? Does it increase your optimism about your own abilities?

A final point. This candidate was obviously well taught and he knew the novel thoroughly. His 'exam technique' – for example, the way in which quotations are integrated into his analysis of the text – is excellent.

Above all, however, his essay is impressive because it expresses his own response to Tess in his own voice. The purpose of this book has been to help you to do the same.